AIJA Law Library

Protection of Minority Shareholders

Other titles in the AIJA Law Library:

Commercial Agency and Distribution Agreements: Law and Practice in the Member States of the European Community and the European Free Trade Association (2nd edn.), G. Bogaert, U. Lohmann (eds.)
ISBN 1 85333 785 4

Evidence in International Arbitration Proceedings, Peter V. Eijsvoogel (ed.)
ISBN 1 85333 964 4

Sale of Private and Public Companies by Auction, C. Grayston, W. F. Schmitz and G. Abbatescianni (eds.)
ISBN 90 411 0925 0

Due Diligence for Corporate Acquisitions, Winfried F. Schmitz (ed.)
ISBN 1 85966 064 9

Please order by title or ISBN

AIJA Law Library

Protection of Minority Shareholders

Series Editor

International Association of Young Lawyers
Association Internationale des Jeunes Avocats

Volume Editor

Matthias W. Stecher

KLUWER LAW INTERNATIONAL
LONDON–THE HAGUE–BOSTON
and

Association Internationale des Jeunes Avocats
International Association of Young Lawyers

Published by
Kluwer Law International Ltd
Sterling House
66 Wilton Road
London SW1V 1DE
United Kingdom

Sold and distributed in the USA and Canada by
Kluwer Law International
675 Massachusetts Avenue
Cambridge MA 02139
USA

Kluwer Law International Ltd incorporates the publishing programmes of
Graham & Trotman Ltd,
Kluwer Law & Taxation Publishers
and Martinus Nijhoff Publishers

In all other countries sold and distributed by Kluwer Law International
P.O. Box 85889
2508 CN The Hague
The Netherlands

ISBN 90-411-0661-8
Series ISBN 1-85333-905-9

First published 1997

British Library Cataloguing in Publication Data and Library of Congress Cataloging-in-Publication Data is available

Typeset by On Screen, West Hanney, Oxfordshire

Printed and bound in Great Britain by CPI Antony Rowe, Eastbourne

CONTENTS

ABOUT AIJA

THE INTERNATIONAL ASSOCIATION OF YOUNG LAWYERS (AIJA: *Association Internationale des Jeunes Avocats*) is a non-political organization founded in 1962 to encourage cooperation and mutual respect among young lawyers from all countries. With some 3,000 members, aged 45 and under and from more than 60 countries on every continent, AIJA is active on a variety of fronts.

An annual week-long meeting, held in late summer, brings together hundreds of AIJA members for the study of issues of interest to both veteran and novice international practitioners. Recent venues have included New Delhi, Barcelona, London, Amsterdam, Rio de Janeiro and Washington, DC; the 1996 annual meeting took place in Montreux, Switzerland. Throughout the year, seminars in cities from Mexico City to Hong Kong focus on the latest developments in specific fields.

AIJA also works actively in human rights and freedom of practice issues, taking a leading role, for example, in on-site representation of lawyers detained by local regimes for nothing more than a faithful representation of their clients. Social issues are on the agenda as well; recent sessions have addressed contemporary questions including sexual harassment and surrogate mothers.

Beyond its activities in continuing legal education and safeguarding lawyers' right to practise freely, AIJA takes as a primary goal the creation of a forum to allow young lawyers from around the world simply to come together and make friends across borders. To that end, AIJA events always include communal meals, receptions and other social opportunities so that participants can become well-acquainted on a personal as well as professional level.

Information about joining AIJA and about upcoming activities may be obtained from:

AIJA
Avenue Louis Lepoutre, 50-Box 20
B-1050 Brussels
Telephone: +32 2 347 2808
Fax: +32 2 347 5522

OFFICERS OF AIJA

President Jean-Yves Feltesse (France)
Immediate Past President Guy Harles (Luxembourg)
President-Elect Horacio Bernardes-Neto
Secretary-General Etienne Rocher
Treasurer G.-Bernard van Parys

A WORD FROM THE PUBLICATIONS COMMITTEE

This is the fifth title in the AIJA Library. An international team consisting of Anita de Jong (The Netherlands), Clare Grayston (United Kingdom), Matthias W. Stecher (Germany) and Joren de Wachter (Belgium) prepared and guided the academic part of an AIJA seminar under the title of the book in Madrid in November 1995. One of the results of the wonderful efforts of the team was the general report included in this publication.

Whoever has edited a book besides the regular professional work knows the additional burden and effort to be undertaken to get a book completed. Special thanks for leading the book through to its production is made to the volume editor, Matthias W. Stecher, who did an outstanding job to get the book done.

This is the first year of the undersigned as President of the Publications Committee. Many thanks go to my predecessor Marc Jobert from Paris who patiently advised and looked after the authors and volume editors of earlier AIJA publications. The Publications Committee of AIJA is looking forward to many more books in the AIJA Library.

Dusseldorf, February 1997

Winfried F. Schmitz
President of AIJA's Publications Committee

PREFACE

As a consequence of the continuing globalization of the economy, more and more even medium-sized and small companies enter into cooperation with foreign enterprises. This cooperation often goes beyond a mere exporter–importer relationship and involves a direct participation in the other company or the formation of a joint venture. If the participation in the foreign company is 50% or less, the new shareholder will want to learn about the rights afforded to him by the law of the foreign country in the event that a conflict arises between him and his co-shareholder(s). The aim of this book is to provide a shareholder investing in a foreign company (and the shareholder's legal advisers) with practical information on the various means of protection and the ways in which such protection can be judicially enforced in the respective foreign country. The book deals with almost all major European jurisdictions and the United States.

This book is the result of a seminar which was organized in November 1995 in Madrid by a team consisting of the editor and other members of the International Business Law Commission of AIJA. The reports by the various countries were based on the questionnaire prepared by the organizers' team (see p. xxxix). In addition, Annex II contains a speech on the London Takeover Panel made by Noel P. Hinton. In view of the seminar's success, the International Business Law Commission is planning further seminars on interesting aspects of international corporate law (and also further publications like the present one).

The editor wishes to thank all the authors for their fine work and their efficient cooperation within the team, Isabel-Clara Canals whose organizational work in Madrid made the seminar possible (and thus also this publication) as well as Claudia Seibel, the President of the International Business Law Commission who supported this project. My personal thanks also go to Karin Etzelsbeck who greatly contributed to the editing of this book.

Matthias W. Stecher
Editor

LIST OF CONTRIBUTORS

VOLUME EDITOR

Matthias W. Stecher

Born Heidelberg, 1958. University of Tübingen (law degree 1984). Law studies at New York University (M.C.J.), 1987–88. Bar exam of the State of New York, 1988. With law firm Brosio, Casati e Associati, Milan, 1991. Areas of practice: corporate and commercial law; unfair competition law. With Beiten Burkhardt Mittl & Wegener, Munich office.
Tel: (49) 89 350 6500.

GENERAL REPORT

Anita de Jong

Born 1959. Utrecht University (law degree 1985). Areas of practice: company law; labour law. Partner, Caron & Stevens/Baker & McKenzie, Amsterdam office.
Tel: (31) 20 55 17 434.

Clare Grayston

Born Wirral, Merseyside, 1960. Qualified, 1985. Areas of practice: mergers and acquisitions; general corporate finance. Partner and Head of Corporate Finance, Lewis Silkin Solicitors, London office.
Tel: (44) 171 227 8000.

Matthias W. Stecher See above.

Joren de Wachter

Born Roeselare, 1966. University FNDP Namur 1984–86, KUL Leuven 1986–89 (law degree 1989). European Law at the Institut d'Etudes Européennes, Brussels, 1989–91. Admitted to the Brussels Bar, 1990. European Young Lawyers Course (London), 1993. Qualified as Solicitor of the Supreme Court of England and Wales 1997. Areas of practice: corporate law; commercial contracts. Partner, De Backer & Bastin, Brussels office.
Tel: (32) 2 374 5777.

AUSTRIA

Christoph Petsch

Born Vienna, 1957. University of Vienna (law degree 1981). Internship with law firms Jacques Mauro and Doise, Martinez et Coutard, Paris, 1983–84. Bar exam in Vienna, 1986. Areas of practice: corporate law; general commercial law; distribution and trademark law. With Petsch, Frosch & Partners, Vienna office.
Tel: (43) 1 586 21 80.

BELGIUM

Joren de Wachter see above.

FINLAND

Pauliina Tenhunen

Born Pihtipudas, 1966. University of Helsinki (law degree 1990). Court practice 1990–91. With law firm Kalliala & Järvensivu, 1990. Areas of practice: litigation; insolvency law. With Castrén & Snellman, Attorneys at Law, Helsinki office.
Tel: (358) 9 228581.

FRANCE

Patrick Peguet

Born Annemasse, 1960. University Robert Schuman of Strasbourg (law degree 1982). French bar exam 1983. Luxembourg bar exam 1990. Areas of practice: banking and finance law; company law; arbitration. With ASA law firm, Strasbourg office.
Tel: (33) 88 56 56 49.

Nathalie Carbiner

Born Forbach, 1968. University Robert Schuman of Strasbourg (law degree 1991). French bar exam 1994. With ASA law firm, Strasbourg office.
Tel: (33) 88 56 56 49.

Jean-Christophe Sabourin

Born Strasbourg, 1968. University Robert Schuman of Strasbourg (law degree 1991, DEA EU LAW 1993). French bar exam 1995. With ASA law firm, Strasbourg office.
Tel: (33) 88 56 56 49.

GERMANY

Matthias W. Stecher see above.

IRELAND

Gerard Coll

Born Dublin, 1957. University College Dublin (law degree 1978). Professional law studies at The Incorporated Law Society of Ireland, 1978–81. University of Amsterdam (Europa Institute), 1981–82. Areas of practice: mergers and acquisitions; joint ventures; corporate finance and venture capital. With Eugene F. Collins, Dublin office.
Tel: (353) 1 676 1924.

Jacqueline Ennis

Born Dublin, 1969. Trinity College Dublin (LL.B., 1991). Professional law studies at The Incorporated Law Society of Ireland, 1991–94. Qualified, 1994. Areas of practice: acquisitions and joint ventures; venture capital. With Eugene F. Collins, Dublin office
Tel: (353) 1 676 1924.

ITALY

Massimo Audisio

Born Milan, 1960. Catholic University of Milan (JD, 1984). Assistant of International Organization at the University of Milan. Visiting foreign lawyer, Radcliffes & Co. Solicitors, London, 1992. Specialization in law and economy of the European Community, University of Milan, 1993–95. Areas of practice: commercial law; company law; labour law. With Scamoni e Associati, Milan office.
Tel: (39) 2 48 01 11 71.

LUXEMBOURG

Pierre Schleimer

Born Luxembourg, 1968. University of Brussels (Master of Laws 1992). Institut d'Etudes Européennes Brussels (Master's Degree in Community Law 1993). Advanced Course of Law Luxembourg. Areas of practice: banking; corporate; contract law. With Zeyen Beghin Feider Loeff Claeys Verbeke, Luxembourg office.
Tel: (352) 46 89 46.

NETHERLANDS

Anita de Jong see above.

Paul W. J. Coenen

Born 1964. University of Nijmegen (law degree). University of Münster (LL.M. in International Law). University of Hamburg and Max Planck-Institute for International Law, Hamburg. Institute for International Business Law, Münster (Ph.D.). Areas of practice: international business law. With Caron & Stevens/Baker & McKenzie, Amsterdam office.
Tel: (31) 20 55 17 434.

PORTUGAL

Miguel de Avillez Pereira

Born Lisbon, 1965. University of Lisbon (law degree). University of Edinburgh (LL.M.). With law firm Maclay, Murray & Spens, Edinburgh, 1992. Author: "Arbitration Issues in EC Law", *Review of Documentation and Comparative Law of the Attorney General's Office* (BGDDC), 1984, No. 57/58 and Separata; "The Right of Action of Third Parties against EC Commission's clearance of Mergers", BGDDC, 1995; "The Position of EC Banks and non-EC Banks under the Second Banking Directive", BGDDC, 1996. Areas of practice: corporate; business; commercial law, mergers and acquisitions. Partner, Avillez Pereira & Associados, Lisbon office.
Tel: (351) 1 353 7002.

SPAIN

Coloma Armero Montes

Born Madrid, 1954. University of Madrid (Licentiate in Law 1977). Areas of practice: corporate law; stock market and securities; mergers and acquisitions. With Bufete Armero, Madrid office.
Tel: (34) 1 431 3100.

SWEDEN

Hans Ramberg

Born Helsingborg, 1963. University of Lund (law degree 1989, MBA 1994). With law firm Lindahl 1989–95. Consulting in information technology law and corporate law, 1996.
Tel: (49) 8 411 5565

SWITZERLAND

Felix R. Ehrat

Born Schaffhausen, 1957. Universities of Lausanne and Zurich (law degree 1982). McGeorge School of Law, Sacramento/USA (LL.M. 1986). Thesis on contractual law, 1990. Admitted to the Bar in Switzerland, 1985. Secondments to Semmes, Bowen & Semmes (Baltimore/USA), 1985/86, and to Ughi e Nunziante (Rome/Italy), 1989. Areas of practice: commercial law; corporate law; international arbitration. Partner, Bär & Karrer, Zurich and Lugano offices.
Tel: (41) 1 261 5150.

UNITED KINGDOM

Andrew P. Johnstone

Born Australia, 1960. University of Sydney (B.A. Hons). University of Queensland (LL.B). Admitted as a solicitor in England, 1991. Areas of practice: company law. With Sinclair Roche & Temperley, London office.
Tel: (44) 171 452 4000.

USA

Catherine Habermehl

State University of New York at Buffalo. Clerk for United States District Court Magistrate in the Western District of Michigan. Areas of practice: litigation of complex liability matters; insurance coverage; international trade issues. Founding member, Altreuter & Habermehl
Tel: (1) 716 853 1150.

David R. Koepsell

State University of New York at Buffalo. Areas of practice: computer law, intellectual property and litigation. With Altreuter & Habermehl, Buffalo office.
Tel: (1) 716 853 1150.

TAKEOVER PANEL

Noel P. Hinton

MA (Cantab.) in Modern and Medieval Languages. M.Sc. in Finance. Seconded to the Takeover Panel from the Bank of England, 1984. Permanent member of the Panel staff since 1986, Deputy Director General since 1991.
Tel: (44) 171 382 9026.

QUESTIONNAIRE

The following questionnaire was given to the authors as a basis for their country reports. For easier reference the questions will be repeated, in a slightly shortened form, in each report.

1. Majority Requirements for Shareholders' Resolutions

1.1 What are the majority requirements in general?
1.2 Which resolutions require a greater majority?
1.3 To what extent can they be modified by the Articles of Association?

2. Influence on the Decision-Making Process

2.1 Do minority shareholders have the right to call a shareholders' meeting?
2.2 Do they have the right to put matters on the agenda?

3. Rights for Information, Independent Auditing and Supervision

3.1 To what extent do the (minority) shareholders have a right to be informed on company matters?
3.2 Do minority shareholders have the right to demand independent auditing or to initiate the supervision of company matters by an independent institution?

4. Capital Increases and Distributions

4.1 To what extent do (minority) shareholders have the right to participate in capital increases?

4.2 Do minority shareholders have the right to demand dividends or other distributions?

5. Derivative Actions

5.1 Can (minority) shareholders enforce rights that the company has against (a) other shareholders, (b) directors, or (c) third parties?

6. Other "Formal" Rights

6.1 Do minority shareholders have any other specific rights comparable to those mentioned in 2–5 above?

7. Extension of These Rights by Statute or Shareholders' Agreements

7.1 Can the Articles of Association provide for additional rights of the minority shareholders (eg to appoint directors)? If not, can such rights be provided for in shareholders' agreements? Are these options commonly used?

8. Remedies Where a Shareholders' Resolution or Other Action Impairs the Rights of Minority Shareholders

8.1 What are the requirements for such remedies (eg unfair prejudice against the interests of the respective shareholder)?

8.2 When do the courts of your country accept these requirements?

8.3 What remedies are available to the claimant (eg avoidance of the resolution; injunctive action; setting aside actions already taken; compensation; buying-out the injured shareholder; winding-up the company)?

9. Specific Protection if the Company is Controlled by Another Company

9.1 What are the rights and remedies (see 8.3) of a shareholder of Company A when Company B gains control over it (by acquiring the majority of its shares or otherwise)?

9.2 What are the shareholder's rights and remedies when Company B exerts its control over Company A in a way which damages the interests of the latter?

GENERAL REPORT

Matthias W. Stecher, Anita de Jong, Joren de Wachter,
Clare Grayston

PROTECTION OF MINORITY SHAREHOLDERS

EDITOR MATTHIAS W. STECHER

GENERAL REPORT

Matthias W. Stecher, Anita de Jong, Joren de Wachter, Clare Grayston

Preamble

The purpose of this report is to explain in general terms how various important jurisdictions approach the problems of minority participation in corporations. Following each topic/question contained in the questionnaire the common themes, important differences and general trends are outlined. Consequently this report does not summarize all the details contained in the country reports – this rather is the purpose of the comparative charts (see Annex I).

The reader should be aware that, wherever certain observations are made referring to specific jurisdictions, it does not necessarily mean that such observations are not to be applied to other jurisdictions. It is only that the national reporters of jurisdictions referred to highlighted these observations and others may not have done so. The term "common law countries" is used herein to mean the United Kingdom, Ireland and the United States. The term "civil law countries" refers to all other countries covered by the national reports.

Introduction

The protection of minority shareholders' investments in both private and quoted companies is an area of uncertainty. Apart from embedded legal rights under company law, which are detailed in the various reports summarized in the comparative charts, the questionnaire sent to the reporters sought to establish whether there is any more general protection in situations where the affairs of a company are being conducted either with intent to harm the interests of minorities (perhaps to encourage them to sell out) or merely with a general disregard for their interests.

By and large, it would be fair to say that minority shareholders in publicly quoted companies tend to have a higher level of protection than those in private companies. Their position is also helped by the fact that there will generally be a market in the shares giving them an exit route if they are dissatisfied with the management and direction of the company. Most publicly quoted companies wish to enhance the level of investment from institutions; the institutions themselves will want to ensure that they have made a safe investment as they cannot afford to speculate with funds that they hold on trust. Therefore, the market will tend to regulate itself and that regulation may be embodied in law or may merely be a code to be observed if a company is not to be blacklisted. Accordingly, shareholders in quoted companies will have the right to receive regular detailed information on the company in which they have invested, and on the remuneration of the management; they will also know that the management and substantial shareholders cannot enter into material transactions with the company without the matter being approved on an independent vote of the shareholders and that large stakes in the company cannot be sold without their being able to participate. Of course, the level of protection will vary from one jurisdiction to another, being particularly high in both the United States and the United Kingdom.

The level of protection for shareholders in private companies is not necessarily so well established. In the last decade or so the incidence of class actions by groups of minority shareholders has increased and businesses have been established with the sole objective of assisting minority and corporate shareholders in protecting their investments.

Members of the European Union have or are in the process of modifying or extending the rights of minorities in order to comply with directives aimed at doing just that. A certain level of conformity can, therefore, be seen in the reports from those member states.

1. Majority Requirements for Shareholders' Resolutions

1.1 What are the majority requirements in general?

As a general rule, a simple majority is required for shareholders' resolutions, that is, 50% plus one of the votes of the shareholders who are present or represented at the meeting.

However, this rule alone does not indicate how many shareholders are, in practice, needed in order for a resolution to be passed. The US report explains the impact of concepts like quorums and voting rights very well. For example, some countries – not all of them – provide for a quorum: a minimum number of the shares with voting rights must be represented, or a minimum number of the shareholders must be present. If the quorum is 50% plus one of the shares entitled to vote and a simple majority is required for a valid resolution, then (at least in theory) a majority of only 25% plus one of *all* shares in the company is sufficient for a resolution to be passed. One of the countries which requires a quorum for ordinary resolutions is Spain (one-third in the case of an SL).

If a large proportion of the shareholders is not interested in the management of the company and therefore does not attend the shareholders' meetings, it may be difficult to reach the required quorum. Therefore, it is often provided that a lower quorum (or no quorum) applies if the shareholders' meeting is convened for a second time. Thus in the Luxembourg Sàrl, a majority of the members representing more than 50% of the share capital is necessary in the first, but not in the second meeting.

1.2 Which resolutions require a greater majority?

Certain resolutions typically affect the rights and interests of the shareholders in a fundamental way. In order to protect the minority shareholders, they must at least have a say in these resolutions even though they may not be able to block "ordinary" resolutions. Each of the countries represented in this book has, therefore, developed a catalogue of subjects which require a greater majority. The most common example is the amendment of the Articles of Association: the necessary majority is, in most cases, three-quarters, sometimes two-thirds. Exceptions are the Iberian countries where – at least in the second meeting – a simple majority is sufficient, and only certain quorum requirements apply. Further examples of resolutions which may require a greater majority are:

- changes in the rights attached to the shares or certain categories of shares (Sweden, Netherlands, Finland);
- merger, demerger or dissolution of the company (Portugal, Netherlands, Germany, Finland, Austria, USA);
- conversion into another legal entity (Netherlands);
- alteration of share capital (Netherlands, Belgium, Austria);
- transfer of the company's assets (Austria, USA).

1.3 To what extent can they be modified by the Articles of Association?

In all countries, the shareholders have the right to modify the majority requirements by appropriate provisions in the Articles of Association. This allows minority shareholders to strengthen their powers: If a capital increase, for instance, requires a majority of more than 90% of the votes, a shareholder holding 10% has a veto power. On the other hand, this freedom to adapt the articles to the structure of the individual enterprise may not be used to weaken the minority protection afforded by (statutory) law. Therefore, in almost all countries, the majority requirements may only be strengthened and not weakened.

2. Influence on the Decision-Making Process

2.1 Do minority shareholders have the right to call a shareholders' meeting?

Unless minority shareholders are represented on the board of directors, they can influence the decisions to be taken in the company only by their participation and their voting in the shareholders' meeting. In most jurisdictions, therefore, shareholders representing a certain percentage of the shares have the right to request that the board of directors or its chairman convene such a meeting. The required percentage is usually 5% or 10% of the voting rights. The only exception seems to be Luxembourg where no such right exists.

Since this right is exercised by the minority specifically in cases of disagreement between the minority and the board, the law must also provide for a way of enforcing the right if the board refuses the request. In fact, in many of the jurisdictions the minority may turn to the courts. If the requirements are met, the court itself will convene a shareholders' meeting (eg Sweden), or will appoint a representative to convene the meeting on behalf of the board (eg Netherlands, France), or will authorize the minority shareholders to convene the meeting themselves (eg Austria, German AG). Minority shareholders in Ireland or of a German GmbH are in an even better position: if the board does not comply with their request within a certain period of time, they may themselves call the shareholders' meeting without having to go to court. Some countries specifically provide that the costs of convening the meeting are to be borne by the company.

2.2 Do they have the right to put matters on the agenda?

Even if the board convenes a shareholders' meeting, its agenda may not contain all the points which the minority wants to be treated. In a few jurisdictions, therefore, a minority (usually the same percentage as discussed above) may request that certain items be added to the agenda. Usually the minority must make such a request a certain minimum period before the meeting is to take place. Somewhat surprising is the situation in Switzerland where a minority holding a share capital of SFR1 million may request matters to be put on the agenda – in smaller companies, therefore, this right is excluded simply for practical reasons.

3. Rights of Information, Independent Auditing and Supervision

3.1 To what extent do the (minority) shareholders have a right to be informed on company matters?

Generally, shareholders have the right to receive the annual report and accounts. Furthermore, they have the right to ask questions in the general meeting. The board of directors may refuse to answer a question if answering is detrimental to the company (eg Sweden). Elsewhere, the chair has a discretion not to take questions at a meeting. In some jurisdictions, further investigative rights are provided for, particularly if there are only a few shareholders or in case of private limited companies.

A specific feature exists under Italian law: a "board of auditors" controls whether the company is managed and, more specifically, whether the books are kept in a formally lawful manner (it does not, however, examine business decisions on the merits). The intention of the legislature was that this control be performed specifically in the interests of the minority shareholders.

3.2 Do they have the right to demand independent auditing or to initiate the supervision of company matters by an independent institution?

Shareholders normally have the right to call for an independent investigation. In some countries they have the right to request an audit, in other countries a court decision is needed to perform an independent investigation. It may be required that the shareholders represent a certain percentage of the shares. In the Netherlands, shareholders representing at least 10% of the issued capital may request the Enterprise Chamber of the Amsterdam Court of Appeals to appoint one or more independent investigators. Such a request must be justified by serious reasons (such as apparent mismanagement). The Enterprise Chamber may impose certain sanctions if the company has been grossly mismanaged. In Ireland, a judicial order for an investigation may also be obtained if there is a prima facie case that the company's affairs have been conducted in a fraudulent, unlawful manner.

The shareholders of a German private limited company (GmbH) do not have the right to (independent) auditing or supervision. In England, the investigators are not appointed by a court, but by the Department of Trade and Industry. Under US law, the court may place the company in receivership and wind it up or appoint a temporary receiver. By-laws may provide for periodic access of, auditing by and the communication of the financial statement to, the shareholders.

4. Capital Increases and Distributions

4.1 To what extent do (minority) shareholders have the right to participate in capital increases?

The basic rule is that shareholders have the right to participate in capital increases. Obviously, this right is essential for any minority as, without it, the majority could, at its discretion, dilute shareholdings and thus the voting power of the minority.

However, this right can be excluded in certain circumstances particularly if expressly provided for in the constitution in relation to a particular class of share. Furthermore, the majority of countries allow the shareholders' meeting to exclude the right by resolution relating to the capital increase in question. In almost all cases this resolution must be taken with a qualified majority (the Netherlands and Spain seem to require only a simple majority). Additionally, some countries require a justified interest for the exclusion of the right by the majority (Austria: objective reasons; Finland: weighty economic reasons; Germany: prevailing interest of the company; Portugal: justified interest; Spain: in the company's interest). This kind of test gives the minority the possibility of having a resolution, which excludes their participation rights, reviewed by the courts. It is then up to the courts to develop rules as to when the interest or the reason is strong enough to justify the exclusion. It seems that German courts apply a particularly high standard in this respect.

4.2 Do minority shareholders have the right to demand dividends or other distributions?

Most countries either do not provide for a shareholder's right to demand dividends or they allow such a right to be excluded from time to time by a shareholders' resolution. Again, some countries allow this resolution, or a refusal on the part of the board of directors to declare a dividend, to be challenged, normally applying a reasonableness test (Belgium and Germany: interest of the company; Netherlands and Luxembourg: abuse; Ireland: oppression). The courts will need to balance the working capital requirements of the company against the general interest of shareholders in receiving a return on their investment. In Portugal, shareholders have a somewhat stronger position in that the right to demand a dividend for a given fiscal year can be excluded only by a qualified majority.

Sweden and Finland have developed a specific instrument for the protection of the minority: one-tenth of the shareholders can demand that one-half of the profit, but not more than 5% of the equity, be distributed. This seems to give a minority the strongest position of all countries covered. Finally, in Germany, shareholders of a stock company (AG) have a right to a minimum dividend of 4% of the share capital held by them.

5. Derivative Actions

5.1 Can (minority) shareholders enforce rights that the company has against other shareholders, directors, or third parties?

The general principle must be that where a company is capable of enforcing its rights itself, then no one shareholder, nor indeed the body of shareholders, will be able to stand in its shoes. A company is a legal person, its management carrying its objects and powers into effect. On that basis, only the company, acting by its directors, should have redress for wrongs done to it unless, either

- the management fails without proper cause to enforce the company's rights; or
- the management itself is guilty of some form of wrongdoing.

In each case, the shareholders, as a body, would be entitled to remove offending directors, replacing them with new management which would be able to enforce the company's rights. The basis of any derivative action would, therefore, normally imply some form of collusion between the directors and the controlling shareholders.

Equity would dictate that, in the case of negligence or default on the part of the directors, non-controlling shareholders should be able to obtain some form of redress to protect the interests of the company and their investment. However, the rights of shareholders to bring derivative actions vary quite markedly from one jurisdiction to another. In the United Kingdom and Ireland, the common law provides relief, by way of exception to the above-mentioned principle, in the following circumstances:

- the company being forced to take action which is either illegal or *ultra vires*;
- invalid resolutions, for example, where a special majority is required and only a simple majority is obtained;
- infringement of members' personal rights;
- "fraud on the minority";
- where "justice otherwise requires".

The last element gives the court a very wide discretion to apply general rules of equity. The test, however, is whether with any other action/remedy, a wrong to the company would otherwise go unremedied. It is not necessary to show a tort at common law but the fraud or oppression must involve unconscionable use of the majority's power resulting in loss or in unfair or discriminatory treatment of the minority. The wrong must also be more serious than a mere failure on the part of the majority to act in the interest of the company as a whole. It is not necessary to show harm or loss to either the company or the complainants, but grossly unfair and oppressive action. The right of action is really against the majority shareholders but it would be going too far to suggest that shareholders owe a fiduciary duty to one another. In the United States it has been held that the majority shareholders *do* owe fiduciary duties to the minority and are, therefore, liable to compensate them for loss suffered in consequence of the majority transferring control of the company to persons whom they know are likely to misapply its assets.

Derivative actions may also be brought in the United Kingdom and Ireland against the directors who control the company for, say, misappropriating company funds, allotting shares to themselves, depriving the company of a business opportunity which they take for themselves, removing shareholders' powers of control. Action may also be taken against the promoters of a company on similar grounds.

In the United States, the right of shareholders to bring derivative actions is well established and is governed largely by state, rather than federal, law. A cause of action may lie against other shareholders, the management or third parties.

The position in civil law countries is, perhaps, less favourable to the minority shareholder and, as between civil law countries, there is a significant variance in the rights conferred. In Sweden, 10% of the membership can bring an action for *gross* breaches of company law or the Articles of Association either against other shareholders or, if damage has been caused to the company, against the management. Action can also be taken against the auditors by some part of the membership; but, otherwise, the shareholders have no cause of action against third parties.

In Spain, there is a specific right of action on the part of 5% of the membership against the management but no cause of action against other shareholders or third parties.

Under Netherlands law, shareholders have no right to bring derivative actions other than in exceptional circumstances where there has been an infringement of those shareholders' personal rights; in such a situation action may be possible against other shareholders, management or third parties. Further, in the Netherlands equity also has a part to play as shareholders may, in exceptional circumstances, have a cause of action against the management for wrongs done.

In Germany, the concept of *actio pro socio*, effectively a partnership concept, applies in limited liability companies, but not stock corporations, giving a cause of action against other shareholders; but does not extend to actions against either the management or third parties.

In Finland, the right of action rests with the members in the general meeting. If the majority veto action against the management or other shareholders, then the holders of 10% or more of the equity will be able to bring a derivative action, but not against third parties. (Contrast the above situation in Luxembourg, where there is absolutely no right to bring derivative actions, the shareholders having no remedy other than as a body against the management personally.)

Whether or not there is a cause of action, the cost implications must be borne in mind. In most jurisdictions, those bringing the action will normally have to fund the proceedings with a right of reimbursement only if ultimately successful. They may even have to provide security for costs. Where lawyers can and do accept instructions on a contingency basis, there will, in all likelihood be a greater incidence of derivative suits. In jurisdictions where contingency fees are not possible, as in most of Europe, cases are more likely to arise as class actions where the cost can be spread.

6. Other "Formal" Rights

6.1 Do minority shareholders have any other specific rights comparable to those mentioned in 2–5 above?

In addition to the rights explained above (ie the right to have a shareholders' meeting called, to receive information on company matters, to have the management and the bookkeeping checked by an independent authority, to participate in capital increases, to receive dividends, to enforce claims of the company on its behalf), minority shareholders may have further rights which are comparable to those listed above. These can be called "formal" rights since they do not require any conduct on the part of the majority or the management which is, in its substance, prejudicial to the minority (this latter aspect will be discussed under 8 below). Some reports list numerous rights of this type (see, eg Austria, Ireland and Spain). A few examples are the rights

- to appoint one member of the supervisory board (Austria) or of the board of directors (Spain);
- to petition for removal of supervisory board members (Austria);
- to demand the appointment of an auditor (Finland);
- to petition for the replacement of an auditor (Austria);

- to demand adjournment of a shareholders' meeting or, at least, of the resolution on certain items (Austria, Spain);
- to demand the preparation of separate accounts for various companies belonging to one group of companies (Austria);
- to prevent the shareholders' meeting from settling or waiving an action against the administrators for breach of duty (Spain);
- to oppose the company's giving financial assistance for the purchase of its shares (Ireland).

Some other rights discussed in the reports under this heading have a close connection with question 8, such as the lock-out and opt-out rights under Belgian law which require a "valid reason", the dissolution and buy-back rights under Swiss law which are given on "important grounds" and Rule 10b 5 of the US Securities Exchange Act which provides for a private right of action as a means of challenging deceptive acts which are detrimental to investors.

7. Extension of These Rights by Statute or Shareholders' Agreements

7.1 Can the Articles of Association provide for additional rights of the minority shareholders? If not, can such rights be provided for in shareholders' agreements? Are these options commonly used?

In most jurisdictions, both the Articles of Association and shareholders' agreements can be used to provide additional rights for minority shareholders.

Various ways in which the rights of minority shareholders can be strengthened through appropriate provisions in the Articles of Association have already been discussed above, for example:

- increase of required majorities; introduction or increase of quorum requirements (question 1);
- extension of information rights (question 3);
- clauses creating or strengthening a right to participate in capital increases or to receive a minimum share of the profits (question 4).

In some countries shareholders enjoy a high degree of freedom in shaping the rights provided for in the Articles to suit their interests. Sometimes this depends on the type of company, thus, in a German GmbH, the shareholders have a great deal of leeway, whereas in an AG the Articles may deviate from statute only if the statutory provisions themselves expressly allow such deviation. In other countries, deviation is allowed only to a limited extent or, at least, not used in practice (eg France, Portugal and Sweden).

Typical minority rights which can be included in the articles are the following:

- pre-emptive rights (Belgium, Germany);
- limitations on the transfer of shares, for example by requiring a shareholders' resolution (Germany, Luxembourg, United Kingdom);

- right to appoint members of the board of directors or of the supervisory board (Austria, Belgium, Germany, Luxembourg);
- requirement of a shareholders' resolution or even the approval by certain shareholders for certain business decisions (Austria, Germany, Ireland, Luxembourg);
- super-voting powers (Austrian private limited liability company);
- introduction of classes of shares (France, Netherlands – "priority shares" and "letter shares").

The use of shareholders' agreements is widespread. Only in a limited number of cases is the validity of shareholders' agreements *per se* called into doubt.

In practice, shareholders' agreements between all shareholders will only be present in smaller companies because the larger the body of shareholders the more difficult it is, logistically, to get them to sign such an agreement whereas, by taking shares in a company either through subscription or acquisition, a shareholder is, by implication, to be taken as accepting the rights and restrictions set out in the constitution of the company.

A different type of shareholders' agreement is one between a select group of shareholders, also known as voting or pooling agreement. Here the parties concerned will normally agree to cast their votes and exercise their other powers in the same manner and to provide rights of first refusal over each others' shares. These agreements, generally speaking, will tend to exist in larger companies, even publicly quoted companies, where the constitution does not, for example, provide preemption rights on transfers of shares.

In some jurisdictions, shareholders' agreements are far more frequently used to protect minorities' rights than the Articles of Association.

Since shareholders' agreements are concluded between shareholders personally, they are subject to contract law and to the rule of privity of contract which may make them more readily enforceable. There may be another benefit in that a shareholders' agreement will not necessarily be a registrable document open to public inspection.

The company will normally not be bound by the provisions of the shareholders' agreement unless it becomes a party to it. However, the company is not always free to do so, because in certain jurisdictions, such as the United Kingdom, shareholders' agreements cannot fetter the statutory powers of the company or its organs.

The remedy for breach of a shareholders' agreement will be based on contract law, giving the possibility for specific performance, injunctive action and damages, but will not necessarily be enforceable against or otherwise affect the company, especially if the company is not a party. The passing of a resolution by a vote in breach of a shareholders' agreement may well be a valid corporate act, even though the prejudiced shareholder may seek damages against the shareholder in breach of contract.

The result of a choice between both techniques will be very different from one country to another for a variety of reasons such as non-disclosure, available remedies, enforceability by or against the company and whether or not it can act to override statutory provisions or the Articles of Association.

8. Remedies Where a Shareholders' Resolution or Other Action Impairs the Rights of Minority Shareholders

In all of the countries covered by this book, shareholders have the right to challenge shareholders' resolutions which violate the law or the Articles of Association. Even though it may sometimes be difficult to determine whether the formal requirements for a valid resolution have been met (eg whether the meeting was correctly convened or the necessary majority was reached) or whether specific rights have been violated, these cases are of lesser interest in a comparative study like this. It is much more interesting to examine how minority shareholders can defend themselves against actions of the majority which, even though formally valid, nevertheless affect their rights and interests.

It would not be possible to specify succinctly the various types of conduct that could be complained of and which may affect minority shareholders. Common examples of such conduct might be:

- passing of a resolution to disapply pre-emption rights and subsequently issuing new capital in which issue the minority shareholder is not invited to participate and which significantly dilutes his holding;
- in the absence of such a resolution, but with general authority, to issue shares, making a new issue of shares at a price that the minority shareholder cannot afford to take up his entitlement;
- paying a management charge to a parent company as a disguised dividend thus diminishing the dividend entitlement of the minority shareholder;
- entrenchment of controlling shareholder directors through long term service contracts;
- through exercise of management control, entering into contracts with related parties other than on arm's length terms which may not require members' authorization or, if they do, which require only a simple majority.

As we have seen above, shareholders, either individually or as a specific minority, may have rights enshrined in national or regional legislation to overturn certain actions of the controlling shareholders or to force action to be taken where the majority refuse to act. In Austria, for example, we have seen that, particularly in relation to joint-stock companies, minority shareholders have a very extensive set of rights, in particular instances, to regulate an unlawful action/omission.

However, a number of other jurisdictions appear not to have a general underlying principle of oppression of minorities nor mechanisms to enable an effective long-term resolution to be obtained. In the United Kingdom, on the other hand, minority shareholders are entitled to petition the court for an order on the grounds that the company's affairs are being or have been conducted in a manner which is "unfairly prejudicial to the interests of its members generally or some part of its members ... or that any actual or proposed actual remission of the company ... is or would be so prejudicial". If the case can be established then the court has a wide range of powers to remedy the situation including a requirement that the prejudiced shareholder be bought out either by the other members or by the company itself.

In Ireland, there is a similar provision although the wording used is different. However, the position in the United States is quite contrary to the position in the United Kingdom and Republic of Ireland. Here the federal courts refuse to engage in disputes between shareholders, leaving it to the state courts to intervene. Even then, it would appear that state law will normally only be invoked if there is harm to the company as well as to the minority shareholders and there will be a difference in approach as between states. Malfeasance or some other form of impropriety would also need to be shown.

The position in civil law countries is just as varied. Germany recognizes some form of fiduciary duty as existing between shareholders, breach of which duty may be actionable. In Belgium, where the law has recently been changed in favour of minority shareholders, it is unclear precisely what is the basis of the new rights – whether they are founded in contract or equity. Other civil law jurisdictions, while perhaps recognizing some form of fiduciary duty, do not provide any general remedy for breach, although the Austrian report suggests that, though not expressly regulated, there might be some form of remedy for grave interference with implied rights even though there might not have been a breach of the constitution of the company or of specific law.

8.1 What are the requirements for such remedies?

In terms of general remedies UK law refers to conduct "unfairly prejudicial". Irish law refers to "oppression" or, as a separate ground, action in "disregard of a member's interests". In the Netherlands the law imposes on shareholders a duty to act reasonably and fairly; reference is made in the Civil Code to "abuse of power" and "abuse of majority power". However, this particular duty attaches only to shareholders, not the directors.

In Germany, reference is to a breach of fiduciary duty (*Treupflicht*) owed by one shareholder to another, the level of duty increasing according to the position and control of the aggressor. Indeed, it is the existence of a fiduciary relationship which appears to be the basis of any general underlying rights that may exist in civil law jurisdictions. The Belgian reporter commented on the current uncertainty as to the basic legal grounding of the newly extended rights introduced in that jurisdiction. Does the right to be treated fairly and equally as a shareholder stem from contract law or equity, the doctrine of good faith? Do rights exist as between shareholders or only as between directors and shareholders? The position appears somewhat unclear.

8.2 When do the courts accept these requirements?

Aggrieved shareholders must first of all show that they have *locus*.

Who can bring an action? In the United Kingdom, only registered members can normally bring an action on general unfair prejudice ground; it is not sufficient merely to show that one is beneficially entitled to the shares; nominee shareholders would need to be joined in any action. In the United Kingdom it was also previously the case that something which prejudiced the members as a whole would not necessarily be grounds for the bringing of a minority action. This position would obviously be open to abuse as a majority shareholder could be compensated in a manner not affecting it *qua* shareholder, for example through payment of a management charge as referred to above. The position was clarified in 1989 so that the relevant legislation now refers to conduct "prejudicial to the interests of its members generally or of *some part* of its members".

Irish law provides that any member may bring an action. In fact, it has been held that, in the case of "oppression", the plaintiff/petitioner need not be the one to have suffered; a member could bring an action in his capacity as director to protect other members. An action based on disregard of members' interests must be brought by a member and he must show that he has suffered in his capacity as member and not in any other capacity.

What actions can be complained of? In the Netherlands, the "reasonableness and fairness" principles need to be interpreted. As mentioned above, the remedy here lies only against co-shareholders *qua* shareholders and not against the management. Case law seems clear in the arena of conflicts of interest. Using one's powers to prefer one's personal interests to the detriment of the interests of the company (the members as a whole) is one situation which may give a cause of action. The general test is whether, in the circumstances and with proper consideration, the same decision could reasonably have been reached. The same concept would apply in the United Kingdom and Ireland. In each of these jurisdictions, it would be up to the courts to determine what is "reasonable" in the circumstances. Accordingly, each case would need to be regarded on its own merits. In jurisdictions such as Germany, where a fiduciary relationship exists between shareholders, conflicts of interest could also be the basis of an action. The existence of a fiduciary duty owed by directors to the members is well established in many jurisdictions. There is no reason why controlling shareholders (whether with actual power or merely the power to be obstructive) should not also be in the same position. They will be trustees of the other members' investment. In such a situation they cannot prefer their own interests.

But should there be a wider duty/responsibility for controlling shareholders? Certainly, evidence of general *mala fides* could be the basis for an action in many jurisdictions and, almost certainly, all jurisdictions where there is a suspicion of fraud. That apart, it might be considered inappropriate to impose a greater duty on shareholders beyond that which they have expressly agreed to accept under the terms of the constitution of the company; they are not in the same position as the management who are the appointees of and responsible to the members.

German case law suggests that whatever rights there may be are better defined in private companies as opposed to quoted companies. Perhaps this is because of the quasi-partnership nature of many private companies where a duty to act *bona fide* would generally apply. In quoted companies, shareholdings tend to be more widespread and the interests of investing institutions more likely to be protected so that they will have rights against the management but will have few responsibilities themselves.

8.3 What remedies are available to the claimant?

The remedy available in each case will normally depend on the facts and the gravity of the situation. In the United Kingdom, the remedies for a successful action under section 459, Companies Act 1985 are at the discretion of the court. In many jurisdictions the courts have the ability to order that the complainant's shares are bought in by the company (subject to company law restrictions on funds to be applied) or for the respondent to buy the minorities' shares. In a very severe case, the courts may order the dissolution/winding up of the company; but this is a draconian measure and, certainly in the United Kingdom would only be used where there was effectively a quasi-partnership where relations between the "partners" had broken down and were irretrievable. Examples of situations in which such an order could be made are:

- deadlock between the shareholders;
- lack of probity of directors, where controlling shareholder/directors disregard their duties as directors and run the business for their personal interests alone;
- breakdown of mutual trust and confidence;
- failure of substratum where the business cannot be run as intended, for example where the company failed to obtain a vital patent;
- exclusion from management.

The winding up remedy would only be available where the court considered it "just and equitable" to do so, this concept being derived from partnership law as that is one of the statutory grounds for dissolution of a partnership under English law.

In Switzerland, it would appear that the buying-out mechanism and dissolution are remedies available only as a consequence of a derivative action.

In some jurisdictions, such as Luxembourg, the courts could order the appointment of a receiver/administrator to take over the running of the business and find a buyer for it; again, a draconian measure.

In some jurisdictions, a distinction is made between private and quoted/listed companies, so the dissolution remedy in Germany, for example, is available only in relation to a GmbH. The right to demand to be bought out is an automatic right of shareholders in a private company (Lda) in Portugal in certain circumstances, such as merger, new issues of shares available to third parties, change of objects, etc.

Injunctive relief is an interesting area. Pre-emptive action will, often, only be taken by the courts where there is a prospective breach of law or of the constitution of the company with very serious consequences. In Switzerland, injunctive action is only available under cantonal, and not federal, law. In the United States, pre-emptive action is possible if the applicant can show a strong case that is likely to succeed on its merits, if the balance of equity lies in the applicant's favour and where irreparable harm is likely in the absence of a restraining order, that is to say restitution would not be possible. However, where proposed action is unlawful, injunctive action will be possible regardless of whether or not the damage could be undone at a later stage.

Specific performance is another possible remedy where the management, for example, refuses to take action against one of their own; this being, effectively, a derivative action enforcing the rights of the company.

Both injunctive relief and specific performance would tend to be interim measures and not exclusive of other remedies, because such action is quite draconian and indicative of a breakdown of trust between the litigating parties.

Table A summarizes the remedies which may be available in the various jurisdictions reported on. But, be warned, these remedies may not be available to all claimants and the right may be very limited.

Table A Summary of remedies available

Country	Void resolution	Void transaction	Injunctive action	Specific performance	Damages	Buy-out	Receiver	Dissolution
Austria	yes		yes		yes			
Belgium	yes	yes	yes	yes	yes	yes	yes	yes
Finland	yes		yes		yes	yes		yes
France	yes				yes		yes	yes
Germany	yes		yes	yes	yes	yes*		
Ireland	yes	yes	yes			yes		yes
Italy	yes							
Luxembourg	yes		yes		yes			
Netherlands	yes		limited right			yes		
Portugal	yes	yes	yes		yes	yes		
Spain	yes	yes	yes		yes	yes		
Sweden	yes				yes	yes		yes
Switzerland	yes	yes	yes		yes	yes		yes
UK	yes	yes	yes	yes	yes	yes	yes	yes
United States	yes		yes	yes	yes			yes

* GmbH only

9. Specific Protection if the Company is Controlled by Another Company

The formation and ever-increasing establishment of company groups is an important feature of today's economy. National or international groups of companies expand their activities (or restrict them to their core business), owners of private companies wish to cooperate with a strong partner or to retire and sell their shares to a competitor. These are only some of the cases where control in one company (let us call it "Company A") passes to another company ("Company B").

Few problems arise where 100% of the shares in Company A change ownership. Where, however, this is not the case, the interests of the minority shareholders of Company A conflict with the interests of the new controlling shareholder, Company B. When acquiring the controlling interest, Company B may wish to pay a premium to a controlling shareholder but not to other shareholders who also wish to sell their shares. In day to day life, Company B has an interest in passing business opportunities of Company A to itself and to shift profits and losses between Company A and itself by charging a "management fee" or higher prices for supplies, etc. The reports show various approaches to resolve these problems.

9.1 What are the rights and remedies of a shareholder of Company A if Company B gains control over it (by acquiring the majority of its shares or otherwise)?

A number of countries do not grant minority shareholders any specific rights when control is acquired by another company (Austria, Italy, Luxembourg, Netherlands).

Another approach is to grant to the minority a right to be bought out by Company B (which is, in most cases, combined with a right of Company B to buy out the minority shareholders of Company A even if they do not want to sell). The situation seems to be quite similar in Belgium, Finland, Ireland, Portugal and Sweden where this right (or obligation) of the minority shareholders is triggered where Company B acquires at least 90% (Ireland: 80%) of Company A's shares. In Finland, Ireland, Portugal and Sweden this rule also seems to apply where Company A is a private company. Lower thresholds are provided for by the laws of Spain (25% and 50%) and the UK (30% and an additional 2% where the previous shareholding was between 30% and 50%).

Since most of the reports do not elaborate on the price which must be paid to the selling minority shareholder, it is unclear to what extent they can participate in a "block premium" paid by Company B to the previous holder of the controlling shares. Only the United States report explains that in some states, the block holder may required by the court to redistribute the premium among the minority holders. The Switzerland report expressly states that no right to participate in such premium exists.

The German legal system distinguishes between public and private companies, on the one hand, and contractual and *de facto* "concerns" on the other hand which makes the system somewhat complicated. While the formation of a contractual group (eg by way of a management contract) gives the minority the right to choose between a guaranteed dividend or a right to be bought out, the mere acquisition of control requires a resolution by the shareholders of Company A in order to be valid (in the case of a private company, the prevailing opinion even requires their unanimous consent which, obviously, gives the minority a very strong position).

Finally, Portugal combines the 90% threshold (see above) with the "German" right of choice between a guaranteed dividend and a buy out.

9.2 What are the shareholder's rights and remedies when Company B exerts its control over Company A in a way which damages the interests of the latter?

In almost all countries covered by the reports, no specific protection of the minority shareholders of Company A is provided where Company B exercises its control to the disadvantage of Company A. In these countries, the rights of the minority are limited to those discussed under 8.

One exception is Ireland where minority shareholders can apply to the High Court to have Company A wound up if "this is just and equitable" or if the company's affairs are being exercised in a manner oppressive to any member or in disregard of his interest as a member. This remedy is appropriate specifically for smaller private companies.

In Switzerland, a majority shareholder who forces its will and decisions upon Company A may be deemed a corporate body of the latter (board of directors) and, therefore, be liable in the same way.

In the USA, a minority shareholder of Company A may sue Company B for any damage done to the subsidiary if there is no independence between parent stockholder and the subsidiary (double derivative theory).

We have already seen above that Portugal takes an approach which is similar to Germany's approach. In fact, the German law of company groups has been used as a model for the Brazilian legislation of 1986, and the Brazilian system, in turn, was the basis for the Portuguese legislation of 1986. It is, therefore, not surprising that both Germany and Portugal give Company A the right to be compensated for any disadvantages arising from Company B exercising its influence to the detriment of Company A. The practical problem is, obviously, to determine which disadvantage was caused by a given measure, that is, what the position of Company A would be had the measure not been taken. For German private companies, therefore (where this problem is not regulated by statutory law), courts have developed the rule that a dominating corporation is completely barred from injuring a dependent corporation. In case of breach, Company A can seek to reverse the measures, have the measure ceased and also seek damages. The minority shareholders of Company A can start a derivative action (*actio pro socio*) to pursue the claims that Company A may have against Company B.

Conclusion

Generally, in all jurisdictions reported on, the principle of majority rule applies while, at the same time, recognizing that the minority requires a certain level of protection from the excesses of the majority. It is not for the courts to intervene in the normal running of a business; that is something which is delegated to the management which owes duties to the members. If the management abuses its position then it is, generally, open to the membership to take action for breach of duty. The problem arises when the controlling shareholders, either directly or via the management which they control, take action which serves only their interests, which disregards the interests of the minority and their investment or which, in some cases, is positively intended to harm their interests. The minority deserves some level of protection. The problem for the legislature and for the judiciary is how to strike a balance between the competing interests; excess regulation will be an undue fetter on the company's ability to function, whereas insufficient protection will discourage investment in businesses. This point is particularly important when considering the high level of investment made by institutions on the various stock exchanges around the world. Where the law is seen as insufficient to protect institutional investment, these markets will tend to regulate themselves.

The law on protection of minority shareholders is a mixture of basic corporate constitutional law and general civil and trust law. The level of protection offered to minorities varies significantly from one jurisdiction to another. None the less, by and large, equity has its place, however described, in almost every jurisdiction, although this does not necessarily mean that the majority owes a fiduciary duty to the minority. Minority or non-controlling shareholders in a company will not, necessarily, be able to obtain relief merely because they can show *mala fides* or negligence on the part of other shareholders or the management. While the Articles of Association of a company may constitute a contract between shareholders, it is often the case that rights are limited in their scope and even if a right has not been observed, the complainants may hold too small a percentage of the voting rights to have the necessary *locus* to bring an action. In a private company which has the character of a *quasi* partnership, shareholders, at a practical level, would be well advised to document their rights *inter se* wherever possible in the form of a shareholders' agreement giving them additional, contractual rights.

The law in this area is, potentially, a minefield. The rights of the minority can be contained in a series of specific rights. Alternatively, or perhaps in addition, there may be a general equitable layer of protection the applicability of which and the remedies available thereunder need to be determined according to the merits of the particular case, thus exposing the parties to the action to the discretion of the judiciary, guided by case law.

aija

AUSTRIA

Christoph Petsch

Petsch, Frosch & Partners
Vienna

PROTECTION OF MINORITY SHAREHOLDERS

***EDITOR* MATTHIAS W. STECHER**

AUSTRIA

Christoph Petsch

1. Majority Requirements for Shareholders' Resolutions

1.1 What are the majority requirements in general?

Joint stock company According to Article 113 AktG,[1] shareholders' resolutions in the general meeting of shareholders require a simple majority of the votes polled unless the law or the articles of association require a greater majority or other requirements exist.

Private limited company The Private Limited Company Act (GmbHG)[2] has in its Article 39 para. 1 an analogous provision which basically requires a simple majority.

1.2 Which resolutions require a greater majority?

Joint stock company In joint stock companies a majority of three-quarters of the share capital represented in the shareholders' meeting is required in the following most important cases:

---

1 AktG – *Bundesgesetz über Aktiengesellschaften* (Corporation Act)
2 GmbHG – *Gesetz über Gesellschaften mit beschränkter Haftung* (Private Limited Company Act).

- modification of the Articles of Association (Article 146, para. 1 AktG);
- ordinary capital increases (Article 149, para. 1 AktG);
- creation of authorized capital (Article 196, para. 2 AktG);
- capital increases by capitalization of reserves, profits and other funds (nominal capital increase) (Article 2, para. 1 KapBG);[3]
- non-application of pre-emptive rights (Article 153 para. 3 AktG);
- ordinary capital reduction (Article 175, para. 1 AktG);
- issue of convertible or dividend bonds (Article 174, para. 1 AktG). The same applies to the granting of special dividend rights (*Genußrechte*);
- non-application of pre-emption rights on an issue of convertible bonds, dividend bonds and special dividend rights (Article 174, para. 4 AktG);
- dissolution of the company (Article 203, para. 1 figure 2 AktG);
- continuation of a dissolved company until the conclusion of the liquidation proceedings (Article 215 AktG);
- amalgamation (*Verschmelzung durch Aufnahme*) (Article 220 para. 2 AktG). This kind of merger consists of a fusion of companies via universal succession without a liquidation taking place;
- consolidation (*Verschmelzung durch Neubildung*) (Article 233, para. 1 AktG). In such a merger the merged companies form a new company which acquires the assets of the transferring companies via universal succession, thereby granting their shareholders adequate share rights;
- merger of a joint stock company with a private limited company (Article 234, para. 2 AktG). In such a case the joint stock company takes over the private limited company;
- de-merger of the company (Article 6, para. 1 SpaltG);[4]
- conversion of a joint stock company into a private limited company (Article 239, para. 2 AktG).

Private limited company In private limited companies a majority of three-quarters of the share capital represented in the shareholders' meeting is required especially in the following cases:

- amendment of the Articles of Association (Article 50 GmbHG). The articles of association can provide further requirements. Since the increase or reduction of the original capital requires the amendment of the articles (Articles 52, para. 1 and 54, para. 1 GmbHG), these resolutions can only be adopted with a special majority;
- premature revocation of the appointment of a member of the supervisory board (Article 30b, para. 3 GmbHG);
- complete sale of the company's assets by a single legal transaction during liquidation proceedings (Article 90, para. 4 GmbHG);
- amalgamation into a joint stock company (Article 234, para. 3 AktG);
- conversion into a joint stock company (Article 245, para. 2 AktG).

---

3 KapBG – *Kapitalberichtigungsgesetz* (Capital Adjustment Act).

4 SpaltG – *Spaltungsgesetz* (Demerger Act).

Unanimity is necessary in the following cases:

- an amendment of the objects of the business requires a unanimous resolution unless the Articles of Association have provided otherwise (Article 50, para. 3 GmbHG);
- a unanimous resolution regarding the merger of the transferring company is also necessary in the case of an amalgamation with a second private limited company (Article 96, para. 1 second phrase GmbHG);
- a resolution to increase a shareholder's obligation or rights as provided by the Articles can only be adopted with the consent of all shareholders concerned. This applies in particular to resolutions which seek to amend provisions regarding the extent of the liability to pay the original capital share (Article 50, para. 4 GmbHG).

A majority of 90% of the original capital is needed in two cases:

- conversion by merger which transfers the assets of the private limited company to the main shareholder (Article 2, para. 1 UmwG);[5]
- conversion through the transfer of assets to a mercantile partnership or a limited partnership requires a majority of three-quarters of the votes represented at the meeting and the consent of 90% of the overall share capital (Article 7, para. 2 UmwG).

1.3 To what extent can they be modified by the Articles of Association?

Joint stock company In all of the above-mentioned cases the majority requirements can be increased.

In the case of a conversion under the Conversion Act, it is also necessary that a sufficient number of the shareholders who were absent in the general meeting give within three months' certified notice of consent so that a majority of nine-tenths of the whole share capital is attained.

In the following cases the Articles of Association can merely require a simple majority:

- ordinary capital increase (Article 149, para. 1 AktG);
- capital increase by capitalization of reserves, profits and other funds (nominal capital increase) (Article 2, para. 1 KapBG);
- issue of convertible or dividend bonds (Article 174, para. 1 AktG) and of special dividend rights;
- amalgamation (Article 220, para. 2 AktG). The Articles of Association of a company which takes over another company can provide the same majority as for a capital increase.

Private limited company In all of the above mentioned cases the majority requirements can be increased.

---

5 UmwG – *Umwandlungsgesetz* (Conversion Act).

In the following cases the Articles of Association can also provide a mere simple majority:

- appointment of a member to the supervisory board (Article 50, para. 2 GmbHG);
- reduction of the remuneration of the managers or members of the supervisory board (Articles 50, para. 2 and 31, para. 1 GmbHG);
- premature revocation of a member's appointment to the supervisory board (Article 30b, para. 3 GmbHG).

In the following cases the articles of association can reduce the majority requirement to three-quarters of the original capital:

- amendment of the objects of the business (Article 50, para. 3 GmbHG).
- merger of the transferring company in the case of an amalgamation with another private limited company (Article 96, para. 1 second phrase GmbHG).

2. Influence on the Decision-Making Process

2.1 Do minority shareholders have the right to call a shareholders' meeting?

Joint stock company Under Article 106, para. 2 AktG, a minority of 5% of the share capital is entitled to call the shareholders' meeting by indicating in writing the purposes and reasons for such. It is normally the board of management which convenes the general meeting. If the management board does not grant the request to call the general meeting, the minority has the right (Article 106, para. 4 AktG) to file a petition with the competent commercial court requesting that the court authorize the shareholders themselves to call the shareholders' meeting. Simultaneously, the court must determine the chairman of the meeting. The right to call the meeting is independent of the right to vote.

Private limited company Pursuant to Article 37, para. 1 GmbHG, a minority of 10% or an even smaller part of the original capital (if so provided in the articles) is entitled to call a general meeting by indicating in writing the purpose of the meeting. If the management board does not grant the request or if such a board does not exist the minority itself can call the general meeting by indicating the relevant circumstances.

2.2 Do they have the right to put matters on the agenda?

Joint stock company A minority of 5% is also entitled (Article 106, para. 3 AktG) to request in writing (indicating the purposes and the reasons) that further items be put on the agenda (supplement of the agenda) or that such items be brought before a shareholders' meeting already convened. The general meeting can only take decisions on a matter of which the shareholders were duly notified. Matters which require a decision by a simple majority must be notified a week before the day of the general meeting. If the matter requires a majority of three-quarters of the represented share capital (eg capital increase, exclusion of the subscription right), the notification has to be made at least a fortnight before the date of the general meeting.

The point of the agenda "discharge" covers the demand for the voting on a special examination but not the voting on claims for compensation against members of the managing board or the supervisory board. These items must be announced separately. Only after completion of the rest of the agenda can demands for the inclusion of matters not yet announced be put to the meeting. If such a demand is not met, the minority can file an application with the court stating that it is itself authorized to raise the items on the supplementary agenda.

Private limited company A minority of 10%, or an even smaller part of the original capital if so provided in the Articles, is entitled (Article 38, para. 3 GmbHG) to request in a signed petition, indicating the reasons, that items be included and published in the notice of the next general meeting. Such demands must be raised within three days after the posting of the notice of the general meeting.

3. Rights of Information, Independent Auditing and Supervision

3.1 To what extent do the (minority) shareholders have a right to be informed on company matters?

Joint stock company According to Articles 125, para. 6, 126 para. 2 and 127, para. 2 AktG, every shareholder has the right to examine, within 14 days before the annual shareholders' meeting and on the business premises, the published annual accounts, the consolidated financial statement (Article 244 HGB),[6] the report of the supervisory board, the proposal of the managing board for profit distribution and the report on the financial situation of the company. The shareholder can have an expert examine these documents. The ordinary general meeting takes place annually. It usually takes note of the annual accounts, decides on the profit distribution, discharges the members of the managing and the supervisory boards and appoints the auditors of the company.

Every shareholder who takes part in the general meeting can examine (Article 110, para. 1 phrase 3 AktG) the register of shareholders before the first voting. The names, domiciles, amounts of represented shares and share types for each shareholder present or represented are indicated in the register of members.

Every shareholder has the right to examine the register of shareholders where, according to Article 61, para. 1 AktG, the named holders of shares are registered. Only registered shareholders are considered shareholders of the company.

---

6 HGB – *Handelsgesetzbuch* (Commercial Code).

Private limited company. When the annual accounts and the report on the financial situation of the company have been drawn up, the management board is required to send copies to every shareholder without delay. The shareholder has the right to inspect the books and documents of the company during the 14 days before the shareholders' meeting in order that consideration of the annual accounts takes place within the term fixed for a shareholders' written resolution. A provision that the shareholders do not have the right of inspection, that the right has to be exercised within a shorter period or which creates any other limitations is only permitted by law if a supervisory board is appointed (Article 22, para. 2 GmbHG). In such cases every shareholder must immediately receive the report concerning the financial situation of the company, the proposal of the managers for the distribution of profits, the audit report and the group audit report.

3.2 Do they have the right to demand independent auditing or to initiate the supervision of company matters by an independent institution?

Joint stock company According to Article 118, para. 2 AktG, a minority of 10% of the share capital is entitled to file an petition with the commercial court demanding that a specially arranged examination be carried out by a nominated auditor if the general assembly has refused to nominate auditors to examine an event pertinent to the founding, or a matter of management, which does not date back more than two years. The goal in such a case would be to determine through external independent auditors whether the leading organs of the company had fulfilled or neglected their duties and whether they have acted in the interests of the company and its shareholders. The result of the special examination can imply compensation rights against certain organ members to be raised afterwards. Normally a general meeting decides, with a simple majority, on the special examination and the nomination of the auditors. The petition to nominate special auditors need not be expressly announced in the agenda if the shareholders' meeting is to decide on the discharge of the leading organs.

The petition of the minority has to be granted only if the applicant is able to show evidence of dishonesty or severe violations of the law or of the Articles of Association.

According to Article 118, para. 3 AktG, a minority of 10% of the share capital is entitled to file a petition with the court for the nomination of auditors other than those nominated in the general meeting. The nomination of other auditors does not depend on other requirements, but the court shall not grant such demand of the minority unless it is satisfied that there are grounds for concern regarding the auditors nominated by the general meeting. This right must be exercised within two weeks following the date of the general meeting.

According to Article 270, para. 3 HGB, a minority of 10% of the share capital is entitled to file an application with the court that other auditors be nominated if there is an important complaint against the auditor nominated by the general meeting. Normally the auditors are nominated by the ordinary general assembly for the next business year. The applicant shareholders must lodge a protest against the nomination at the time of the decision of the general meeting. The application must be filed within a month from the nomination of the auditors by the general meeting.

Private limited company If a demand to nominate expert auditors to examine the last annual accounts has been refused by a shareholders' resolution (Article 45, para. 1 GmbHG), a minority of 10% or of a nominal amount of 10 million schillings can file an petition with the commercial court which has jurisdiction for the business seat of the company to appoint one or several auditors. The shareholders must show dishonesty or that gross violations of the law or of the Articles of Association have taken place. During the audit the applicant shareholders cannot assign their shares without the consent of the company. The auditors have the right to access all books, documents, invoices and stocks, the right to demand information from managers, members of the supervisory board and every employee entrusted with keeping company information, and the right to obtain explanations regarding the accuracy of the last annual accounts. Finally, they may investigate the company cash in hand, securities, debt documents and merchandise. The requested explanations and information must be given without delay and must be precise and correct.

4. Capital Increases and Distributions

4.1 To what extent do (minority) shareholders have the right to participate in capital increases?

Joint stock company To the minority shareholder, as to every other shareholder, new shares must be issued on his demand, in proportion to his existing shareholding. For the exercise of such a right a period of at least two weeks is required.

The managing board is required to publish the issue price together with the term in the official gazettes.

This subscription right exists in the case of an ordinary capital increase with approved capital, but not in the case of a conditional capital increase. With a nominal capital increase, ie, the conversion of capital resources into share capital, the new shares automatically accrue to the shareholders by virtue of law. The subscription right exists for all types of shares. Every shareholder can demand the allotment of convertible dividend bonds and special dividend rights (Article 174, para. 4 AktG). Exclusion of the subscription right requires a majority of 75% of the share capital and requires objective grounds (eg new business possibilities, reorganization of the company). The exclusion must be clearly notified at least two weeks before the shareholders' meeting.

Private limited company In the absence of a different provision in the Articles of Association or in the resolution regarding the capital increase, the shareholders have the right to take over the new shares within four weeks from the day of the resolution (Article 52, para. 3 GmbHG). The shareholders are entitled to new shares in proportion to the originally held shares.

The subscription right can, however, be excluded with a majority of 75% of the share capital. The admissibility of such exclusion must be examined above all from the point of view of the principle of equal treatment. Also to be considered carefully are the interests of the company that are thereby infringed, as well as those of the concerned shareholder. The principles of necessity and proportionality have been developed by the leading cases. The subscription right can therefore particularly be excluded if the aim pursued by the capital increase cannot be reached otherwise, but its realization is indicated by objective reasons in the interest of the company.

4.2 Do minority shareholders have the right to demand dividends or other distributions?

Joint stock company Every shareholder has the right to receive dividends, defined as the distribution of the net profit shown in the annual accounts (Article 52 AktG). Normally the managing board prepares the annual statement of accounts which will then be adopted with the approval of the supervisory board. If authorized by the Articles of Association (Article 126, para. 3 AktG), the shareholders' meeting can take a decision on the partial or total transfer of the net profit to reserves. As soon as the general meeting has determined the distribution, the shareholder has a right to claim the distribution from the company. The amount of the claim depends on the nominal amount of his participation and his membership in a certain type of share.

A minority shareholder is by principle not entitled to demand payment of dividends. The Articles of Association can provide, however, that the shareholders will receive extra dividends (bonus, super-dividend) under certain conditions. In the case of shares that are not paid in the same proportion the shareholders receive an anticipated maximum dividend of 4% corresponding to the effectively paid-in share (Article 53 AktG).

Private limited company According to Article 82, para. 1 GmbHG, shareholders cannot claim back their capital shares. As long as the company exists they only have the right to receive the net earnings (shown in the balance sheet as surplus of assets over liabilities) so long as the shareholder is not excluded from distribution by the Articles of Association or by a shareholders' resolution. The distribution of the profit occurs, in the absence of a specific provision in the articles, in proportion to the paid-up capital shares. Interest for shareholders may be neither stipulated nor paid out.

The distribution of profit is not guaranteed and can therefore only be demanded if its refusal is not justified by objective reasons, not in the interests of the company or is in the exclusive interest of the majority shareholders.

5. Derivative Actions

5.1 Can (minority) shareholders enforce rights that the company has against other shareholders, directors, or third parties?

Joint stock company According to Article 122, para. 1 AktG, a minority of 10% of the share capital can demand that the company raise valid claims against the founders, members of the managing or supervisory boards or other persons responsible for the foundation, post-formation or management for actions taken by the responsible persons, when such actions are not based on decisions of the general meeting. The claims are made on behalf of the company and not on behalf of the demanding shareholders. If the claims stem from an examination report, even a minority of 5% of the share capital is entitled to propose a motion. Normally, such claims are raised if the general meeting has taken the decision by a simple majority. If the agenda of the forthcoming general meeting already contains the assertion of compensation claims or the report of special auditors (Article 121, para. 3 AktG), a special announcement of the minority demand is not necessary. However, the announcement of the agenda item "discharge" is not sufficient. If there is no connection with an announced agenda item the minority must demand in a timely manner (seven days) the announcement (Article 106, para. 3 AktG) of a corresponding agenda item or must demand the legal authorization of an announcement. In case of necessity the minority can file a petition with the court (Article 106, para. 2 AktG) to obtain the authorization to call a general meeting. The shareholders must prove that they have held shares for at least three months before the day of the general meeting which refused the assertion of compensation claims and that they have deposited their share certificates with the court or in a notary's office.

According to Article 122, para. 2 AktG, a minority of 10% of the share capital can designate court nominated persons to prosecute the claims of the company. The court must grant the petition if the claim is not obviously unjustified.

Pursuant to Article 124 AktG, a minority of 10% of the share capital is entitled to oppose a waiver or a settlement of compensation claims raised by the company on the demand of the minority. As long as the minority shareholders do not approve, a waiver or a settlement it is not valid. The waiver or the settlement must basically be decided by the general meeting.

Private limited company A minority of 10% or of the nominal amount of 10 million schillings of the share capital is entitled to raise compensation claims which the company has on the basis of Articles 10, 25, 27 and 33 GmbHG against the managers and members of the supervisory board if the prosecution of these claims has been refused by shareholders' resolution or if a petition was not submitted to a resolution, even if the managers were notified in a timely manner. The minority must file the suit on behalf of the company within three months from the day of the adopted or frustrated resolution. During the litigation the suing shareholders cannot assign their capital shares without the company's consent. On demand of the defendant the plaintiffs must lodge security for imminent damages which the court can fix by discretion. If the lawsuit was unjustified the applicants are liable for damages to the company if they acted with intent or with gross negligence (Article 48 GmbHG).

A legal action of a shareholder as an *actio pro socio* is discussed by the doctrine but so far the courts have not recognized such a right. According to the legal comments the legislature had the clear intention of limiting the right of action to a certain participation quota and not to offer rights for individual shareholders.

6. Other "Formal" Rights

6.1 Do minority shareholders have any other specific rights comparable to those mentioned in 2–5 above?

The shareholders of a joint stock company are additionally vested with the following rights:

- Pursuant to Article 206, para. 2 AktG, a minority of 5% of the share capital can file an application with the court to nominate and remove a liquidator for an important reason.
- According to Article 211, para. 3 and para. 5 AktG, a minority of 5% or 5 million schillings of the share capital can file a petition with the court that a final examination of the annual accounts and opening balance of the liquidation be ordered for important reasons.
- A minority of 5% of the share capital is entitled to annul a decision of the shareholders' meeting (Article 196, para. 2 AktG) regarding depreciation, write-offs, reserves or special reserves which exceed the degree admissible by the law or the articles of association.
- A minority holding at least 10% or 20 million schillings, and, under certain conditions, 5% or 10 million schillings of the share capital of a subsidiary company which is only included in foreign group accounts can demand from the group the preparation of separate accounts for the various parts of the group. Such demand should occur at least six months before the end of the business year (Article 245, para. 1 last phrase HGB).
- A minority of 10% of the share capital can file a petition with the court (Article 88, para. 4 AktG) that a delegated member of the supervisory board be removed for an important reason.
- A minority of 10% of the share capital can demand (Article 125, para. 7 AktG) the adjournment of the shareholders' meeting at which the annual statement of accounts, the group accounts, the profit distribution and the discharge are to be considered once certain entries in the annual accounts are criticized.
- Pursuant to Article 270, para. 3 HGB, a minority of 10 million schillings of the share capital can file a petition with the court for another auditor to be nominated if there are well-founded concerns regarding the person who was nominated auditor by the shareholders' meeting (eg lack of technical qualification, concerns of prejudice). The petitioning shareholders must have lodged a protest against the nomination decision in the general meeting.

- According to Articles 43, 84 para. 4, 99 and 100, para. 4 AktG a minority of 20% may object to a decision of the shareholders' meeting regarding the waiver or settlement of compensation claims against founders, persons liable with them (auditors), members of the management or supervisory board and other persons who exercised harmful influence in order to obtain a special advantage.
- According to Article 87, para. 1 AktG, a minority of one-third of the share capital can elect a member of the supervisory board if at least three members are elected at the same time and the vote of each member occurs separately.

In a private limited company the minority shareholders have, in addition to the above, the following rights:

- a minority of 10% of the share capital can file a petition with the court to dismiss a member of the supervisory board for an important reason (Article 30c, para. 4 GmbHG).
- pursuant to Article 89, para. 2 GmbHG, a minority of 10% or the nominal amount of 10 million schillings (or an even smaller part if so provided in the articles) can, for an important reason, file a petition with the court to appoint liquidators in place of those already appointed by the company.
- in large private limited companies which have supervisory boards, a minority of 5% can, for an important reason, lodge a protest against the selection of the auditors of the annual accounts (Article 270, para. 3 HGB).
- if at least three members of the supervisory board are to be elected at the same general meeting a minority of one-third of the original capital represented in the general meeting can demand that the election of each member take place separately.
- with cause, and with a court order any shareholder (including minority shareholders), is entitled to call for the dismissal of a manager who is also a shareholder (Article 16, para. 2 GmbHG).

7. Extension of These Rights by Statute or Shareholders' Agreements

7.1 Can the Articles of Association provide for additional rights of the minority shareholders? If not, can such rights be provided for in shareholders' agreements? Are these options commonly used?

Joint stock company The Articles of Association can provide additional rights even for minority shareholders. Since the supervisory board nominates the members of the management board it is important to have a representative in this organ. The right to appoint up to one-third of all supervisory board members who represent the shareholders can be reserved to certain shareholders. These members can normally only be removed by the designating shareholders. Only for important reasons would a minority shareholder also have a right to recall the member. Furthermore, important resolutions can require the approval by certain and even minority shareholders because multiple-vote shares are forbidden by law without exception (Article 12 AktG). Such rights can be also provided for in shareholders' agreements. These options are used in formerly state-owned companies which have been step-by-step privatized but where the Austrian state still insists on retaining influence. There are no statistics as to the extent to which additional rights of minority shareholders are stipulated by shareholders' agreements. It is, however, not common.

Pure agreements between shareholders such as voting trust agreements are effective and valid unless they are not *contra bonos mores* or detrimental to the company. No special form is required for such agreements. Such instruments can, of course, also be used to strengthen the rights of minority shareholders. Such agreements however, commit only the shareholders and not the company. This means that a vote which infringes the shareholders' agreement is valid and also that the avoidance of such a shareholders' resolution is excluded. Although it is possible to file an action to enforce such agreements it will normally fail from the beginning because the vote will take place before the court has rendered a definite decision. An interim injunction cannot normally be used as remedy because specific performance is inappropriate. It is therefore strongly advisable to secure shareholders' agreements through penalty stipulations.

Private limited company Only additional rights ("privileges") provided to the minority shareholders by the Articles of Association obligate the company.[7] An explicit and complete definition of these rights is required. It is, for instance, possible to confer upon a shareholder more voting rights ("rights of domination"), higher profits than he would have in conformity with his capital share, or a fixed profit ("economic rights"). A shareholder may also have the right to be a manager. Article 30c, para. 1 GmbHG offers the possibility of conferring the right to appoint members of the supervisory board to certain shareholders or the owners of certain capital shares. Since the overwhelming number of companies adopt standard articles and the minimum corporate capital, additional rights of minority shareholders are rarely stipulated.

As far as agreements between shareholders are concerned, the legal environment corresponds to the outline given above regarding the joint stock company.

8. Remedies Where a Shareholders' Resolution or Other Action Impairs the Rights of Minority Shareholders

8.1 What are the requirements for such remedies?

Remedies for the infringement of minority shareholders' rights require a violation of legal provisions or the Articles of Association. Remedies are also available for resolutions or actions which fundamentally interfere with the rights of minority shareholders. Even though not expressly regulated, such actions include disregarding the object of the company, the principle of equality or duties of loyalty.

---

7 NZ 1990, 35.

Shareholders must be loyal to the company.[8] The level of this duty depends on the real structure of the company and the power base in each case.[9] Generally a shareholder is obliged not to damage the company. For private limited companies the leading cases now adopt the principle that there is also a duty of loyalty between shareholders.[10] The doctrine may also apply to shareholders in joint stock companies as well.

8.2 When do the courts of your country accept these requirements?

Violations of the main object of the company do not at the present time suffice as a ground for nullification. Within the framework of admissible modification of the articles, the shareholders have a (renounceable) right of equal treatment. If a resolution violates this principle it may be annulled.[11] The order for equal treatment does not forbid a differentiation but rather only an arbitrary unequal treatment.[12] Such arbitrariness exists if the unequal treatment has no objective justification.[13] This is the case, for instance, where not all shareholders participate equally in a concealed distribution of profits. On the other hand, it is admissible to privilege shareholders who make additional contributions.

Votes in breach of good faith are not null and void but may be voidable.[14] The duty of loyalty includes the obligation to respect the interests of the company, which includes both the purpose of the company and the interests of all other shareholders. A special case is Article 195, para. 2 AktG which allows a resolution to be annulled if a shareholder exercises his right to vote with the intent to obtain for himself or a third person special advantages thereby damaging the company or its shareholders. An example of this was a case where certain shareholders acted in concert to engineer a take over of the going concern of a company.[15] In another case no unjustified special advantage was found when a shareholder voted for the employment of his son in the company as there was adequate need, he had the required qualifications and the employment was at a reasonable salary.[16]

Otherwise it is, however, not possible to define the nature or the extent of a general duty of loyalty. Most importantly, there is no principle which is generally applicable for all elements of a resolution.

The Supreme Court examines infringements of shareholders' membership rights under the criteria of necessity and reasonableness.[17] Therefore, the legal pre-emption rights of shareholders on the occasion of a capital increase are part of the gen-

---

8 JBl 1989, 253.
9 JBL 1989, 253.
10 JBL 1992, 597; EvBl 1992/103; WBl 1989, 222; SZ 60/285.
11 SZ 54/15; SZ 53/172; SZ 52/158; SZ 37/35; SZ 29/52; and SZ 6/263.
12 SZ 54/15; SZ 53/172.
13 Compare apart from SZ 54/15 and SZ 52/158 also SZ 29/52.
14 JBl 1989, 253; EvBl 1992/103; GesRZ 1984, 217.
15 SZ 27/276, compare BGHZ 76, 352.
16 JBl 1989, 253.
17 GesRZ 1986, 38; SZ 53/172.

eral membership rights. The non-application of pre-emption rights must be in the interests of the company and only for justifiable means. The defendant bears the burden of proof to show that there are circumstances which justify an infringement of the membership right.

In cases of decisions which do not involve infringement of membership rights, but concern special issues such as matters of management, the shareholders are strictly bound to follow the purposes of the company.[18] Since such decisions are often guided by considerations of expediency, the shareholders have wide latitude in evaluation which is only limited where the purpose of the company is interfered with. Legal control is therefore reduced to questions concerning the abuse of discretion.[19] Such an abuse of discretion arises, for example, when, in pursuit of his own interests, a shareholder vetos a decision to extend the company activities as he wants to carry on this business on his own.

At the bottom of the scale of the voidable decisions, which neither interfere with the membership rights of single shareholders nor frustrate the purpose of the company, are decisions regarding the distribution of profits. In principle, no one is obliged to vote in favour of the retention of profits even if it is contrary to a legal or contractual provision or if the retention is urgently required in the interests of the company.

8.3 What remedies are available to the claimant?

Joint stock company Pursuant to Article 195, para. 1 AktG, a shareholder is entitled to demand the annulment of shareholders' resolutions. With this act of avoidance defects in the resolutions are legally asserted. In such a case the aim is to set aside a valid resolution as, for example, in the cases of breach of the fiduciary duty mentioned above. Avoidance grounds are, for instance, an incorrect counting of votes, wrongful exclusion of a voting right or a mistaken exchange rate in merger transactions. Shareholders who are present in the shareholders' meeting must lodge a protest in the minutes (Article 195, para. 2 AktG). Absent shareholders only have a right to avoid the resolution if they were wrongfully excluded from the meeting, if they were not called duly to the meeting, or if a resolution item was not announced properly. Grounds for avoidance must be raised within one month from the shareholders' meeting or such resolutions will remain valid. The court of first instance in commercial matters has jurisdiction.

Compensation claims can only be raised if the shareholder himself and not the company suffered damage. In most cases the shareholder suffers damage only indirectly, whereas the direct damage is found in the company assets.

The winding up of the company can only be decided by a shareholders' resolution with a qualified majority. Beyond this the single shareholder has no right to dissolve the company by termination. Such a right is not only not found in the law but it is also incompatible with the principles of joint stock company law.

Private limited company According to Article 41 GmbHG every shareholder has the right to file a petition with the commercial court to nullify a shareholders' res-

---

18 JBl 1989, 253.
19 WBl 1988, 3; GesRZ 1987, 127f.

olution if the decision is clearly not compatible with law or the Articles of Association, if the decision violates compulsory legal provisions, or if the decision is in conflict with the Articles of Association and its provisions regarding amendment of the articles were not respected. It is therefore possible for a resolution to be annulled for procedural defects or substantive defects which do not violate procedures, such as breaches of good faith or duty of loyalty which are nevertheless detrimental to a shareholder's interest.

A shareholder who was present in the general meeting must have lodged a protest against the resolution in the minutes. Any shareholder who was unjustifiably excluded from the general meeting, or who was prevented from attending by defects in the invitation is also authorized to file a claim.

The statement of claim must be filed within a month from the day of the registration of the resolution in the minute book. Claims must be directed against the company. The court for commercial matters has exclusive jurisdiction for the action. The court can defer the execution of a contested resolution by interim injunction if the plaintiff can provide evidence that irretrievable damage threatens the company.

The shareholder can claim damages if the resolution was successfully annulled and if he personally suffered damages. Indirect loss suffered as a result of a damage to the company assets is excluded.

The winding up of the company can in principle only be decided in a shareholders' resolution. A simple majority will suffice. Even when the articles do not provide a right of termination, the leading cases give every shareholder at least the right to dissolve the company by termination in light of circumstances that render their membership unacceptable. The remaining shareholders have the right, however, to continue the company but they must pay to the retiring shareholder the value of his shares according to the Articles of Association and, respectively, the winding-up balance sheet.

9. Specific Protection if a Company is Controlled by Another Company

9.1 What are the rights and remedies of a shareholder of Company A when Company B gains control over it (by acquiring the majority of its shares or otherwise)?

Article 15 AktG and Article 115 GmbHG define a group of affiliated companies as either legally independent enterprises which are united by a unified management for economic purposes or, by virtue of participations or otherwise directly or indirectly, as a legally independent enterprise which is under the controlling interest of another enterprise.

In Austria such group law is not as regulated as in Germany, although the laws for joint stock and private limited companies in both countries are very similar. Therefore the group is essentially only *de facto* recognized. The legislature has only introduced a definition in order to consider certain actual situations and to connect with it several single provisions which are scattered in different laws. The organizational structure of a joint stock company is already sufficient to obtain influence in the sense of the legal definition of a group, through such means as adequate participation.

The pure possibility of unified management is not sufficient for consideration as a group. The management functions must be exercised *de facto*. Pure control functions do not create a unified management. Conversely, the requirement of the controlling interest is already fulfilled if the pure possibility of domination exists.

Since a unified management in a group requires a modification of the purpose of the company as provided in the Articles of Association, in practice, group clauses are used by both the dependent as well as the dominant enterprises. Modification of the Articles must respect the protection of minority shareholders who will not participate in the advantages of the creation of a group. Furthermore, the principle of equal treatment must be observed. Only if the creation of a group is objectively justified by the well-being of the company, and especially the long-term existence of the enterprise, will a group clause then be admissible if the minority faces discrimination. Compensation is not necessary if it is clear that the minority would not be in a better position without the creation of the group. However, a submission which threatens the existence remains in any case barred. Apart from such cases a group clause must normally offer, or at least provide for adequate compensation for detrimental effects to minority shareholders.

Austrian law has not regulated the controlling agreement as a type of contract. Since it normally contains the right to give instructions it is highly controversial whether or not such an agreement is admissible. The commitment of a joint stock company to instructions on the basis of a controlling agreement would violate Article 70 AktG which regulates the compulsory management of the company by the self-responsibility of the management board. The board-members are liable for damages as they must always observe the well-being of the company.

9.2 What are the shareholder's rights and remedies when Company B exerts its control over Company A in a way which damages the interests of the latter?

For the above-mentioned reasons the dominant enterprise is liable for damages to the subordinate enterprise and to its minority shareholders if enterprise agreements or other contracts in favour of third parties are violated. However, a special group liability has been refused where a group of enterprises do not form a unified liability association.[20]

In jurisprudence it is so far undecided whether, as an exception, direct liability of directors or shareholders is possible. In doctrine, cases concerning abuse or evasion of law are discussed, especially in the framework of a group where shareholders exert influence directly or indirectly on the management of a company. In such cases they may act only with the same duties which the law also provides for the board of management.

Thus the remedies for a minority shareholder are limited to those already described in the preceding sections.

---

[20] GesRZ 1983, 156.

BELGIUM

Joren de Wachter

De Backer & Bastin

Brussels

PROTECTION OF MINORITY SHAREHOLDERS

***EDITOR* MATTHIAS W. STECHER**

BELGIUM

Joren de Wachter

Introduction

In Belgium, the protection of minority shareholders has been changed many times in the recent past. The Companies Act has been considerably amended in the last 10 years, and a number of statutory provisions have given substantial rights to minority shareholders.

In order to understand the balance of powers and rights between parties however, one should be aware of the theory of the conflicting rights and interests of the parties concerned. Belgian legal theory has developed the concepts of the "interests of the company" and the "interests of the shareholders".

The interests of the company are more than just the sum of the individual shareholders' interests. The interests of the company exist as an independent concept, and concern the existence of the company as a business. They take into account (but do not merely consist of) the interests of several parties who are linked with the business, such as employees, creditors, the group to which the company belongs (if applicable), etc. The interests of the shareholders (eg obtaining dividends) may be contrary to those of the company (eg investing the profits).

The shareholders (majority shareholders to a larger extent than minority shareholders), have a limited duty towards the company to ensure its survival of the company, even if contrary to their own immediate interests.

The balance between the interests (and rights) of the company, and those of the shareholders is not defined by statutes, but is wholly dependent upon the definition given by the courts as the "interests of the company".

However, the courts will never provide a description or accurate definition of the interests of the company. They only define this concept in a negative way, that is, they state that a certain behaviour of shareholders is clearly contrary to the interests of the company. Thus, only the limits of the interests of the company are indicated, not the actual content.

1. Majority Requirements for Shareholders' Resolutions

1.1 What are the majority requirements in general?

The basic rule is that there are no rules, except those specifically provided by the Companies Act. The Act mentions several majority requirements (and the necessary quorum) for different kinds of decision that can be taken by the shareholders' meeting, but does not state a general – or common – rule of majority, with the exception of Article 74bis, §1 of the Companies Act, which states that, unless provided otherwise in the Articles of Association, the generally applicable rules are those of meetings of bodies. This refers to the internal regulation adopted by Parliament.

According to these regulations, the common majority is a simple majority of 50% of the votes plus one. Only the votes cast will be taken into consideration, without abstentions.

Common majority requirements will apply to all decisions that are within the powers of the shareholders' meeting,[1] and for which no specific majority or quorum has been established. Such requirements will apply irrespective of the number of shares present or represented. In case of a tie, the proposal fails.

1.2 Which resolutions require a greater majority?

There are two major exceptions to the common rule explained above. First, for certain decisions a quorum based on a percentage of shares being present or represented is necessary. This quorum can apply to different categories of shares, or to combinations of categories.[2] Second, certain decisions require a special majority of

[1] It should be noted that the shareholders' meeting can only use the powers specifically given to it according to the Companies Act and the Articles of Association, and that the residual power lies with the board of directors.

[2] Eg non-voting shares, voting certificates (which do not represent a share in the company's capital), or other kinds of securities.

the votes cast. For certain decisions, a combination of quorum and special majority is applied.

Non-voting shares will not be taken into account for determining the quorum or the majority, unless the vote involves rights attached to such shares, or unless they have acquired the right to vote under the Companies Act.[3]

The most important special majorities are the following.

1.2.1 Majority to modify the Articles of Association[4]

At least 50% of the shares representing the capital must be represented. If this is not the case, a new meeting must be called within a reasonable period of time. At the new meeting there is no quorum requirement.

A resolution proposing such modification requires 75% of the votes cast.[5]

1.2.2 Majority to modify the objects of the company

The 50% quorum applies to all classes of shares. If this quorum is not reached, a new meeting will be called (where no quorum applies) but at least one share representing part of the capital must be represented. The majority required is 80% of the votes cast.

The Companies Act states that shares which do not represent a share in the capital will each have one vote, notwithstanding the provisions of the Articles of Association. They cannot represent more than two-thirds of the total of votes cast by shares representing the capital.

1.2.3 Specific applications of the majority required to modify the Articles of Association

1.2.3.1 Majority to modify the rights attached to specific classes of shares

The General Meeting of shareholders always has the right to modify the rights attached to certain classes of shares. If such modification is proposed, the holders of shares in the class concerned will always have a vote, and the rules applicable to modifications of the Articles of Association (quorum and majority) will apply to the class meeting vote, as well as for all shares normally having voting rights.

1.2.3.2 Reduction of the capital

The quorum and majority requirements for a modification to the Articles of Association must be met. However, if applicable, the provisions as explained under 1.2.3.1 will apply, and different sub-majorities may be required.

---

[3] Non-voting shares have to be preferential shares (for the purposes of dividing profits) and will become voting shares under certain conditions (if dividends have not been paid in full for three successive years) or for certain decisions (liquidation of the company and division of the company, modification of the object, reduction of capital).

[4] This includes any modification to the capital.

[5] It has to be noted that the invitation to be present at the meeting has to indicate in detail the proposed alterations to the Articles of Association.

1.3 To what extent can they be modified by the Articles of Association?

The Articles of Association can provide for specific majorities. These can be defined according to the kind of resolutions to be passed. Only one general rule is applicable, namely that the majorities provided for in the Companies Act may only be increased, not reduced.

The Companies Act provides for a specific alteration of the use of voting rights, namely, it is possible to determine in the Articles of Association that each individual shareholder may only cast a specific number of votes even if he holds more shares. The only condition is that this rule must be applied without any discrimination between the different classes of shares.[6]

2. Influence on the Decision-Making Process

2.1 Do minority shareholders have the right to call a shareholders' meeting?

The Companies Act states that shareholders owning 20% of the shares representing the capital of the company may call a shareholders' meeting. Such a request must be sent to the board of directors, which is obliged to call a shareholders' meeting within a reasonable period of time.[7]

2.2 Do they have the right to put matters on the agenda?

Minority shareholders have the right to determine which matters will be put on the agenda of a shareholders' meeting which they wish to call. This right does not formally exist for the agenda of any other shareholders' meeting (ie one which is not called by the minority of 20%), but such requests will normally be honoured. Moreover, the board of directors always has the right to add matters to the agenda of any shareholders' meeting, as long as such matters are mentioned in the notice sent to the shareholders.

---

6 The rule explained above will apply as from the coming into effect of the modified Companies Act (Art. 76). It modifies the previous Act which determined that the Articles of Association can limit the number of votes to be cast by an individual shareholder to one-fifth of the votes existing and two-fifths of the votes cast. This rule in its turn was a change, introduced in 1991, to the previous rule which determined that in any case, no individual shareholder could cast more than one-fifth of the existing votes, or two-fifths of the votes cast.

7 When this reasonable period of time is not observed, the minority can ask the president of the court to set a date, with penalties per day of delay. Breach of this rule will also cause the directors to be liable for breach of the provisions of the Companies Act. A reasonable period of time will always have to take into account the formalities to be respected to call the shareholders to the meeting (as the case may be, publication in the Official Journal).

3. Rights of Information, Independent Auditing and Supervision

3.1 To what extent do the (minority) shareholders have a right to be informed on company matters?

The notice to attend the shareholders' meeting will mention the points of the agenda. Each shareholder has the right to obtain, free of charge, a copy of the balance sheet and accounts of the company, a copy of the report of the board of directors, and a copy of the report of the auditors.

According to the provisions of the Companies Act, the board of directors has a duty to answer questions asked by shareholders at the shareholders' meeting.[8] However, it is generally accepted that the board does not have a duty to answer questions if this would be contrary to the interests of the company.[9]

3.2 Do they have the right to demand independent auditing or to initiate the supervision of company matters by an independent institution?

Belgian law makes a basic distinction regarding the shareholders' right to be informed. This distinction is based on the size of the company, which is determined by such criteria as average number of staff, yearly turnover and balance sheet total.[10] In companies falling below these criteria each individual shareholder has a full and unconditional right to send an accountant to the company to have an audit performed. The accountant's fee will be paid by the company if it agrees with the audit, or if so determined by the court. In companies which exceed at least two of the criteria indicated, the Companies Act creates an obligation for the nomination of an independent auditor. Each year, the auditors present a special report to the shareholders' meeting.

Auditors are appointed by the shareholders' meeting by simple majority. Auditors must be officially recognized and regularly approved by the Institute of Auditors, an independent body which supervises their activities. Auditors are also subject to professional liability.

---

8 Art. 70ter, Companies Act.

9 A classic example would be the situation where a direct competitor has acquired one share, and wishes to obtain information of a private, secret or privileged nature. The courts have the power to take into account the reasonableness of the request of the shareholder or of the refusal of the board to submit information.

10 Art. 12, §2 of the Act of 17 July 1975. The criteria applicable at this date are as follows: if more than one of the following criteria is exceeded, the company will be considered as a "large" company (the term "large company" does not as such exist in the statutes): (i) average number of personnel fifty; (ii) turnover (excluding VAT) BEF170 million; (iii) balance sheet total amount BEF85 million.

In practice, the right of minority shareholders to have audits performed has proved rather limited. For this reason, Parliament amended the Companies Act to grant minority shareholders the right to have specific audits performed. Thus, a shareholder or group of shareholders holding at least 1% of all existing shares, or holding shares representing an amount of capital of at least BEF 50 million, may ask the court to appoint an auditor.[11] The interest of the company, as defined by the courts, is the criterion for the performance of an audit.

The application for an audit must indicate the reason for the audit, and is often introduced within the framework of a liability claim against directors (see 5.1.2 below), or a claim to nullify decisions of the shareholders' meeting.

The court will determine the areas to be audited. These are not limited to financial issues, but may include all the company's records. The court will also decide who will bear the cost of the audit. This implies that if the claim succeeds, the minority will not normally be ordered to pay the costs. However, they may often have to advance such costs.

4. Capital Increases and Distributions

4.1 To what extent do (minority) shareholders have the right to participate in capital increases?

The general rule is that all shareholders have a preferential right to participate in a capital increase according to the number of capital shares they own.

The shareholder must use his preferential right within a period of 15 days following the opening day of subscription to the capital increase as determined by the shareholders' meeting. The capital increase must be communicated to the shareholders prior to the opening day of the subscription period. Shareholders have the right to sell or transfer their preferential right. The preferential right of each shareholder to participate in a capital increase cannot be limited by the Articles of Association.

There is one exception to this rule, namely, in the case of a capital increase by means of authorized capital, by decision of the board of directors. The Articles of Association can limit the preferential right of shareholders for capital increases by use of the authorized capital by the board of directors.[12] This limitation cannot be used in favour of subsidiaries of the company, unless it has been specifically provided for in the Articles of Association, through authorization for an increase in capital by means of authorized capital. Moreover, the board must justify its deci-

[11] Art. 191, Companies Act.

[12] Normally, the share capital can only be increased by decision of the shareholders' meeting. The Articles of Association can, however, provide for the board of directors to increase the capital ("authorized capital"). The Companies Act sets certain limits and conditions on the use of authorized capital.

sion to limit the preferential right in a report which is subject to an auditor's report. A copy of this report must be deposited with the court.

The preferential right can be limited or excluded by a shareholders' meeting which decides on a capital increase with the same majority necessary for modification of the Articles of Association (75%, subject to quorum in the first meeting). The proposal for limitation or exclusion must be mentioned in the notice to the respective shareholders' meeting.

Other special conditions must be fulfilled if the modification of the preferential right is effected in favour of staff of the company or subsidiaries.

4.2 Do minority shareholders have the right to demand dividends or other distributions?

Decisions on profit distribution fall within the power of the shareholders' meeting, decided by simple majority. However, as seen above,[13] the interests of the company may limit the options available to the majority. Moreover, a majority may not openly abuse its right to decide on profit distribution, for example, by continuously refusing to pay dividends, while the company simultaneously pays unreasonable amounts under commercial contracts (eg consultancy) to its majority shareholders.[14]

5. Derivative Actions

5.1 Can (minority) shareholders enforce rights that the company has against other shareholders, directors, or third parties?

Only the company itself may enforce rights against other shareholders. For minority shareholders, the only cause of action is a personal claim against another shareholder for breach of a duty. The claimant must show a personal interest independent of his position as a shareholder of the company. The shareholder cannot represent the company, or claim rights belonging to the company as such.

Article 66bis Companies Act, introduced in 1991, gives minority shareholders holding individually or together 1% of the existing shares (no matter what kind of shares), or holding capital shares representing at least BEF 50 million of the company's capital, the right to introduce a claim against directors.[15] Such a claim can

---

13 See Introduction on "the interests of the company".

14 Abuse of majority is a well established concept in legal theory and is applied by the courts. See Cass., 19 September 1983, TBH, 1984, 250–253, F. Van Neste, "Misbruik van recht", TPR, 1967, 339 ev; P. Van Ommeslaeghe, "Abus de droit, fraude aux droits des tiers et fraude à la loi", with Cass., 10 September 1971, RCJB, 1976, 318.

15 This claim is based on the liability of directors towards the company, based on the provisions of the Companies Act, the Articles of Association and the fiduciary duty of directors towards the company.

only be introduced by shareholders who have refused to or who have not validly[16] discharged the directors at the shareholders' meeting. The claim remains valid even if the individual shareholder or the group of shareholders who introduced the claim lose their right to initiate such a claim afterwards.

The claim is introduced on behalf of the company by a special representative appointed by the claimant(s). If the claim is successful, all costs paid by the minority shareholders will be reimbursed by the company. This is provided by a direct reference to the right to have an audit performed through an injunctive procedure (as discussed above).[17]

Claims against third parties can only be introduced by the company. An individual shareholder may, however, be able to introduce a personal claim based on an interest different from his interests as a shareholder, but such claim will not be on behalf of the company.[18]

6. Other "Formal" Rights

6.1 Do minority shareholders have any other specific rights comparable to those mentioned in 2–5 above?

The Companies Act provides a number of other rights for minority shareholders.

6.1.1 Nullity of decisions taken by a shareholders' meeting

Under certain conditions, the Companies Act confers the right to have decisions of the shareholders' meeting declared void.[19] This right is not only given to shareholders, but to all others having an interest in such a claim.

The claim may be based upon any irregularity or breach of the Articles of Association or the Companies Act, abuse of power, or breach of the limits of power *ultra vires*.

No claim can be introduced by a shareholder who has approved of the decisions taken by the shareholders' meeting in question. The claim must be introduced against the company, within six months after the date of the shareholders' meeting.[20]

---

16 This may be the case if the board has omitted to give relevant information, or has given wrong, false or insufficient information to the shareholders, thus making it impossible to decide validly on discharge of directors.

17 See point 3.2, referring to Art. 191 of the Companies Act.

18 The question of who will collect the proceeds of such a claim is a delicate one, where individual shareholders may collect monies through such a claim that would normally befall the company. In practice, such claims are very rare, and the company will normally follow the individual shareholder in his claim to safeguard its rights.

19 Art. 190bis, Companies Act.

20 Or within six months after the claimant was informed of the decisions of said shareholders' meeting.

6.1.2 Liquidation of the company[21]

If the company's net assets fall below one-half of the share capital, the board of directors must call a shareholders' meeting to decide on the continuation of the company.

If the net assets fall below one-fourth of the share capital, a 25% majority of votes cast at the shareholders' meeting can decide to put the company into liquidation.

6.1.3 Lock-out and opt-out

Since the integration of the new "Reparation Act" in the Companies Act, minority shareholders have acquired two new rights: the right to buy out other shareholders ("lock-out"), and the right to have their shares bought by the majority ("opt-out").[22] These rights only apply to private companies.

6.1.3.1 Lock-out

It may seem surprising to see this right mentioned as the right of a minority, but the law sets as a minimum the ownership of 30% of the shares. Theoretically, a minority of 30% may force a majority of 70% to sell its shares.

As a consequence of the new provisions of Article 190ter of the Companies Act, a group of shareholders may ask the court to order that another group (which does not need to consist of all remaining shareholders) sell their shares at a price set by the court. The "lock-out" claim can never be introduced by the company itself or any of its subsidiaries.

The court will only award the claim if there is a "valid reason"[23] to do so. This implies that there must be a basic, fundamental disagreement between the different groups of shareholders which endangers the ability of the company to continue its activities on a normal basis.

Claims are justified by showing that defendants have seriously refused or omitted to fulfil their duties to the company. It must be stressed that the court will only take into account the interests of the company, and not the personal interests of the claimant shareholders. It appears likely that the low requirements set by the Act for the starting of a lock-out action will provide the courts with ample opportunity to define valid reason, and to further develop the concept of "interests of the company".[24]

For minority shareholders, abuse by the majority may be a valid reason, but often use of the "opt-out" solution may be more appropriate.

---

[21] Art. 103, Companies Act.

[22] These possibilities have been introduced in the new Art. 190ter and 190quater of the Companies Act. Act of 13 April 1995, BS, 17 June 1995. They entered into force in July 1996.

[23] The French version of the Act (which limits the linguistic discussion that is possible on the basis of the Dutch version, which is unclear) speaks of a *juste motif*.

[24] The typical example, given by legal theory, is breach by a shareholder of provisions of the Articles of Association. As to how much this might afterwards lead to a claim in liability by the company against the individual shareholder is not clear, but the possibility should not be excluded.

The procedure follows the rules for injunctive orders, which should guarantee a rapid decision. The court will determine the value of the shares, hence the purchase price of the shares. The decision will contain an order for claimants to purchase the shares of the locked-out shareholders at the price set by the court.

It should be noted that a lock-out action does not provide claimants any certainty as to the purchase price which will be ordered. The risk that this amount will be too high to be interesting for the claimants cannot be excluded.[25]

6.1.3.2 Opt-out

The new Companies Act also confers the right to opt out, that is, to force another shareholder to take over the shares of the claimant at a price set by the court. There is no limit or minimum on the number of shares one must hold in order to start the claim.

Again, the claim must be based on a valid reason. The example given by Parliament was abuse of majority, through the systematic refusal to pay dividends, and retention of profits by the company without valid reason.[26] The procedure is the same as for the lock-out option.

7. Extension of These Rights by Statute or Shareholders' Agreements

7.1 Can the Articles of Association provide for additional rights of the minority shareholders? If not, can such rights be provided for in shareholders' agreements? Are these options commonly used?

Provisions in both the Articles of Association and shareholders' agreements can modify or specify the rights of groups of shareholders, but not in a way that the minority would completely take over the company or would have a "lion's share" of profit or other benefits.[27]

The Articles of Association and a shareholders' agreement can contain such provisions, of which the most commonly used are:

- appointment of directors by minority groups;
- specific majorities necessary within the board of directors for certain decisions, normally in combination with the previous right;

---

[25] Moreover, defendants (if they own 30% of the shares) might introduce a counterclaim to have the original claimants locked-out, where the original claim will be held as a "valid reason" !

[26] *Gedr. St. Kamer*, 1005 (1992–93), no. 19, 70.

[27] This is an application of the civil law origin of company law, where the company originally was created as a contract between partners. A basic and fundamental unfair treatment of a "partner" can be held void by the courts. This system also applies to companies, but its applications and criteria are set completely by jurisprudence.

- pre-emptive rights, follow-me rights in the event of sale of shares, rights of first refusal;[28]
- special (increased) majorities at shareholders' meetings for specific decisions;
- specific determination of the powers of the board of directors, of the directors in charge of the daily management, and of the shareholders' meeting.

Whether such provisions should be contained in the Articles of Association or in a shareholders' agreement will depend on the different legal status of each technique.

A modification of the Articles of Association needs approval by a majority of 75%. A shareholders' agreement can only be modified unanimously (by the shareholders who are a party to it).[29]

The Articles of Association are published in the Official Journal whereas a shareholders' agreement can (and often will) contain a non-disclosure provision.

Shareholders' agreements are recognized as valid by the Companies Act, but they must be for a limited period of time (which may be extended for additional terms if no party gives notice of termination). There is no such obligation for the Articles of Association.

Under the provisions of the new Companies Act,[30] shareholders' agreements must be *at all times* in the interests of the company. This ambiguous provision has suddenly made shareholders' agreements more uncertain from a legal point of view. No one can define or foresee what the interest of the company will be at any given moment in the future, so there is always a risk that the shareholders' agreement, at the moment a party wishes to have it enforced, will be declared as contrary to the interests of the company.

A breach of a shareholders' agreement will render the person in breach liable on the basis of contract law. A breach of the Articles of Association will often lead, under the Companies Act, to the nullity of the act considered in breach of the Articles of Association. Moreover, such a breach (if committed by a director, which will often be the case) may create liability according to the provisions of the Companies Act concerning liability of directors. The latter can also be more easily considered a valid reason for a lock-out or opt-out claim.

The choice between these two techniques will depend on factual and individual circumstances, but it is important to be aware of the consequences of either possibility. In any event, both are commonly used to adjust the balance of power within a company according to the position of the respective groups of shareholders.

---

[28] A limitation to the possibility to sell shares (such as rights of first refusal) must always be limited in time, and can never have as an effect that it is totally impossible to sell shares to a non-shareholder.

[29] Contract law applies to shareholders' agreements.

[30] New Art. 74ter.

8. Remedies Where a Shareholders' Resolution or Other Action Impairs the Rights of Minority Shareholders

8.1 What are the requirements for such remedies?

The Companies Act does not provide a specific remedy for the protection of minority shareholders' rights in general. Minority shareholders have at their disposal the specific rights and remedies as explained above.[31] The Companies Act sets the requirements for each type of remedy in the provision containing the respective rights of the (minority) shareholder. The minority shareholder will therefore have to analyse the situation, and, according to the facts, determine which remedy is the most appropriate for the situation.

Generally, it is important for the (minority) shareholder to ensure that the minutes of the different meetings which he has attended contain the information necessary to prove what has happened. In this respect, it might be important for the (minority) shareholder to have counsel assist him at the shareholders' meeting.[32]

While the Companies Act does not provide minority shareholders with a general rule of protection against unfair prejudice, legal theory has developed a general theory of the importance of fair treatment for minority shareholders. This theory is based on concepts found in the Companies Act which are vague and impossible to define with complete certainty, such as "the interests of the company", "valid reason", and "justifiable serious reason".[33] These concepts must be defined in specific situations according to the facts related to them. Courts will, however, not give an explicit definition, but will indicate the limits of these concepts by indicating that action allegedly in breach of a duty is "manifestly" contrary to the interests of the company, or is "clearly", "beyond reasonable doubt" a justifiable serious reason.

8.2 When do the courts of your country accept these requirements?

The notion of "interests of the company" has been introduced in the statutes very recently, and at this time there is no jurisprudence. Previously, the courts

[31] See answers to questions 2–6 above.

[32] There is substantial jurisprudence on the question whether or not the (minority) shareholder may be assisted by counsel at the shareholders' meeting. The general rule that non-shareholders may be refused access to the meeting will in such cases be set aside by the Courts. It is important to stress that the rule as to who may appear as proxy-holder of a shareholder at a shareholders' meeting is determined in the Articles of Association. An essential element for minority shareholders to defend their interest will therefore often be the insertion of a provision in the Articles of Association that a proxy-holder need not be a shareholder.

[33] The *juste motif.*

used the expression without giving a proper definition, but by indicating its limits.[34]

On this basis, legal theory states that majority may not act in a way that is considered "abusive".[35] This "abuse of majority" concept derives from general tort law,[36] but is a specific application of the contractual obligations of a shareholders.

In regard to the definition of "justifiable serious reason", there exists jurisprudence indicating the borders of this concept. The mere fact that minority shareholders are unable to have the prevailing view at shareholders' meetings cannot be considered a justifiable serious reason.

A good example is the decision of the Court of Brussels of June 12 1973,[37] where the Court decided that a majority continuously acting against the interests of the company, and thus constantly impairing the powers of management as well as the interests of minority shareholders, would be considered a justifiable serious reason.

According to the courts, a serious and continuous impairment of minority shareholders' interests (which are not the same as the formal rights protected under the statutes) would be a justifiable serious reason.

The courts will normally refrain from taking over the management of the company or from suggesting what should have been done instead.

8.3 What remedies are available to the claimant?

The specific remedies as set out above are available if the conditions set out in the statutory rules are fulfilled.

Besides these specific remedies, there are a number of other remedies not specifically provided for in the Companies Act that have proven effective. They can be divided into the following categories.

---

[34] See introduction on "the interests of the company". See also Cass., 19 September 1983, TBH, 1984, 250–3. No specific definition is given, the courts will only decide that a specific action is "manifestly" or "obviously" contrary to the interests of the company.

[35] See P. Coppens, *L'abus de majorité dans les sociétés anonymes*, Gembloux, Duclot, 1947, no. 56, p. 83; J. Ronse, "Nietigheid van besluiten van organen van de naamloze vennootschap", *Preadvies voor de Vereniging voor vergelijkende studie van het recht in Belgien Nederland*, Zwolle, 1966, 25; C. Del Marmol, "Protection des actionnaires minoritaires en droit belge, évolution récente", in *Etudes offertes à R. Houin*, Paris, Dalloz, 1985, 172.

[36] See 8.3.2. Also, W. Van Gerven, *Algemeen deel*, no. 69, p. 181, and no. 70, p. 191. In fact, tort law is introduced via the duty of care of the owner of shares. Abuse of ownership rights can be considered as a breach of duty of the owner (see Cass., 10 September 1971, RCJB, 1976, 300). Specifically for companies, it has been decided that abuse of rights (such as the rights granted to majority shareholders under the Companies Act), has to be considered as a breach of contract (Cass., 19 September 1983, Pas., 1984, I, 55; RW, 1983–84, 1480; TBH, 1984, 276; JT, 1985, 56; RCJB, 1986, 282). This is however merely a point of discussion for legal theory, since the requirements for an action under tort or under contract law are almost identical (breach of duty, causality, damage).

[37] Pas., 1973, III, 75 (see also M. Coipel, "Dispositions communes", *Rep. Not.*, no. 497, p. 208; J. Van Ryn en P. Van Ommeslaeghe, RCJB, 1981, no.93, p. 434.)

8.3.1 Injunctive order – specific performance

Under the provisions of Article 584 of the Judicial Code, the President of the Commercial Court can take any measure he considers necessary in case of urgency. In practice, this provision is often used in cases of obvious mismanagement, complete deadlock of the management, or shareholders' resolutions or management decisions which clearly infringe the rights of minority shareholders. Urgency is a crucial element necessary to obtain a decision of the President.

Orders have been sought for the following:

- suspending the effects of decisions taken by shareholders' meetings;
- calling a meeting of the board of directors;
- appointment of a provisional director;
- specific orders to the management.[38]

The courts are often reluctant to apply such a remedy, so claimants must present clear evidence of immediate and irreparable damage if the request for the injunctive order is not awarded.[39]

8.3.2 Damages

As seen under 8.1 above,[40] the general rule of liability, be it under tort or contract law[41] applies to all actions or omissions by either shareholders or management.

The conditions necessary are fault, causality and damage. Practically, it is the condition of fault that will be specifically interpreted according to the provisions of the Companies Act. For certain specific duties, the causality will also be defined by the Companies Act, thereby providing which party bears the burden of proof.[42]

For the management, duties are found in the rules of liability of directors[43] which are based on the specific duties of directors contained in the Companies Act,[44] and the general fiduciary duty of directors.[45]

Moreover, both majority and minority shareholders have a duty to respect the interests of the company.[46] Any action or omission that is obviously against the interests of the company may be considered a breach of duty, creating liability for the party in breach.

---

38 Eg an order not to sell specific assets.

39 Two typical situations, where the author has been able to obtain such remedy, are the refusal of the board of directors to meet (hence to call the shareholders' meeting), and the danger of all assets of the company disappearing to an off-shore company in the West Indies, owned by the majority shareholder.

40 See no. 37.

41 Art. 1382 C.C. for tort, Art. 1134 C.C. for contractual liability.

42 Eg the provisions of Art. 103, where the failure of directors to call a shareholders' meeting will be considered to have caused any damage resulting for the shareholders.

43 Art. 62, Companies Act.

44 Eg the duty to call a shareholders' meeting if the conditions of Art. 103 (net assets below one-half of share capital) are fulfilled.

45 Eg to respect the provisions of the Articles of Association.

46 A typical example could be the refusal of a minority holding 30% of voting shares to allow an increase in share capital (eg because they have not the means to follow such increase, which would

The duty of a shareholder may be considered a fiduciary duty,[47] but its implications will depend on the situation of the shareholder at a given moment.

8.3.3 Liquidation of the company[48]

Liquidation is a drastic and final solution, which the courts are reluctant to apply. The right to have the company liquidated by court order is, however, specifically provided for by Article 102, Companies Act. This right is based on fundamental misbehaviour of one (or more) shareholders, and requires not just a "valid reason", but a "justifiable serious reason".[49] As explained above, a common example of a justifiable serious reason is a situation where majority shareholders continuously and seriously impair the rights of minority shareholders.

9. Specific Protection if the Company is Controlled by Another Company

9.1 What are the rights and remedies of a shareholder of Company A when Company B gains control over it (by acquiring the majority of its shares or otherwise)?

The most important specific remedy offered to a minority shareholder in the case where control of the company is taken over exists in the situation of an acquisition of a public company, where two additional rights are provided: An obligation that the company (or person) taking over make a public offer on all the shares of the company if it has acquired control of the company,[50] and the right of minority shareholders, even if they refused the bid, to force the company (or person) taking over the company to purchase their shares at the price indicated in the bid.

---

cont.

then diminish their voting power), thus making it impossible for the company to obtain fresh money. If this refusal is considered to be against the interests of the company, the minority shareholder could be held liable for the subsequential liquidation of the company, and to a certain extent for the debts of the company. On abuse of minority rights, see J. Ronse and K. Geens, "Het misbruik van minderheidspositie", in *Van vennootschappelijk belang (bundel J.M.M. Maeier)*, Zwolle, Tjeenk Willink, 1988, 277; L. Simont, "Réflexion sur l'abus de minorité", in *Liber Amicorum Jan Ronse*, Brussels, Story Scientia, 1986, 307.

47 The words "fiduciary duty" are not quite correct, and the duty of shareholders towards the company is obviously less important than the duty of directors. Moreover, a distinction will be made between majority and minority, where majority will be considered to have more important duties towards the company. The limits of such duties will always have to be considered from case to case.

48 Art. 102, Companies Act.

49 This rule has found its origin in the provisions in the Civil Code, that deal with the company as a specific kind of contract: Art. 1871 C.C.

50 Royal Decree of 8 November 1989, Art. 41.

The former is applicable if 50% of the shares have been acquired in a public company, the latter applies if the bidder has acquired over 90% of the shares of the company taken over.[51]

These rights exist independently of whether the acquirer is a company or not.

9.2 What are the shareholder's rights and remedies when Company B exerts its control over Company A in a way which damages the interests of the latter?

There are no specific provisions applicable to this situation. However, in such a case the distinction between the interests of the company and the interests of the majority shareholder will come into play, together with the interests of the group (which may also be taken into account).[52]

The specific and general remedies as set out above will apply, and the courts may have to check and balance the rights and interests of all parties involved (including the company itself).

[51] Royal Decree of 8 November 1989, Art. 32.

[52] The notion of "interests of groups of companies" has been recognized to exist by the courts. See eg Voorz. Kh. Gent, 18 May 1988, TRV, 1988, 30.

FINLAND

Pauliina Tenhunen

Castrén & Snellman Oy
Helsinki

PROTECTION OF MINORITY SHAREHOLDERS

***EDITOR* MATTHIAS W. STECHER**

FINLAND

Pauliina Tenhunen

Introduction

The most important forms of incorporation for business enterprises in Finland are general partnerships (*avoin yhtiö*), limited partnerships (*kommandiittiyhtiö*), limited companies (*osakeyhtiö*) and cooperative societies (*osuuskunta*). Joint ventures are not treated as separate legal entities.

This report concentrates on limited companies. The answers are based on the Finnish Companies Act of 1978, which is a result of Nordic legal cooperation.

In 1992, Finland signed the Agreement on the European Economic Area. It was agreed that within a transition period of two years from the entry into force all of the existing 10 EC Directives on the Harmonization of Company Law would be incorporated into Finnish company law. Numerous amendments are required in order to meet the demands of the EC Directives. One of the major reforms is the proposed division of limited liability companies into private and public limited companies. However, most of the provisions of the Companies Act, which also includes minority protection, will apply to both companies. The amendments are intended to become effective on 1 September 1997.[1]

---

[1] The amendments to the Companies Act were approved by Parliament on 16 December 1996, in other words, after this report was written. Through the revision of the Companies Act the protection of minority shareholders is improved, for example, their right to receive information from the company is extended.

1. Majority Requirements for Shareholders' Resolutions

1.1 What are the majority requirements in general?

According to the Finnish Companies Act, most decisions require a simple majority of the votes cast. In case of equality of votes, the chairman has the deciding vote. In elections, the person who receives most of the votes is considered elected.

1.2 Which resolutions require a greater majority?

It is provided in the Companies Act[2] that a resolution to amend the Articles of Association requires a greater majority. The decision can be made when the shareholders with at least two-thirds of the votes cast as well as two-thirds of the shares represented at the meeting have supported it.

There are also some resolutions to amend the Articles of Association which require the approval of all shareholders or, in addition to the above mentioned amount (two-thirds), the approval of owners of such shares which the amendments affect. These decisions are as follows:

- to reduce the right of the shareholders to the company's profits or net assets;
- to increase the shareholders' obligatory payments to the company;
- to restrict the right to acquire the company's shares; or
- to otherwise alter the rights attached to shares of the same class.

A resolution to amend the Articles of Association to the effect that more than one-tenth of the profits are to be left undistributed can only be made when owners of shares with at least nine-tenths of the votes represented at the meeting have supported it.

The law also provides that a greater majority is needed when the general shareholders' meeting desires to deviate from the shareholders' order of preference in subscription for shares. According to the law the shareholders of a company have priority in the subscription of the new shares in the same proportion as the amount of shares they already own. Exceptions to this principle may be made if there is a strong reason to do so from the company's point of view and the majority of shareholders support the exception. The majority needed is the same as that stated in the first paragraph (two-thirds).

A greater majority is also required when a decision is made on the formation of a company. The company is formed when subscribers representing a majority of the votes cast and two-thirds of the shares represented at the meeting vote in favour of the formation. This provision is applicable in situations where the charter of foundation and subscription of shares are made separately. After this the decision

---

2 Chapter 9, s. 14.

of the foundation of the company is made at the constituent meeting. At the constituent meeting the subscribers check whether the amount of subscribed shares corresponds to the minimum capital stock and confirm whether the subscribers support the foundation of the company. If the qualified majority cannot be obtained, the foundation of the company will lapse.

A greater majority may also decide on liquidation and merger. Normally, a decision concerning liquidation merely requires a simple majority of the votes cast. If the company does not have to be dissolved in accordance with the Companies Act or a regulation provided by the Articles of Association, a greater majority is required. The decision is valid only when the shareholders holding at least two-thirds of the votes cast and of the shares represented at the meeting have supported it. The same majority is required in the case of the assigning company merging with another company, so that the assigning company is dissolved without going into liquidation and its assets and liabilities are taken over by the acquiring company.

A share in the company which is owned by the company itself or by its subsidiary shall not be taken into account when an approval of all shareholders or of a specific majority is required for making a valid decision or for exercising a special right. This also applies to shares belonging to a group pension fund.

1.3 To what extent can the majority requirements be modified by the Articles of Association?

According to the law, the majority requirements in general can be modified by the Articles of Association. However, the Articles of Association may not include any stipulations, except those regarding elections, by which the majority requirement under the Companies Act could be reduced.

2. Influence on the Decision-Making Process

2.1 Do minority shareholders have the right to call a shareholders' meeting?

According to the Companies Act,[3] the shareholders holding at least one-tenth of the shares have the right to call a shareholders' meeting. A lower threshold can be provided by the Articles of Association. It can even be provided in the Articles of Association that every shareholder has a right to call a shareholders' meeting.

Shareholders have to make a written request for the convening of a shareholders' meeting for a specified purpose. According to established legal practice it is not possible to request a shareholders' meeting for a matter which has been dealt with and decided on at the general shareholders' meeting some time earlier.

---

[3] Chapter 9, s. 6.

The law also provides that when a general shareholders' meeting must be held in accordance with the Companies Act, the Articles of Association or a decision of the general meeting, but the meeting has not been properly convened, a shareholder can ask the County Administration to authorize him to convene the meeting at the company's expense. Directors, the supervisory board and auditors have the same right.

2.2 Do they have the right to put matters on the agenda?

The law[4] provides that every shareholder has the right to have a matter dealt with at a general meeting. The shareholder must make a written request to the board of directors in a timely fashion so that the matter can be included in the notice convening the meeting.

3. Rights of Information, Independent Auditing and Supervision

3.1 To what extent do the (minority) shareholders have a right to be informed on the company matters?

According to the Companies Act,[5] all shareholders have the right to inquire about company matters at the general meeting. The board of directors and the managing director must before the meeting provide such factual information as may affect the assessment of the company's annual report, financial position, or other matters dealt with at the meeting. The obligation to give such information also covers the relationship with another company in the same group of companies and, where the company is a parent company, any consolidated accounts.

The board of directors is not required to disclose information which it considers prejudicial to the company.

If the information requested by the shareholder is not available at the general meeting, it must be supplied within two weeks in writing. The answer must be made available for the shareholders at the company's head office. It must also be sent to the shareholder who submitted the request for information.

Shareholders do not have the right to be continuously informed about company matters. They have no right to see book-keeping, correspondence or agreements made by the company.

It is also provided in the Companies Act that when a general meeting is to deal with annual accounts, the documents concerning the accounts or copies thereof shall be made available for inspection by shareholders at the company's head office. They are also to be sent to a shareholder immediately upon request.

---

4 Companies Act, chapter 9, s. 7.

5 Chapter 9, s. 12.

3.2 Do they have the right to demand independent auditing or to initiate the supervision of company matters by an independent institution?

First, minority shareholders may require that an extra auditor be appointed to take part in the audit together with the incumbent auditors. The proposal has to be made at the general meeting at which the election of the auditors takes place. If the owners of at least one-tenth of all shares or one-third of the votes represented at the meeting support the proposal, the auditor must be elected.

However, it is provided in the Companies Act that an auditor may not provide an individual shareholder with information about the company's affairs which he has obtained in the performance of his examination if such information is prejudicial to the company. The auditor may provide the general meeting with all the information requested unless this would be materially prejudicial to the company.

The Companies Act[6] also provides that a shareholder may require a special examination of the company's books and accounts for a specific past period or for a specific measure or matter. If the minority shareholders who own at least one-tenth of all shares or one-third of shares represented at the meeting support the proposal, the independent audit must be carried out. If there are difficulties the shareholder can request that authorities (the county government) appoint an examiner.

4. Capital Increases and Distributions

4.1 To what extent do (minority) shareholders have the right to participate in capital increases?

Under the Companies Act,[7] all shareholders of the company have pre-emptive rights on a new issue of shares pro rata to the number of shares they already own. If there are various classes of shares in the company, the order of priority is specified in the Articles of Association.

However, the general meeting of the shareholders may resolve to vary these rights if there are, from the company's point of view, strong economic reasons for the deviation. The decision is valid only if those shareholders who possess not less than two-thirds of the votes cast and of the shares represented at the general meeting have supported it.

---

6 Chapter 10, s .14.
7 Chapter 4, s. 2.

4.2 Do minority shareholders have the right to demand dividends or other distributions?

The minority shareholders have the right to demand dividends. It is provided in the Companies Act[8] that such a request must be made at the annual general meeting before the decision on the allocation of the profit by the members representing at least one-tenth of all shares. A smaller percentage may be provided for in the Articles of Association.

If these conditions are fulfilled, the general meeting must decide to distribute as dividends at least one-half of the sum of the profit for the financial period which remains, less any deductions required by the law and any transfers provided for in the Articles of Association. However, the shareholders may not require that more 5% of the company's stockholders' equity be distributed as dividends.

5. Derivative Actions

5.1 Can (minority) shareholders enforce rights that the company has against other shareholders, directors, or third parties?

The Companies Act[9] provides that, as a rule, the bringing of an action for damages on behalf of the company must be approved by the company in a general meeting. Directors, auditors and other shareholders may be liable to the company for any loss that they may have caused the company.

However, when discharge from liability has been granted at the general meeting or when it otherwise has been decided not to bring an action for damages, the minority shareholders may bring legal action on behalf of the company. The required minority are the owners of at least one-tenth of all shares or at least one-third of the shares represented at the meeting. They have to vote against the decision made at a general meeting.

The shareholders who have brought the action are liable for the expenses of the proceedings. They are, however, entitled to reimbursement from the company to the extent that the costs are covered by the amount received by the company through the action.

Shareholders cannot enforce rights on behalf of the company against third parties.

8 Chapter 12, s. 4, subs. 2.
9 Chapter 15, s. 5.

6. Other "Formal" Rights

6.1 Do minority shareholders have any other specific rights comparable to those mentioned in 2–5 above?

Some provisions of the Companies Act may be regarded as minority protection. For instance, the law provides that every shareholder may be accompanied by an advisor at the general meeting.

The law also provides other rights. Shareholders who own at least one-tenth of all shares can demand that decisions concerning adoption of the accounts, the source and application of funds and discharge of the directors from responsibility be adjourned to another meeting. Through this action the shareholders can get more time to examine the matters in question.

The owners of at least one-tenth of all shares can require that an authorized auditor be appointed even if it is not compulsory according to the law.

7. Extension of These Rights by Statute or Shareholders' Agreements

7.1 Can the Articles of Association provide for additional rights of the minority shareholders (eg to appoint directors)? If not, can such rights be provided for in shareholders' agreements? Are these options commonly used?

The Articles of Association can provide for additional rights of the minority shareholders. According to the Companies Act, the Articles of Association may, for instance, provide that one or some of the members of the board of directors, though less than half of them, be elected other than by the company in the general meeting. For example, the Articles of Association may authorize particular members (such as a parent company) to name the members, or the Articles of Association may provide that a person or persons in certain positions automatically become members of the board of directors.

Generally, it can be stated that the inclusion of special stipulations in the Articles of Association makes it possible to deviate from the procedures that are not compulsory according to the law. Apart from appointments to the board, such procedures can, for example, cover the appointment of the managing director, the method of electing the chairman of the board, the quorum for meetings and the votes required at the meetings of the board and of the members in the general meeting. In such cases additional rights for the minority shareholders can be provided.

In legal literature it has been stated that other clauses can also be included in the Articles of Association, provided that they are not contrary to the Companies Act or other law. Further, it has been stated that the Articles of Association should not include detailed information concerning the agreements for the administration and financial operations of the company made between the founders and the shareholders, but that such agreements should be included in a separate shareholders' agreement.

For example, the shareholders can enter into a so-called shareholders' agreement which determines the voting rights of the shares in general meetings. The agreement is binding on the parties to the agreement, but does not obligate the company, unless the company has separately bound itself to the contract. Even if the company has bound itself, the legal validity and significance of each provision of the contract in company law and/or law of contracts will, however, be considered separately as far as the company and its organs are concerned.

A judgment of the Supreme Court, dated 29 August 1990 No. 1567, provides an example of this legal practice. Here the company, according to an agreement approved by the board of directors on behalf of the company, was under an obligation to make interim accounts signed by all the shareholders.

Shareholders' agreements are commonly used in order to ensure a certain composition of company management, as evidence of agreement upon the guidelines of the company's administration, or as an aid for the resolution of disagreements in the management of the company.

Shareholders' agreements are common, especially in family-owned companies, in joint venture companies and in situations in which the majority shareholders sell their majority ownership to another, while they themselves remain in the company as minority shareholders. Such agreements are also used in order to obtain or maintain the command over the company in which no individual shareholder alone has majority of votes.

In shareholders' agreements, additional rights for the minority shareholders can be provided.

Details of shareholders' agreements do not appear in any public register.

8. Remedies Where a Shareholders' Resolution or Other Action Impairs the Rights of Minority Shareholders

8.1 What are the requirements for such remedies?

There exists a so-called "general clause" in the Companies Act which provides that the general meeting may not pass a resolution by which certain shareholders or third parties manifestly obtain an unjustified benefit at the expense of the company or other shareholders.[10] Any shareholder who believes that the majority has infringed his rights in this way may appeal to the court in order to have the resolution declared null and void.

The purpose of the general clause is to shield individual shareholders and minority groups from prejudicial acts of the majority. Such practices may take many

[10] It is also provided in the Companies Act that the board of directors or other representatives of the company may not enter into such legal actions or undertake other measures which may cause undue benefit to a shareholder or a third party at the company's or another shareholder's expense.

forms. The majority shareholders can "exhaust" the minority by producing accounts that repeatedly show loss or insignificant profits, thereby making the distribution of profits to the shareholders impossible. At the same time, the majority can obtain advantages that the minority cannot obtain by exploiting the services of the company or through other means. Remuneration of board members that the majority has elected from among themselves can be confirmed at an unreasonably high level, or an increase in the share capital can be sought when such an increase actually only benefits the majority.

8.2 When do the courts of your country accept these requirements?

The burden of proof lies with the plaintiff. The plaintiff must prove the events that have taken place and that such events have been illegal or harmful. The judgment of the court depends also upon the demands that the plaintiff makes. For example, the violation of the general clause does not necessarily demand intent on the part of the management of the company or the persons who have taken part in the decision of the general meeting. The general clause can also be applied when an express intention to violate the general clause cannot be proved. Other remedies, for example, an obligation to pay damages, depend, however, on the intent or negligence of those guilty of the violation.

The requirements for the most drastic remedies such as liquidation are great. In the preparatory materials of the law it is stated that the substantiation of the malpractice is not in itself adequate as a ground for a liquidation judgment, but the company can be placed in liquidation only in the case of an extremely serious situation for which there are no other alternatives. The court of justice must consider the length of the period of malpractice, its seriousness and consequences.

There are a few examples in the legal practice in which the demands presented in the action for annulment of the judgment have been approved (see below, 8.3). On the other hand, there is no legal practice concerning the liquidation judgment:

> "The company's branch of industry was the production of marketing and administrative services for those of its shareholders who had made co-operation and service agreements with the company. After the company had given notice of termination of a co-operation agreement with shareholder A, who had owned more than one-third of the shares of the company, the general meeting decided to increase the capital stock of the company. New shares could be subscribed at a very high rate. To preserve his relative share in the company and the minority shares based on it, A would have been forced to invest a remarkable amount of money in the company and in fact only the shareholders who were entitled to the company's services would benefit from this investment. Thus, the decision of the general meeting was considered to give unjustified benefit to the other shareholders and was declared null and void."[11]

[11] Supreme Court 1991: 46.

8.3 What remedies are available to the claimant?

When a resolution of the members in a general meeting has not been made in due order or where it is otherwise contrary to the Companies Act (eg against the general rule mentioned above), a shareholder may bring legal action against the company for annulment or amendment of the resolution.

The plaintiff can also apply to the court for a precautionary measure in order to prevent the enforcement of the harmful resolution. The court can, for example, forbid the adverse party to do something, force them to do something, order the adverse party under penalty of a fine to do something, entitle the claimant to do or have something done or can give an order for an action that is needed to protect the rights of the claimant. A precondition for a precautionary measure is that the claimant prove the likelihood that he has a certain right against the respondent, and that the danger exists that the respondent by taking an action, by neglecting something or in some other way can prevent or impair the realization of the plaintiff's right or decrease its value or significance.

Generally, a precautionary measure is connected with the action for annulment mentioned in the first paragraph. If, on the other hand, the decision made by the company is null and void, an actual action for annulment is not necessary because the board of directors of a company may not enforce an invalid decision.

The claimant can also be paid compensation for damages. Majority shareholders are liable for losses they have caused minority shareholders by assisting in a violation of the Companies Act or the Articles of Association, either intentionally or by gross negligence. Generally, the liability to compensate for damages arises from the participation in a specific decision of the general meeting. In practice a shareholder can, however, contribute to the loss in other ways than through participation in the general meeting. A majority shareholder can, for example, press the board of directors or the managing director to act contrary to the Companies Act or Articles of Association. In cases such as this, the shareholder's liability for damage always presupposes express action.

Minority shareholders can also demand compensation from those members of the management who are guilty of malpractice.

Furthermore, the Companies Act contains a special rule giving shareholders the right to apply to the court for the winding up of the company if other shareholders have co-operated in a decision conflicting with the general rule, or have otherwise wilfully abused their influence in the company. The law provides that an order to wind up the company can be made only if there are exceptional reasons for doing so. Alternatively the court may, upon the request of the aggrieved party, order the company to redeem the shares held by the plaintiff at a reasonable price.

In the explanatory materials of the law, an example of the previously mentioned malpractices is a long-term "war of attrition", the intent being to force the minority to sell its shares to the majority below market value. Examples include the misuse of the clause of consent, and hiding the yearly profit in over-large reserves and write-offs or in revenues paid to the majority. A winding up order is used only as a last resort in such a situation where no other legal means are available to the minority. There is so far no case law concerning the application of this legal provision.

Instead of ordering the winding up of the company, a court may oblige the company to redeem the shares of the plaintiff. In principle the preconditions for the redemption are the same as those for a liquidation order. In practice, however, the redemption may be more easily carried out. While considering the consequences the court of law should take into consideration the interest of the company's work force and its creditors.

9. Specific Protection if the Company is Controlled by Another Company

9.1 What are the rights and remedies of a shareholder of Company A when Company B gains control over it (by acquiring the majority of its shares or otherwise)?

If the minority shareholder's stockholding is at least 10% of the total, the minority can, in cases where the majority rule is being misused, resort to the previously mentioned protective provisions of the Companies Act. The minority can require that an extraordinary general meeting is convened, that an extra auditor is appointed or that a special audit is made. Furthermore, the minority can begin to carry on an action on behalf of the company against the management of the company.

All the measures mentioned in 8.3 can be used by the minority shareholders.

The Companies Act[12] makes provisions for cases where a company alone or together with its subsidiaries acquires more than nine-tenths of all the shares in a subsidiary and such shares represent more than nine-tenths of all votes. First of all, the parent company is entitled to purchase the remaining shares at a current price from the other shareholders in the subsidiary. On the other hand, a shareholder whose shares are subject to such right has a right to require the parent company to purchase his shares.

As a preliminary, the right to purchase and the price should be agreed between the parties. If the parties cannot reach an agreement, a dispute about the right to purchase and the price will be settled by arbitration. A dispute about the right to purchase can, for example, arise if a shareholder believes that the parent company does not have the necessary amount of shares in its possession. Arbitration also becomes necessary in situations where some of the shareholders of the subsidiary cannot be reached and thus will not receive the demand for redemption.[13]

According to the law, shares must be redeemed at market value. No other more precise valuation principles have been provided by the law. In arbitration some principles have arisen, for example, that the redemption price must be determined by dividing the market value of the company by the number of the shares. The value of the company is determined at the time of the demand for redemption. Depending on the situation, the basis for the determination of value can be the net capital of the company (net asset value), the net income that can be expected from the company (income value), the realization value of the company, or the combination

[12] Chapter 14, s. 8.

[13] Koski-af Schultén, *Osakeyhtiölaki selityksin II*, p. 345–6.

of these three. The basis for the valuation can also be the earlier trade prices of the shares of the company.

The Securities Market Act includes provisions for the redemption right of minority shares in a publicly quoted company. The obligation to redeem arises when the ownership of a shareholder exceeds two-thirds of the total votes of the shares of the company after the stock has been publicly listed. When the share of the votes is calculated, apart from the shares that the shareholder owns directly, the shares owned by corporations under his authority must also be taken into account.

Listed companies may tighten the obligation to redeem by including in the Articles of Association a stipulation according to which the obligation to redeem arises when the shareholder owns, for example, one-third of the total votes.

9.2 What are the shareholder's rights and remedies when Company B exerts its control over Company A in a way which damages the interests of the latter?

In the Companies Act there are no special provisions concerning situations in which shareholder companies misuse their authority and cause damage to the company and other shareholders. The measures specified in 8.3 are available to the minority shareholders.

In Finland there is no case law on the subject. On the other hand, the Articles of Association may include an arbitration clause. In such cases the disputes do not become public.

FRANCE

Patrick Peguet, Nathalie Carbiner,
Jean-Christophe Sabourin

ASA Law Firm

Strasbourg

PROTECTION OF MINORITY SHAREHOLDERS

***EDITOR* MATTHIAS W. STECHER**

FRANCE

Patrick Peguet, Nathalie Carbiner, Jean-Christophe Sabourin

Introduction

French company law[1] provides for six types of commercial company:

- general partnerships;[2]
- limited partnerships;[3]
- limited liability companies;[4]
- corporations;[5]
- stock partnerships;[6] and
- simplified stock companies.[7]

---

1 Company law no. 66-537 dated 24 July 1996, hereinafter "CL".
2 *Société en nom collectif* or "SNC".
3 *Société en commandite simple.*
4 *Société à responsabilité limitée* or "Sàrl".
5 *Société anonyme* or "SA".
6 *Société en commandite par actions.*
7 *Société par actions simplifiée* or "SAS".

Among these, partnerships[8] which are characterized by the strong *intuitu personae* binding the associates are normally distinguished from stock companies[9] whose concept is not based on the associates' personality.

The strictness of the strong *intuitu personae* rarely allows the issue of minority rights to develop within partnerships; therefore, partnerships will not be included in this report. Similarly, the simplified stock company that has many features of a partnership although it formally constitutes a stock company, will be excluded.

The original distinction between power and capital institutionally organized within the stock partnership, renders the issue of minority rights less substantial with regard to these companies.

Therefore, the issue of minority shareholders' rights under French law will be considered with regard to statutory provisions governing corporations and limited liability companies which are the two most common types.

1. Majority Requirements for Shareholders' Resolutions

1.1 What are the majority requirements in general?

In corporations, the ordinary general meeting approves the annual accounts, the appointment or replacement of directors, control or supervisory boards of the company and all other decisions which do not come under the competence of the extraordinary meeting. A majority of the votes held by those present, or represented, shareholders is required.[10]

The extraordinary general meeting, which is solely entitled to amend the Articles of Association and by-laws of the company, requires a majority of two-thirds of the votes held by the present, or represented, shareholders.[11] Special meetings which convene the holders of a certain category of shares require the same majorities as extraordinary general meetings.

With respect to limited liability companies, ordinary decisions are carried out by an absolute majority vote, that is, a total number of votes corresponding to more than half of the shares on first consultation and by a majority of the votes cast upon second consultation.[12]

Amendments to the Articles of Association and by-laws are generally decided by associates representing three-quarters of the shares.[13]

---

8 General and limited partnerships.
9 Corporations and stock partnerships.
10 Art. 155, 3 CL.
11 Art. 155, 3 CL.
12 Art. 59, CL.
13 Art. 60, 2 CL.

1.2 Which resolutions require a greater majority?

With regard to both corporations and limited liability companies, specific majority requirements are provided for certain extraordinary decisions. The required majorities are sometimes reduced, but are more commonly increased.

In particular, an increase of shareholders' liabilities must be decided by a unanimous vote. Thus, the transformation of the company into a general partnership in which the partners are jointly and severally liable for all corporate debts requires unanimous agreement of the shareholders.[14] A unanimous vote is also required for a capital increase through raising the nominal amount of shares that must be paid up by new contributions.[15]

The transformation into a limited partnership or a stock partnership requires, in addition to a two-thirds majority, unanimous agreement from the future general partners who also will become jointly and severally liable for all corporate debts.[16]

Although not justified by any increase in a shareholder's liability, unanimity is also required for transformation into a simplified stock company.[17] Unanimity is understood to be a necessary counter-balance to the contractual freedom from which the partners profit by the drawing up of the simplified stock company Articles and by-laws.

Finally, transformation into a limited liability company must be decided with the same majority necessary for the amendment of the Articles and by-laws of a limited liability company, that is, three-quarters of the registered capital.

In limited liability companies, a unanimous vote of the associates is required in order to decide:

- a change of nationality of the company;[18]
- a transformation of the company into a simplified stock company;[19] and
- an increase of the associates' liability.[20]

Moreover, admission of new associates is subject to the consent of a majority of partners who represent three-quarters of the shares.[21]

1.3 To what extent can they be modified by the Articles of Association?

With respect to the collective decision process within limited liability companies, the Articles and by-laws, pursuant to Article 59 CL, may impose an absolute majority vote requirement for the second meeting. However, Article 60 CL prohibits any

[14] Art. 238, 1 CL.
[15] Art. 178, 3 CL.
[16] Art. 238, 2 CL.
[17] Art. 262-4 C.L.
[18] Art. 60, 1 CL.
[19] Art. 261-1, 2 CL.
[20] Art. 60, 1 CL.
[21] Arts. 45 1 and 46 CL.

provision in the Articles or by-laws requiring a greater majority for extraordinary resolutions.

For corporations, the law is silent with regard to modifications of majority rules. Quorum rules are, however, imperative. Consequently, it is generally admitted by analogy that the majority rules are also imperative which means that the articles and by-laws shall not depart from them.

2. Influence on the Decision-Making Process

2.1 Do minority shareholders have the right to call a shareholders' meeting?

Minority shareholders of corporations do not have a direct right to convene a meeting. However, pursuant to Article 158 CL, it is possible to petition the court for the appointment of an agent instructed to call a meeting. In the case of an emergency, such a petition may be filed by any interested person, hence even by a minority shareholder.[22]

In the absence of an emergency, such a petition may be filed by one or more shareholders who represent at least one-tenth of the registered capital if a general meeting is petitioned for,[23] or by one or more shareholders who represent at least one-tenth of the shares of the class concerned if a special meeting is petitioned for.[24]

With regard to limited liability companies, one-fourth of the associates or one or more associates holding one-fourth of the shares can require the manager to convene the meeting.[25] If the manager refuses, any associate can then obtain from the court the appointment of an agent instructed to convene the meeting regardless of the registered capital percentage they hold.

According to case law, however, the purpose of such a petition must be consistent with the corporate interest.[26]

2.2 Do they have the right to put matters on the agenda?

In a corporation or limited liability company, the content of the agenda is decided by the person responsible for the convocation.

However, shareholders of corporations holding a certain percentage of the registered capital may put a resolution on to the agenda. Such a resolution is compulsorily submitted to the meeting.[27]

---

22 Art. 158 2ème CL.
23 Art. 158 CL and 122 of Company decree no. 67-236 of 23 March 1967 hereafter "CD".
24 Art. 122 CD.
25 Art. 57, 3 CL.
26 *Cassation commerciale* 9 June 1990, Bulletin IV, no. 186.
27 Art. 131, 2 CD.

This prerogative is granted to any shareholder holding:

- at least 5% of the registered capital, in companies with a registered capital of less than FFR5 million; or
- a capital percentage varying from 4% to 0.5% in companies with a registered capital greater than FFR5 million.

The law is silent on this subject with respect to limited liability companies. Therefore, minority associates may not demand that a resolution be put on the agenda unless the Articles and by-laws expressly provide for such, or if the minority associates petitioned the court to convene the meeting (see 2.1 above).

3. Rights of Information, Independent Auditing and Supervision

3.1 To what extent do the (minority) shareholders have a right to be informed on company matters?

With regard to corporations, any shareholder may "at any time" obtain documents regarding corporate management during the last three fiscal years. These same documents must be provided to any shareholder prior to a meeting, be it ordinary, special or extraordinary.

If the requested information is refused, shareholders may petition that the court order the company to place at their disposal the documents they claim pursuant to Article 168 CL and that the court fix a fine if the company does not fulfil the judgment.

In addition, punitive sanctions are available against the chairman of the board of directors, the directors or the general manager if documents which the shareholders are entitled to examine are not provided.

Prior to a meeting, every shareholder may also submit written questions which the board of directors or the directorate must answer during the meeting. Also, twice per fiscal year, shareholders holding at least one-tenth of the registered capital may question, in writing, the chairman of the board of directors or the directorate about any fact that might endanger the continuation of the business operation.

In stock exchange listed companies, a letter may be sent to keeping them informed of the business, the results and other events which may have an effect on the quotations. Although the *Commission des Opérations de Bourse* (hereinafter "COB") favours the publishing of such information, the shareholders have no right to compel the company to provide them with this.

Within limited liability companies, associates' rights are generally modelled upon those of corporation shareholders.

3.2 Do they have the right to demand independent auditing or to initiate the supervision of company matters by an independent institution?

Within both corporations and limited liability companies, the shareholder or the associate, in exercise of the rights of communication and information, may be assisted by an expert registered on a list kept with the court.[28] Moreover, shareholders or associates holding at least one-tenth of the registered capital may petition the court for the appointment of an expert to report on one or several management operations which he criticizes.

The expert, whose terms of reference are determined by the commercial court, shall submit the report to the court clerk's office. The clerk will then forward it to the petitioner, the manager in limited liability companies, the board of directors or the directorate and the supervisory board in corporations, the auditor, the Attorney General's office (*Ministère public*) as well as the COB if the company makes a public offering. The same report will be annexed to the report drawn up by the auditors for the general meeting.

4. Capital Increases and Distributions

4.1 To what extent do minority shareholders have the right to participate in capital increases?

In limited liability companies, the law allows no pre-emptive subscription right in the case of a capital increase. However, the subscription of shares by a new associate would be subject to the approval of the other associates.

Within corporations, the pre-emptive subscription right is governed by Article 183 CL. This right is available to any shareholder in proportion to the number of their shares regardless of the percentage of capital held.

However, to the extent this pre-emptive right may be cancelled by a decision of the extraordinary general meeting, companies making a public offering often replace it, upon recommendation of the COB, by a priority right. This right, which has a term of 10 stock exchange days, is provided to shareholders in order to enable them to subscribe new shares in priority. The priority right like the pre-emptive subscription right is available to any shareholder. It is not negotiable.

4.2 Do minority shareholders have the right to demand dividends or other distributions?

The ordinary general meeting, after approving the accounts of the past fiscal year and establishing the existence of distributable sums, decides upon the distribution

---

[28] Arts. 33 and 144 CD.

of dividends. Therefore, minority shareholders are not entitled to require the payment of dividends. Indeed, the law does not create for shareholders any direct right to dividends.

However, minority shareholders must be protected against possible abuse from majority shareholders. Courts may intervene if minority shareholders can prove that a take-over of power has been undertaken for an illegal purpose.

The claim of the minority shareholders will be admissible in court if they can prove that a meeting's resolution not to distribute dividends has been taken for the sole "purpose of benefiting the majority members to the detriment of minority members".[29]

Courts have ruled that "the behaviour of managers who had not distributed any dividends during 20 years was abusive ...", and did not correspond to the company's interests.[30]

Minority shareholders are not entitled to demand the payment of dividends unless they can prove that an abuse was committed by the majority shareholders or that the majority shareholders agreed to guarantee a dividend to the minority shareholders pursuant to a shareholders' agreement. It is conceivable that a majority shareholder may agree to distribute, annually, a dividend to the minority shareholders should the profits so allow. Any breach of such a commitment by the majority shareholder may allow for damages as well as judicial termination of the shareholders' agreement.

A minority shareholder cannot demand payment of any other advantages either. Consideration of the example of optional reserves will help to clarify this point.

Very often, the company's Articles and by-laws provide that the general meeting may allocate a certain amount of the profits to the reserves. Since the right to a part of the profits is an individual right of a shareholder, minority shareholders may believe that they are victims of an abuse should the majority shareholders decide to allocate an important part of the profit to the reserves. Minority shareholders will most certainly be able to initiate proceedings if they can prove that the allocation of the profits into the reserves has been decided against the corporate interest and for the sole purpose of benefiting the majority members to the detriment of the minority members.[31]

However, courts are still reluctant to admit and sanction an abuse of right in this regard. Thus it has been said that "judgments confirming the setting apart of reserves in the name of corporate interest are much more frequent than those overruling it"[32] and "the systematic appropriation of the profits into the reserves can only and exceptionally characterize the existence of an abuse of right".[33]

Certain decisions of the French Supreme Court *Cour de cassation* are very illustrative since they consider that the breach of equality and the abuse of rights are realized only if "the building up of profits, year after year, allows the managers to

---

[29] *Cassation commerciale* 18 April 1961, Gazette du Palais, 1961, 2, p. 5.
[30] *Cassation commerciale* 22 April 1976, Dalloz 1977 p. 4 obs. Bousquet.
[31] *Cassation commerciale* 18 April 1961, a-m.
[32] Ripert and Roblot, *Traité de droit commercial*, Vol. 1, 15th edn, LGDJ no. 1507 p.1131.
[33] Reinhard, *Revue Trimestrielle de Droit commercial* 1988, p. 72.

grant themselves excessive compensation which enable them to make investments which should have been made by the company".[34]

5. Derivative Actions

5.1 Can (minority) shareholders enforce rights that the company has against other shareholders, directors, or third parties?

Corporations as well as limited liability companies are represented in lawsuits by their legal representatives who are solely empowered to act on behalf of the company.

Partners or shareholders are not entitled to initiate proceedings on behalf of the company unless their actions are based upon the liability of either the manager or the directors in which case they may initiate a derivative action.

Such an action allows compensation for damages suffered by the company. Starting an action is generally the task of the company's legal representatives. However, should these legal representatives fail to assert the company's rights, a shareholder may individually file the derivative action regardless of the capital percentage he holds. It is possible for shareholders to regroup in order to take such action.

The implementation of this action implies the company's involvement in the lawsuit. The relief that may be granted by the court shall be entirely for the benefit of the company.

As opposed to actions against the directors and managers, minority shareholders are not entitled to act on behalf of the company against another shareholder or a third party.

6. Other "Formal" Rights

6.1 Do minority shareholders have any other specific rights comparable to those mentioned in 2–5 above?

As mentioned above, minority shareholders may, provided that they hold a certain percentage of the registered capital,

- submit written questions to the manager or the board of directors before the session of a meeting;
- petition the court for an agent to be appointed in order to convene the meeting;

---

[34] Rives Lange, "L'abus de majorité", *Revue de jurisprudence commerciale* 1991, special edition, p. 65 *et seq.*

- ask for a resolution project to be put on the agenda;
- petition the court for the appointment of a management expert; and
- bring a derivative action against the directors.

In addition, shareholders of a corporation are also entitled to

- exercise their veto against certain resolutions that require the unanimous vote of shareholders;
- oppose the majority shareholders to grant themselves special benefits, while the beneficiaries of such benefits cannot vote on the resolution with respect to the allocation of the same; and
- apply for dissolution of the company before the president of the commercial court. Such dissolution implies, generally, a halting of the company's operation. However, courts have also pronounced such a dissolution in case of majority abuse.[35]

Finally, provided that the minority shareholders hold one-third of the shares plus one, they are entitled, pursuant to Article 153 CL, to oppose any amendments to the articles and by-laws.

7. Extension of these Rights by Statute or Shareholders' Agreements

7.1 Can the Articles of Association provide for additional rights for minority shareholders (eg to appoint directors)? If not, can such rights be provided for in shareholders' agreements? Are these options commonly used?

While the Articles of Association and by-laws can provide for the protection of minority shareholders, it should be remembered that the majority shareholders' governance is widely institutionalized by various public policy provisions of corporate or limited liability company law.

The result is that there is limited freedom to insert specific rights in favour of minority shareholders into the Articles and by-laws. Thus, it is not possible for the Articles and by-laws to impair the majority rules even to satisfy the minority shareholders (see 1.3 above).

However, the Articles and by-laws can provide for an increased right to information that will benefit all shareholders or even an extension of the right to appoint a management expert.

Finally, in order to institutionalize minority rights, or the rights of certain minority shareholders, it is necessary to resort to the preferred shares mechanism. The

---

[35] *Cassation commerciale* 18 May 1982, *Revues des sociétés*, 1982, p. 804, obs. Le Cannu.

creation of such a class of shares allows holders to be vested with various prerogatives including:

- a right to a priority dividend;
- a preferential right in the winding-up bonus; and
- a right to be represented at the board of directors.

In practice, therefore, shareholders generally prefer to organize control of the corporate management as well as the capital structure in shareholders' agreements. Such agreements are often concluded when an equity capital institutional investor holds part of the shares. The content of these agreements varies greatly.

Certain provisions, for example, voting agreements, organize the distribution of powers inside the company and create consistency within corporate business management. Other provisions seek to guarantee stability of the share ownership or protect the minority shareholders against a change in the control of the company. Such provisions include rights of pre-emption, anti-dilution provisions and the right to withdraw from the company.

In more complex situations, for instance when the company forms an integral part of a group, the agreement can provide for sophisticated provisions such as a "right of pursuit" in the subsidiaries' capital or a preferential right to take a holding in the capital of the parent company.

Thus, it appears that the content of the shareholders' agreement is highly dependent upon the imagination of the parties in accordance with their needs. However, it should be remembered that a shareholders' agreement will not always be allowed to deviate from the public policy rules which govern the organization and operation of stock companies.

In this respect, the French Parliament has recently created a new type of company, the simplified stock company. The organization and operation of the simplified stock company depends greatly upon the parties' will. But such contractual freedom has been considered dangerous enough to be reserved for only the most experienced parties. Simplified stock companies can indeed only be constituted by companies having a registered capital of at least FFR1,500,000.

8. Remedies Where a Shareholders' Resolution or Other Action Impairs the Rights of Minority Shareholders

8.1 What are the requirements for such remedies?

If minority shareholders believe that a resolution is contrary to their rights or interests, but such a resolution is none the less formally correct and therefore not subject to legal sanctions, the shareholders may bring a lawsuit on the grounds of majority abuse.

The requirements for such an action are based on the concept of majority abuse. This concept is not defined by statute, and case law has therefore defined it.

A "resolution taken against the general corporate interest and for the sole purpose of benefiting the majority member to the minority's detriment"[36] is considered abusive. Thus, majority abuse is characterized by two elements:

- interference with the corporate interest; and
- a breach of equality between the shareholders which is characterized by favouring the majority shareholders to the detriment of the minority shareholders.

This breach must be "conscious" or "purposeful". The majority members must be "conscious of favouring themselves, directly or through an intermediary".[37]

Although some legal authors have asserted that breach of equality is the more important of the two elements in the definition of majority abuse, nothing in case law supports this opinion.

8.2 When do the courts of your country accept these requirements?

In addition to systematic appropriation of the profits into the reserves, majority abuse has been upheld in the following cases:

- the assessment of exorbitant compensation for the executives of the company;[38]
- the assumption by a company of the liabilities of its subsidiary if the resolution had the sole purpose of covering up improper management by a member of the majority group;[39]
- the *location-gérance*[40] granted by one company to another company set up by the majority shareholders of the first one since the purpose of the transaction was to permit the transfer of the corporate assets solely to the majority shareholders;[41] and
- the insertion, between a parent company and its subsidiary, of a stock partnership having as general partner and manager as provided by the Articles and bylaws the majority shareholder of the parent company since this transaction secured for the majority shareholder total freedom of action by limiting the intervention powers of the minority shareholder.[42]

---

36 *Cassation commerciale* 18 April 1961, a-m.
37 Hemard, Terre and Mabilat *Sociétés commerciales*, Tome II, Dalloz no. 388.
38 *Cour d'appel Grenoble* 6 May 1964, Gazette du Palais 1964, 2, p. 208.
39 *Cassation commerciale* 29 May 1972, Bulletin IV, no. 164.
40 *Location-gérance* is a means of transferring a *fonds de commerce*, ie the aggregate of personal property, both tangible and intangible, used in a particular business.
41 *Cassation commerciale* 8 January 1973, Bulletin IV, no. 13.
42 *Cassation commerciale* 24 January 1995, *Revue de Jurisprudence de Droit des affaires*, 4/95 no. 439.

8.3 What remedies are available to the claimant?

The measures that may be petitioned and the sanctions that the court can impose differ depending on whether compensation is sought for prejudice suffered by the minority shareholders or by the company (see 5.1 above).

The minority shareholders may achieve the annulment of the abusive resolution taken by the majority shareholders pursuant to Article 360 CL. In addition to such invalidation, they may recover damages if the action is brought against the majority shareholders who perpetrated the fault and the abuse.[43]

To the extent that majority abuse reveals a disagreement between the shareholders, sanctions against the company may also be considered. Thus, courts have pronounced the dissolution of a company pursuant to Article 1844-7 of the Civil Code (see 6.1 above).

In addition, courts have, in some cases, appointed a temporary judicial administrator in order to overcome a crisis brought about by the majority abuse.

9. Specific Protection if the Company is Controlled by Another Company

9.1 What are the rights and remedies of a shareholder of Company A when Company B gains control over it (by acquiring the majority of its shares or otherwise)?

The gaining of control over Company A by Company B does not involve any inequality between shareholders.

As pointed out by a legal scholar, the majority shareholders of the controlled company are most certainly privileged since they may "transfer their rights under more favourable terms". This transfer "does not create by any means a breach of equality between shareholders" but "induces merely a value differentiation of the corporate rights".[44]

Therefore, the minority shareholders of the controlled company may not oppose such a taking over of control on the grounds of the concept of an abuse of right.

The French Supreme Court (*Cour de Cassation*) confirmed this rule in cases where the control of companies had been transferred with the consent of the majority shareholders. The Supreme Court did not find majority abuse since taking over of control is not contrary to the corporate interest.[45]

Generally, minority shareholders are therefore not entitled to any particular protection in case of a transfer of control.

The situation is different with regard to listed companies in which the protection of minority shareholders is provided by various measures:

---

[43] *Cassation commerciale* 6 June 1990, *Revue des sociétés* 1990, p. 606, obs. Chartier.

[44] D. Schmidt, "Quelques remarques sur les droits de la minorité dans les cessions de contrôle" Dalloz 1972, chroniques, p. 223.

[45] *Cassation commerciale* 21 January 1970, RTD Com., 1970, p. 738, obs. Houin.

- If one or more individuals or legal entities hold more than one-third of the capital shares or more than one-third of the voting rights of a French company listed on the official exchange, they shall inform the Securities Exchange Board (*Conseil des Bourses de valeur*, hereinafter "CBV") about the holding and shall file a take-over bid proposal (*offre publique d'achat*, hereinafter "OPA") for the total amount of existing securities which also includes the minority shareholders' securities.[46]
- If one or several persons acting in co-operation hold 95% of the voting rights in the general meetings, the minority shareholders shall be entitled to request the CBV to require the majority shareholders to file an OPA for the minority shareholders' shares.[47]
- If a majority group holds at least two-thirds of the voting rights of a corporation and wishes to transform this company into a limited partnership with shares, this group shall file a public offer of withdrawal (*offre publique de retrait*, hereinafter "OPR") for the minority shareholders.[48]
- If individuals or legal entities have a controlling influence on a modification of the Articles or by-laws of the company, they shall consider, together with the CBV, whether an OPR is necessary.[49]
- Any transaction that would result in the holding of a majority of the capital or voting rights of a company implies an obligation on the part of the control stock purchaser to purchase all securities offered on the market (thus including those of the minority shareholders) at the price for which the securities transfer was carried out.[50]

Besides the above-mentioned protection which allows minority shareholders to transfer their securities in the case of a transfer of control, it must be pointed out that the company (and especially its executives) must inform its shareholders of the identity of individuals or legal entities who hold more than one-twentieth, one-tenth, one-fifth, one-third, one-half or two-thirds of the registered capital or voting rights in the general meetings. Therefore, the minority shareholders, even if they do not hold sufficient shares to oppose the takeover of their company, have none the less the benefit of various measures which protect them in case of a takeover.

Both civil and penal sanctions are of course available, should such measures not be abided by.

9.2 What are the shareholder's rights and remedies when company B exerts its control over company A in a way which damages the interests of the latter?

A takeover of control, as seen above, cannot be avoided by the minority shareholders. However, the subsequent exercise of power may be subject to sanctions. Mi-

---

46 Art. 5.4.1. CBV regulation.
47 Art. 5.5.2. CBV regulation.
48 Art. 5.5.4. CBV regulation.
49 Art. 5.5.5. CBV regulation
50 Art. 5.3.2. CBV regulation.

nority shareholders are always entitled to claim abuse by the majority under the requirements already described (see 8.1 above).

Case law has, however, recently denied minority shareholders the right to oppose the acquisition of the company by its majority shareholder on the grounds of "special advantage".[51]

It has been held that "the fact that the majority shareholder receives the assets and liabilities of the company he/she acquires, whereas the minority shareholders receive only shares of the acquiring company, does not constitute a "special advantage" because within a company, even if each share is treated in the same way with the same voting rights, the majority rule prevails with the minority only being allowed to complain about a majority abuse".[52]

---

[51] *Avantage particulier*; see Arts. 193 and 377 CL.
[52] *Cour d'appel Douai* 7 July 1994, Bulletin Joly 1994, p. 264, obs. Le Cannu.

GERMANY

Matthias W. Stecher

Beiten Burkhardt Mittl & Wegener
Munich

PROTECTION OF MINORITY SHAREHOLDERS

***EDITOR* MATTHIAS W. STECHER**

GERMANY

Matthias W. Stecher

1. Majority Requirements for Shareholders' Resolutions

1.1 What are the majority requirements in general?

For limited liability companies (GmbH) and stock corporations (AG), a simple majority of the votes given is required to pass a shareholders' resolution.[1] Therefore, abstentions and the voting rights of absentee shareholders are not taken into account. In the event of a tied vote, the proposal fails.

Neither the GmbH nor the AG requires a quorum in order to pass a resolution.

The Act on Limited Liability Companies provides for one vote for every interest in the amount of DM100; the Articles of Association can specify otherwise. According to the Stock Corporation Act, every share is entitled to one vote. Under certain circumstances, preferred stock without voting rights may be issued; stocks with multiple voting rights are permitted only in exceptional cases, but have no practical significance.

---

1 §47 I GmbHG, §133 AktG; GmbHG = Act on Limited Liability Companies, AktG = Stock Corporation Act.

1.2 Which resolutions require a greater majority?

In the case of the GmbH, a three-quarters majority of the votes given is required to amend or modify the Articles of Association or to dissolve the corporation.[2]

In the case of the AG, on the other hand, modifications and amendments to the Articles of Association require a simple majority of the votes given in addition to a three-quarters majority of the share capital represented at the meeting.[3] This is especially true for capital increases and the dissolution of the corporation. There are also several additional statutory provisions relating to special majority requirements that shall not be addressed individually in this report. The distinction made between votes given and the capital represented is particularly important in cases in which the votes do not correspond to the shareholders' capital, for example if there are preferred shares without voting rights, or shares with multiple voting rights.

1.3 To what extent can they be modified by the Articles of Association?

GmbH Instead of a simple majority, a greater majority or even unanimity can be specified; moreover, minimum requirements relating to the competency to pass resolutions (a quorum) can be introduced. The three-quarters majority required for amendments or modifications to the Articles of Association can similarly be increased, but not decreased.

AG The general rule is that the Articles of Association may only differ from statutory provisions when the law expressly allows such differentiations.[4] The requirement of a simple majority to pass a shareholders' resolution can be increased in the Articles of Association, but not decreased; for elections, however, a reduction in the number of votes required is also possible.[5] The three-quarters majority necessary to amend or modify the Articles of Association can be increased or decreased.

2. Influence on the Decision-Making Process

2.1 Do minority shareholders have the right to call a shareholders' meeting?

2.2 Do they have the right to put matters on the agenda?

GmbH Shareholders whose interests represent at least one-tenth of the share capital can demand that the management of the company call a shareholders' meeting. In doing so, the shareholders must indicate the agenda and the reasons why they

---

2 §§53 II, 60 I 2 GmbHG.
3 §179 II AktG.
4 §23 V AktG.
5 §133 I and II AktG.

consider such a meeting to be necessary. Should company management refuse to call the meeting, the minority shareholders can call the meeting themselves. With the same share of the votes, they can also demand that certain (additional) items are placed on the agenda.[6]

AG The law corresponds to that of the GmbH; however, a minority of one-twentieth of the share capital is sufficient.[7] The Articles of Association can specify an even smaller minority. Should the board of directors refuse a request to call a meeting, the minority shareholders can seek a court order authorizing them to call a shareholders' meeting.

3. Rights of Information, Independent Auditing and Supervision

3.1 To what extent do the (minority) shareholders have a right to be informed on company matters?

GmbH Every shareholder has the right to request information on the affairs of the corporation and to inspect its financial records and written documents.[8] The financial statements and written documents include accounting documents as well as correspondence, including data stored electronically. The scope of the information depends on the purpose of the request (eg, to evaluate the general position of the corporation, or to evaluate a proposed resolution), and on how, specifically, the request is phrased. In the case of a specific question, the corporation must provide a detailed answer.

The company managers may refuse to provide information or allow inspection if there are grounds to believe that the shareholder will use such information in a manner which is not related to the business activities of the corporation and which would be detrimental to its interests. Such a refusal requires a shareholder resolution. Should the information or inspection be refused improperly, the shareholder can seek a court order to gain access to the information.[9]

AG Every shareholder has the right to receive information from the board of directors, but only upon requesting such information at the general meeting, only and to the extent that the information is necessary for a pertinent evaluation of an item on the agenda.[10] The board can only refuse such a request in extremely limited circumstances, which are described in detail in statutory provisions. Should a request be refused improperly, a shareholder can seek a court order to gain access to the information.[11]

---

6 §50 GmbHG.
7 §122 AktG.
8 §51 a GmbHG.
9 §51 b GmbHG.
10 §131 AktG.
11 §132 AktG.

3.2. Do they have the right to demand independent auditing or to initiate the supervision of company matters by an independent institution?

GmbH The statutory provisions do not provide minority shareholders with any such rights; however, they may be included in the Articles of Association.

AG At the general meeting, the shareholders can, with a simple majority, appoint a so-called "special auditor" (*Sonderprüfer*) to audit the procedures involved with the founding or managing of the AG. Should the votes fall short of the simple majority, minority shareholders whose holdings total one-tenth of the share capital or a nominal value of DM2 million can request the court to order the special audit. The court will grant such a request "when circumstances exist that are grounds for suspecting that the affairs have been conducted dishonestly or are gross violations of the law or the Articles of Association".[12] A gross violation is recognized as such especially when it creates a claim for damages on behalf of the corporation.

The appointment of the special auditor must be with reference to certain affairs (and not constitute a general audit of an entire period). The audit focuses on the actions of the board of directors, but also considers the managing employees and the supervisory board, to the extent that these have influence on the management of the corporation.

Additionally, a minority of shareholders whose holdings constitute at least one-twentieth of the share capital or a nominal value of DM1 million can request the court to order a special audit when there are grounds to assume that certain items are not insignificantly undervalued in the year-end balance sheets or that an appendix to the annual report does not contain all or some of the required information.[13] The general statutory provisions regarding the audit of annual financial statements[14] are independent of this; a shareholders' resolution or a demand on behalf of the minority shareholders for an annual audit is not required.

4. Capital Increases and Distributions

4.1 To what extent do (minority) shareholders have the right to participate in capital increases?

GmbH Since the original capital is specified in the Articles of Association, a resolution to increase the capital represents a modification of the Articles of Association and requires a three-quarters majority (see 1.2 above).

The right to participate in a capital increase can, however, be excluded, either in whole or in part, with a three-quarters majority. This would, however, only be ad-

---

[12] §142 II AktG.
[13] §258 I AktG.
[14] §316 *et seq*. HGB (HGB = Commercial Code).

missible when such an exclusion from participation in the capital increase was in the best interests of the corporation, and there are strict guidelines which determine whether this is the case. For example, an exclusion from participating in a capital increase may be allowed if the purchaser of the new shares is willing to offer more financial backing than the shares are worth, or if the purchaser is only willing to invest if he can acquire a majority of shares. If a capital increase in which only one shareholder is allowed to participate is to be used to acquire valuable contributions in kind, it needs to be considered whether the corporation could instead accomplish the acquisition by means of offering the new shares to all shareholders and simply purchasing the items. Only in extremely limited circumstances can a single, individual (minority) shareholder be excluded from exercising the right to participate in a capital increase.

If a shareholders' resolution in favour of a capital increase violates these general rules, the affected shareholder can challenge the resolution in a court proceeding. If the action is successful, the resolution is considered to have been invalid from the beginning.

AG As is the case generally for amending or modifying the Articles of Association, a simple majority of the votes given and a three-quarters majority of the share capital represented at the vote is required to effectuate a capital increase; this three-quarters majority can be reduced in the Articles of Association.[15]

In contrast to the GmbH, the right of the stockholders of an AG to participate in a capital increase is expressly regulated by statute.[16] For the exclusion of such rights, the same guidelines apply as those which are applicable to the GmbH (described above). Again, there are almost no circumstances in which an individual (minority) shareholder could be legally precluded from exercising pre-emptive rights.

4.2 Do minority shareholders have the right to demand dividends or other distributions?

GmbH Until 1985, the shareholders of a GmbH were legally entitled to the profit of the corporation if the Articles of Association did not specify otherwise. However, the new version of §29 GmbHG provides for the shareholders to determine, by the same majority required for shareholders' resolutions, if all or part of the profits are to remain in the corporation. Minority shareholders are therefore not entitled to demand payment of a dividend. The only exception is a situation in which the non-payment of a dividend is not justified by the interests of the corporation, and particularly benefits only the interests of the majority shareholders, which would be difficult to prove. Therefore, sufficient protection for the minority shareholders is really only possible in appropriate provisions in the Articles of Association, which can specify that a certain share of the profit must be paid to the shareholders, or that the entire profit is to be paid unless a shareholders' resolution, for example, with a qualified majority of the votes, decides otherwise.

---

[15] Exceptions see §182 I AktG.
[16] §§186 *et seq.* AktG.

AG Similarly, in an AG, the shareholders resolve, by a simple majority at the annual meeting, whether the profits are to be paid out to shareholders or are to remain in the corporation.[17] In any case, the stockholders are entitled to a dividend of 4% of the nominal amount of their shareholding unless it is necessary to retain this profit share to further the interests of the corporation "in the opinion of a prudent businessman".[18] A resolution in violation of these rights can be challenged by the stockholders.

5. Derivative Actions

5.1 Can (minority) shareholders enforce rights that the company has against other shareholders, directors, or third parties?

GmbH In the past few years, the courts have recognized that in certain circumstances the shareholders of a GmbH have the right to pursue legal action against other shareholders on behalf of the corporation. This right, which is also known as the *actio pro socio*, exists only if the majority of shareholders does not pursue the claims. This legal action is limited to claims arising out of the shareholder relations, for example, cases such as the payment of contributions which are past due, damages, cessation of competition, but does not include claims resulting from a contract between the corporation and a shareholder. A shareholder who exercises this right and initiates an *actio pro socio* can only demand performance to the corporation directly, and not to himself personally.

The prevailing opinion is that the individual shareholders cannot pursue any claims which the corporation has against directors or third parties.

AG A minority which holds at least one-tenth of the share capital can demand that the corporation pursue certain damage claims against the founders of the corporation or the members of the board of directors of an AG.[19] However, a minority shareholder does not have the right to pursue such claims himself; there is no legal action for the shareholders of the AG which is comparable to the *actio pro socio*. The only exception is in the case of certain damage claims against the controlling corporation of a concern (see 9 below).

6. Other "Formal" Rights

6.1 Do minority shareholders have any other specific rights comparable to those mentioned in 2–5 above?

The right of every shareholder to challenge shareholders' resolutions is of particular importance to the minority shareholder. A challenge to a resolution is accom-

---

[17] §174 AktG.
[18] For details see §254 AktG.
[19] §147 AktG.

plished by means of a complaint filed with the court. The details are governed by §243 *et seq*. of the Stock Corporation Act, and are applied by analogy to the GmbH. According to these provisions, a resolution is initially valid, even if it violates statutory provisions or the Articles of Association; the resolution becomes ineffective only once it has been declared void by the court. A resolution is only void *per se* in the case of certain serious defects.

In the case of an AG, a minority holding one-tenth of the share capital can pursue certain claims on behalf of the corporation (see also 5.1 above). The same minority can demand a vote at the annual meeting on a stockholder's proposal regarding the election of the members of the supervisory board.[20] Shareholders whose interests total one-tenth of the share capital or a nominal value of DM2 million can demand that decisions to exonerate the members of the board of directors or the supervisory board are not to be made for the board as a whole, but rather for each individual member.[21]

For the GmbH, a minority of one-tenth of the share capital can file a complaint against the corporation with the intent to dissolve the corporation. Such a motion will be granted when it has become impossible to fulfil the purpose of the corporation, or when there are other important grounds for the dissolution of the company in the relations among shareholders.[22] The same minority can request that if the corporation is to be liquidated, the liquidator shall not be a managing director or someone selected by the shareholders' meeting, but a person appointed by the court.[23]

7. Extension of These Rights by Statute or Shareholders' Agreements

7.1 Can the Articles of Association provide for additional rights of the minority shareholders? If not, can such rights be provided for in shareholders' agreements? Are these options commonly used?

GmbH The basic rule is that the shareholders are free to provide for any rights and obligations in the Articles of Association unless statutory provisions expressly limit this freedom. Various ways in which the rights of minority shareholders can be strengthened through appropriate provisions in the Articles of Association were discussed above (see 1.1, 1.3, 3.2, 4.2). Additional provisions which are often used include the following:

- The transfer of shares requires a shareholders' resolution in order to be effective (and, as the case may be, also requires a qualified majority).

20 §137 AktG.
21 §120 AktG.
22 §61 I GmbHG.
23 §66 II GmbHG.

- In case of the sale of shares, the remaining shareholders are to be accorded pre-emptive rights.
- A (minority) shareholder is to be the director, without a resolution, or he has the right to appoint a director.
- Certain business transactions (eg the purchase of real property) require a shareholders' resolution (and, as the case may be, also require a qualified majority).

Given the numerous possibilities available in drafting the Articles of Association, shareholders' agreements play a relatively minor role in strengthening the rights of the minority shareholders.

AG As discussed earlier, the Articles of Association of an AG may only deviate from law if the statutory provisions themselves expressly allow it. Specific examples have already been discussed above (1.1, 1.3, 2, 4.1). Beyond this, it is also possible to provide that stock which has been issued in the stockholder's name cannot be assigned without consent of the shareholders at the general meeting.[24] Pre-emptive rights cannot be determined in the Articles of Association, but they can be agreed upon between individual stockholders. The Articles can grant certain stockholders the right to appoint members of the supervisory board.[25] The shareholders do not, however, have any direct influence on the appointment of the board of directors, since its members are appointed by the supervisory board.

Shareholders' agreements in which the shareholders bind themselves to act in a certain manner are effective and valid; such agreements can also be used to strengthen the rights of the minority shareholders. If one party to such a contract does not fulfil his obligations, he is liable for breach and the other party can file a complaint seeking specific performance. Note, however, that a breach of a contract between shareholders does not affect the validity of the vote and the shareholders' resolution.

8. Remedies Where a Shareholders' Resolution or Other Action Impairs the Rights of Minority Shareholders

8.1 What are the requirements for such remedies?

Every shareholder is legally obligated to consider the legitimate interests of the other shareholders in all of his actions (fiduciary duty – *Treupflicht*). This principle was developed with respect to the GmbH, but has since been recognized by the courts for the AG as well.[26] The scope of this duty depends on individual circumstances; particularly relevant is the nature of the relationship among the shareholders, the scope of the investment – the controlling majority shareholders are bound

---

24 §68 II AktG.
25 §101 II AktG.
26 BGH NJW 1988, 1579 *Linotype*.

by particularly extensive fiduciary obligations; the duration of the investment and the necessity and proportionality of a certain action in relation to its effect on other shareholders. A special aspect of the fiduciary duty is the rule of equal treatment of all shareholders.[27]

8.2 When do the courts of your country accept these requirements?

The courts have, in the case of the GmbH, recognized a breach of fiduciary duty:

- when a majority shareholder aims to dissolve the corporation with the intent to continue its operation at the exclusion of the minority;[28]
- when a shareholder, as a result of a serious disagreement with another shareholder, works to dissolve the corporation, even though the other shareholder is willing to assume the shares at their full value;[29]
- when a shareholder refuses to participate in a needed capital increase in order to enforce other rights which are not related to the increase but are only in his personal interests;[30]
- when a shareholder who exercises a certain influence on the management of the company competes against this company through another company.[31]

In the court decisions relating to the AG, the principle of fiduciary duty has played only a limited role. One court held that a majority resolution regarding the dissolution of the corporation is challengeable when the majority shareholder has already arranged with the board of directors of the AG to acquire a significant portion of the assets of the corporation.[32] It has been discussed above (4.1) that preventing the exercise of pre-emptive rights in the case of a capital increase can be valid only under certain circumstances.[33]

8.3 What remedies are available to the claimant?

The following remedies may be available depending on the specific case:

- If the breach of fiduciary duty is the result of a shareholders' resolution, the resolution can be avoided by the affected shareholders like any other resolution which violates statutory law or the Articles of Association (see 6.1 above). Only in extreme cases is a resolution void *ipso iure*.
- Should certain actions be harmful, the shareholders can demand that the actions be ceased. In exceptional cases, the fiduciary duty can result in an obligation to

---

27 See §53 a AktG.
28 BGHZ 76, 352, 355 f.
29 BGH NJW 1985, 1901.
30 BGH WM 1987, 841.
31 BGHZ 80, 69, 74.
32 BGH NJW 1988, 1579.
33 See, for the AG, BGHZ 71, 40.

act affirmatively (eg, to vote in a particular way); in these cases, a claimant can demand specific performance.

- Additionally, a breach of the fiduciary duty can result in claims for damages by the injured minority shareholders.
- The shareholder of a GmbH (not an AG) has a right to be bought out if there is an important ground which makes it unreasonable to expect the shareholder to remain in the company. In this case he can claim payment of an amount equal to the proportionate market value of the company. This right for payment can be restricted but not excluded in the Articles. In Germany there is no statutory right to have the company wound up in such cases.[34]
- In urgent cases, the injured shareholder may also obtain a preliminary injunction aimed at stopping a harmful action or the implementation of a voidable resolution.

9. Specific Protection if the Company is Controlled by Another Company

9.1 What are the rights and remedies of a shareholder of Company A if Company B gains control over it (by acquiring the majority of its shares or otherwise)?

9.1.1 The term "concern"

A key term in the German law of groups of corporations is the "concern". A concern is formed whenever a dominant corporation and one or more dependent corporations are managed uniformly under the management of the dominant corporation.[35] It should be noted that the mere holding of a majority in another company does not necessarily lead to such "uniform management" and, consequently, to the rights explained hereinafter.

A concern can be created when a dependent corporation (hereinafter Company A) contractually grants the dominant corporation (hereinafter Company B) and its board of directors the comprehensive right to make decisions, or is obligated to assign its entire profits to Company B.[36] Although these contracts are regulated by statutory law only in the case of the AG, a GmbH can also make such a contract.

A dominant corporation can also exercise influence on a dependent corporation (AG or GmbH) without a contract, with the intent to bring the corporation under its unified management. Such an exercise of influence, in individual cases, is known as a "*de facto* concern"; if Company B's influence is so extensive that individual,

---

34 See, however, §61 GmbHG and 6.1 above.
35 §18 I 1 AktG.
36 §§291 *et seq.* AktG.

independent directives and their effects are no longer distinguishable, it is known as a "qualified *de facto* concern".

While the law of the AG contains very detailed rules regarding the different types of concerns, the law of concern for the GmbH has developed largely through court decisions and scholarly debate. To some extent, the provisions of the law of the AG are applied analogously, so that it is appropriate to examine these rules first.

The following rules (also those described under 9.2) apply as long as Company A is located in Germany, which includes cases in which Company B is a foreign corporation.

9.1.2.1 Contractual concern with a subordinated AG

The contract is only valid if the general meeting (also) of Company A consents, for which a three-quarters majority of the share capital present is required. The Articles of Association can specify a greater majority, but not a smaller one. Moreover, the contract must contain a dividend guarantee for the benefit of the minority shareholders in order to be valid ("compensation").[37] The minority shareholder has a right to receive those payments which would likely be paid on individual shares, given the corporation's present financial situation and its forecasted profitability. Arguably, the dominant corporation is responsible for fulfilling these obligations. The amount of the payment is determined when the shareholders approve the contract, so that later positive or negative developments will not be taken into consideration. The value of the obligation can also, at the option of the minority shareholders, be measured by the dividends of Company B.[38]

Instead of the dividend guarantee, a minority shareholder can demand that Company B buy him out at a reasonable price.[39] The payment consists of shares of Company B, if this is a domestic AG, otherwise it will be a cash payment.

Not suprisingly, determining the value of the performance owed to the minority shareholders is extremely difficult in practice. First, the expected future earnings of Company A must be calculated. In the case of a buy out, the value of the corporation and the value of the individual stocks must be determined. Should a minority shareholder demand payment based on the dividends of Company B, or to be bought out in exchange for shares of Company B, the exchange ratio and therefore the value of Company B must be determined as well. A special judicial proceeding has been established to audit these valuation issues;[40] while such proceedings generally are time-intensive, they tend to result in the minority shareholders receiving a higher price than that which was initially offered by the dominant corporation.[41]

9.1.2.2 *De facto* concern with a subordinated AG

While the minority shareholders of an AG are only protected against detrimental actions (see 9.2.1), some of the available literature indicates that a *de facto* concern is only legally permissible if it was approved by the same majority that is required

---

37 §304 AktG.
38 §304 II 2 AktG.
39 §305 AktG.
40 §306 AktG.
41 See cases: *VW/Audi-NSU*, BGH AG 1976, 218; *VEBA-Gelsenberg*, BGHZ 69, 334; *Thyssen/Rheinstahl*, OLG Düsseldorf AG 1978, 283; *Langenbrahm/Rüger*, BGH AG 1991, 104.

for modifications and amendments to the Articles of Association.[42] There are no decisions of the Federal Court of Justice ("BGH") on this issue.

9.1.3 Contractual concern with a subordinated GmbH

It is still debatable what majority of the vote is required for a resolution to be valid that would create such a contract in the case of the GmbH. The most common opinion is probably that unanimity is required; the BGH has not yet decided on this question. If a smaller majority is to be sufficient, the general view is that the minority shareholders are to be given a dividend guarantee or be bought out pursuant to § 304 *et seq.* AktG.

9.1.4 De facto *concern with a subordinated GmbH*

The prevailing opinion among scholars is that the formation of a qualified *de facto* concern, in the case of the GmbH, requires a unanimous resolution of the shareholders of Company A. If a smaller minority is to be sufficient pursuant to the provisions of the Articles of Association, the minority shareholders could order an audit to determine whether the resolution is in the best interests of Company A.[43]

9.1.5 Protection of minority shareholders of the dominant corporation

It should not be forgotten that the minority shareholders of Company B could also suffer disadvantage when a concern is formed. For example, if an AG transfers important business activities to a subsidiary, the influence of the shareholders of Company B on such activities is shifted to the board of directors of Company B. For this reason, the BGH ruled, in a well known 1982 case, that such an extensive measure requires the same majority as amending or modifying the Articles of Association, and that in the absence of this majority, the minority shareholders have the right to demand a nullification, even retroactively.[44] The same should be the case for the GmbH, although the specifics are still debatable.

9.2 What are the shareholder's rights and remedies when Company B exerts its control over Company A in a way which damages the interests of the latter?

9.2.1 AG

Contracts to assign profits or assume control exist precisely for the purpose of managing the dependent corporation in a manner which serves the interests of the dom-

---

42 OLG Hamm, NJW 1987, 1030 *Banning*.
43 According to a BGH decision relating to a dependent partnership – BGHZ 80, 39 *Süssen*.
44 BGHZ 83, 122 *Holzmüller*.

inating corporation. Directives are not acceptable, however, if they violate the contract or statutory provisions, or if the existence of the dependent corporation is threatened.

There are stronger protections for the minority shareholders in the case of a *de facto* concern. §311 of the Stock Corporation Act forbids Company B to exercise any influence to the detriment of Company A, unless it provides compensation for any disadvantages. If this is not done by the end of the fiscal year, Company B will be liable for damages.[45]

Even with individual and independent measures that are detrimental to Company A, it is difficult to ascertain the amount of damages, that is, how Company A would have fared in the absence of those measures. It is nearly impossible to calculate the value of damages in the case of a qualified *de facto* concern. For this reason, attempts are generally made to protect minority shareholders at the time the concern is formed, and not only through §311 and 317 of the Stock Corp. Law (see 9.1.2.2 above).

9.2.2 GmbH

Since the protection of minority shareholders provided for in the Stock Corporation Act is not adequate, the courts have attempted to develop specific rules for the GmbH. As early as 1975, the BGH held that the dominant corporation is completely barred from injuring a dependent corporation.[46] Examples of such injuries include the shifting of business from Company A to Company B,[47] an agreement to pay inflated prices for shipments to Company A by Company B, the obligation on the part of Company A to pay a "concern fee" to Company B, etc. In such a case, Company A can seek to reverse the measures, have the measures cease, and also seek damages. Company B has the burden of proving that the injuries to Company A were not the result of an exercise of influence which violated any duty. Importantly for the minority shareholder, he can use the *actio pro socio* to pursue the claims that Company A may have against Company B.

---

45 §317 AktG.

46 BGHZ 65, 15 *ITT*; BGHZ 89, 162 *Heumann/Ogilvy*.

47 BGH NJW 1979, 2104.

IRELAND

Gerard Coll, Jacqueline Ennis

Eugene F. Collins

Dublin

PROTECTION OF MINORITY SHAREHOLDERS

***EDITOR* MATTHIAS W. STECHER**

IRELAND

Gerard Coll, Jacqueline Ennis

Introduction

In Ireland, the legal structure of companies is governed by the Companies Acts, 1963 to 1990 (the "Acts"). The majority of companies formed and registered under the Acts are private companies, accordingly this report focuses primarily on private companies.

1. Majority Requirements for Shareholders' Resolutions

1.1 What are the majority requirements in general?

There are two kinds of resolutions in Irish Company Law: ordinary resolutions and special resolutions.

An ordinary resolution must be passed by a simple majority of 50% plus one vote of those voting in person or by proxy. Seven days' notice must be given of a general meeting at which an ordinary resolution will be proposed.

A special resolution must be passed by not less than three-quarters of the votes cast by such members as are entitled to vote in person or, where proxies are allowed, by proxy at a general meeting of which not less than 21 days' notice, specifying the intention to propose a special resolution, has been given.[1] Special resolutions are used to authorize actions which may be contentious or where they are expressly provided for by law. By its Articles of Association a company may provide that particular resolutions must be passed by a prescribed majority (indeed this is a common feature of shareholder agreements).

1.2 Which resolutions require a greater majority?

Under the Acts, the following resolutions require a 75% majority, (ie to be passed by special resolution):

- to alter the objects of a company's Memorandum of Association;[2]
- to alter the Articles of Association of a company;[3]
- to change the name of a company, (an approval is also required from the Minister for Enterprise and Employment); [4]
- to alter any provision contained in a company's Memorandum which could lawfully have been contained in the Articles of Association;[5]
- s. 60 of the Companies Act, 1963 provides, in essence, that it is not lawful for a company to give financial assistance in connection with the purchase of shares in the company or, where the company is a subsidiary company, in its holding company. This restriction does not apply if the financial assistance is given under the authority of a special resolution of the company passed not more than 12 months previously;[6]
- any preference shares issued by a company before the 5 May 1959 may be redeemed provided the redemption has been authorized by a special resolution of the company;[7]
- a limited company may, by special resolution, determine that any portion of its share capital which has not already been called up shall not be capable of being called up except in the event and for the purposes of the company being wound up;[8]
- subject to confirmation by the High Court, a company limited by shares or a company limited by guarantee and having a share capital may, if so authorized by its Articles of Association, pass a special resolution to reduce its share capital;[9]

---

1 S. 141, Companies Act, 1963.
2 S. 10, Companies Act, 1963.
3 S. 15, Companies Act, 1963.
4 S. 23, Companies Act, 1963.
5 S. 28, Companies Act, 1963.
6 S. 60. Companies Act, 1963.
7 S. 65(d), Companies Act, 1963.
8 S. 67, Companies Act, 1963.
9 S. 72, Companies Act, 1963.

- a limited company, if authorized by its Articles, may by special resolution, alter its Memorandum so as to render unlimited the liability of its directors or of any managing director;[10]
- if a provision is made by the Articles or by any agreement entered into between any person and the company empowering a director to assign his office to another person, any such assignment will only be effective if it has been approved by a special resolution;[11]
- where a company proposes to enter into an arrangement with its creditors or members and three-quarters of the creditors (measured in value) or three-quarters of the members support the arrangement it will, if sanctioned by the High Court, be binding on all creditors or members and also on the company;[12]
- the winding up of a company by the High Court;[13]
- the voluntary winding up of a company if the members so resolve;[14]
- certain transfers of company property in the course of a liquidation; [15]
- the re-registration of a private company as a public company;[16]
- the re-registration of an unlimited company as a public limited company;[17]
- the re-registration of a public limited company as a private company;[18]
- the disapplication of the statutory right of pre-emption on the issue of shares;[19]
- the variation of rights attaching to different classes of shares;[20]
- the conversion of a limited company to an unlimited one and vice versa;[21]
- establishing the re-issue price of any treasury shares;[22]
- the "off-market" purchase by a company of its own shares;[23] and
- the "off-market" purchase of shares by a company in its holding company.[24]

1.3 To what extent can they be modified by the Articles of Association?

The above statutory provisions requiring special resolutions must be adhered to unless otherwise expressly provided in the statutory provisions. For example, any special resolution required under section 38 of the Companies (Amendment) Act,

---

10 S. 198,Companies Act, 1963.
11 S. 199, Companies Act, 1963.
12 S. 201,Companies Act, 1963.
13 S. 213(a), Companies Act, 1963.
14 S. 251(a) Companies Act, 1963.
15 S. 260, Companies Act, 1963.
16 S. 9, Companies (Amendment) Act, 1983.
17 S. 11, Companies (Amendment) Act, 1983.
18 S. 14 , Companies (Amendment)Act, 1983.
19 S. 24, Companies (Amendment) Act, 1983.
20 S. 38, Companies Act,1983 and Model Art. Table A, Part 1, Regulation 3.
21 Ss. 52 & 53, Companies (Amendment) Act, 1983.
22 S. 209, Companies Act, 1990.
23 S. 213, Companies Act, 1990.
24 S. 224, Companies Act, 1990.

1983 (see above), is subject to any alternative provision contained in the Articles of Association of a company dealing with the variation of rights.

2. Influence on the Decision-Making Process

2.1 Do minority shareholders have the right to call a shareholders' meeting?

There are two types of members meetings: Annual general meetings and Extraordinary general meetings. Section 134(b) of the Companies Act, 1963 provides that two or more members holding not less than one-tenth of the issued share capital or where the company does not have a share capital not less than 5% in number of all the members of the company may call a meeting unless the Articles of Association provide otherwise. It is common for the articles of association of private companies to provide for the convening of meetings by the directors alone.

An important right is given by section 132 of the Companies Act, 1963 to members, namely, to require the directors to convene a general meeting. Section 132 provides that the directors must convene an extraordinary general meeting on a requisition of members holding at the date of the requisition not less than one-tenth of such paid-up capital as carries voting rights at a general meeting. In the case of a company not having a share capital, the number of requisitioning members must represent not less than one-tenth of the total voting rights of all the members entitled to vote at general meetings. These provisions cannot be excluded by the Articles.

The requisition must state the objects of the meeting, be signed by the requisitionists and be deposited at the registered office of the company. The directors have two months in which to convene the meeting. If the directors fail to convene the meeting within 21 days from the date of the deposit of the requisition, the requisitionists, or any of them representing more than one-half of the total voting rights of all of them, may convene the meeting. The meeting must be held within three months from the date of the deposit of the requisition.

Every company must hold a general meeting in each year as its annual general meeting. This applies to all types of companies formed and registered under the Acts.[25] Not more than 15 months may elapse between the date of the holding of one annual general meeting and the next. If the company fails to hold the meetings, a government minister has power on the application of any member to call or direct the calling of a general meeting. Again, the minister may give such ancillary or consequential directions as he thinks expedient, including directions altering or supplementing the operation of the articles in relation to the calling, holding or conducting of the meeting.

---

[25] S. 131(1), Companies Act, 1963, but see Regulation 8 of the European Communities (Single-Member Private Limited Companies) Regulations, 1994..

2.2 Do they have the right to put matters on the agenda?

There is no restriction on the rights of members to put matters on the agenda before a general meeting provided the relevant procedural requirements are met. All members and other persons entitled to attend and vote at general meetings may advance proposals which may be resolved upon by the members at such meetings. There are, however, certain notice requirements which must be adhered to. If a special resolution is being proposed, 21 days' notice must be given of the meeting to the members. Seven days' notice is required in the case of an ordinary resolution. However, if all the members of the company entitled to attend and vote at a meeting and the company's auditors consent, a meeting may be called by short notice as specified in the Acts or in the Articles of the company.[26] There are also resolutions for which extended notice must be given. These include resolutions removing a director from office,[27] and resolutions providing that a retiring auditor shall not be reappointed or that another person shall be appointed in place of a retiring auditor.[28]

3. Rights of Information, Independent Auditing and Supervision

3.1 To what extent do the (minority) shareholders have a right to be informed on company matters?

The members have various statutory rights in relation to the company conferred by the Acts. The following are statutory rights conferred on the members:

- to receive a copy of the Memorandum and Articles of Association and any Act of the *Oireachtas* which alters the Memorandum and Articles of Association;[29]
- to inspect the register of debenture holders;[30]
- to inspect and obtain copies of all resolutions and agreements required to be kept by the company;[31]
- to inspect and take copies of the register of members;[32]
- to inspect and take copies of the register of directors and secretaries;[33]
- to inspect the register of directors' and secretaries' shareholdings;[34]
- to receive copies of the balance sheets and directors and auditors reports;[35]

---

26 S. 133(3), Companies Act, 1963.
27 S. 182, Companies Act, 1963.
28 S. 161(1), Companies Act, 1963.
29 S. 29, Companies Act, 1963.
30 S. 92, Companies Act, 1963.
31 S. 143, Companies Act, 1963.
32 S. 119, Companies Act, 1963.
33 S. 195, Companies Act, 1963, as amended by section 51 of the Companies Act 1990.
34 S. 190 of the Companies Act, 1963, as amended.
35 S. 159, Companies Act, 1963.

- to demand and receive the balance sheet of a subsidiary company for the preceding 10 years;[36]
- to inspect the minute book;[37]
- that the balance sheet and profit and loss account be laid before the members at the annual general meetings;[38]
- that group accounts be laid before the members at the annual general meeting. Members have a right to copies of such accounts on request;[39] and
- that the documents required to be annexed to the balance sheet must be laid before the members at the annual general meeting.[40]

By virtue of section 370 of the Companies Act, 1963 all public documents are open to inspection at the Companies Registration Office, Dublin, by any member of the public.

3.2 Do they have a right to demand independent auditing or to initiate the supervision of company matters by an independent institution?

The members in a general meeting have the power to appoint or remove the auditor and to fix his remuneration. An auditor may be removed by ordinary resolution of the members in general meeting and another auditor nominated by any member of the company may be appointed in his place. There is no statutory right of a member to an independent audit.

The members of a company, however, may initiate the investigation of a company's affairs. Section 7 of the Companies Act,1990, confers on the High Court the power to appoint one or more competent inspectors to investigate the affairs of a company. The High Court's jurisdiction is limited to applications made by the following persons:

- in the case of a company having a share capital, not less than 100 members or a member or members holding not less than one-tenth of the paid up share capital;
- in the case of a company not having a share capital, no fewer than one-fifth in number of the persons on the company's register of members; and
- in any case, the company or a creditor or a director of the company.

The High Court also has jurisdiction to order an investigation upon the application of the Minister for Enterprise and Employment. This power can be exercised where the court is satisfied that there are circumstances suggesting:

---

36 S. 154, Companies Act, 1963.
37 S. 146, Companies Act, 1963.
38 S. 148, Companies Act, 1963.
39 S. 150, Companies Act, 1963.
40 S. 157, Companies Act, 1963.

- that the company's affairs are being or have been conducted with intent to defraud its creditors or the creditors of any other person or otherwise for a fraudulent or unlawful purpose or in a manner which is unfairly prejudicial to some part of its members or that any actual or proposed act or omission of the company is or would be so prejudicial or that it was formed for any fraudulent or unlawful purpose; or
- that persons connected with its formation or the management of its affairs have, in connection therewith, been guilty of fraud, misfeasance or of misconduct towards it or towards its members; or
- that its members have not been given all the information relating to its affairs that they might reasonably expect.[41]

The investigation is into "the affairs of the company". The powers are not exercisable simply because of a belief on the part of the members or creditors that the company is about to take some action which they view may damage their interests. The functions of the inspectors are to investigate and report. It is a fact-finding exercise and does not affect the legal rights and obligations of any individual.

On completion of their investigation the inspectors must make a report to the court. The court may make such orders as it deems fit in relation to matters arising from the report including an order of its own motion for the winding up of a company. The court must furnish a government minister with a copy of the report. It may also have the report printed and published and may forward a copy on request and payment of a fee to any member of the company being the subject of the report. The court may also forward a copy to the company's registered office.

4. Capital Increases and Distributions

4.1 To what extent do (minority) shareholders have the right to participate in capital increases?

Section 23 of the Companies (Amendment) Act, 1983 gives the members of a company a statutory pre-emptive right on the allotment of new shares in proportion to their existing shareholding. These pre-emptive rights may, however, be excluded by the provisions of the Memorandum or Articles of Association of a company. A company may provide for its own pre-emption scheme in its Memorandum and Articles and in such cases, section 23 will not apply.

Failure to comply with the statutory requirements as to pre-emption will render the company and every officer who knowingly authorized or permitted the contravention, jointly and severally liable to compensate any person to whom the offer should have been made. Contravention of the statutory provision, however, does not invalidate the allotment.

---

[41] S. 8(1) Companies Act, 1990.

4.2 Do minority shareholders have the right to demand dividends or other distributions?

There is no legal obligation on a company to pay a dividend, even in cases where there are sufficient profits available for distribution, unless it is provided otherwise in the company's constitutional documents.

A shareholder has no right to a dividend while the company is a going concern until a dividend is declared and payable.[42] The Acts contain no provisions as to who should declare dividends nor do they provide when a dividend shall become payable. These are matters for the internal management of a company. Model Article 116 of Table A, First Schedule to the Companies Act, 1963 provides that the company in a general meeting may declare dividends but no dividend shall exceed the amount recommended by the directors. Where model Article 116 or a similar provision is contained in a company's Articles the directors are given the ultimate say as to when a dividend is to be declared and how much is to be available for that purpose.

The failure of the directors to declare dividends may amount to oppression within the meaning of section 205 of the Companies Act, 1963. For example, the directors may use up all the distributable profits which would otherwise be available for distribution as a dividend by paying themselves excessive salaries. The discretion given to the court to award relief for a breach of section 205 of the Companies Act, 1963 may include the power to order the declaration of a dividend. (Section 205 is discussed in more detail under question 8 below.)

5. Derivative Actions

5.1 Can (minority) shareholders enforce rights that the company has against other shareholders, directors, or third parties?

There is a well established rule in Irish company law known as the Rule in *Foss* v. *Harbottle*.[43] This rule provides that where a wrong has been committed against a company, the company and not the shareholder is the proper person to institute proceedings. Also, the individual shareholders may not bring proceedings to overturn a decision of the company where that decision is one which a majority of the members may confirm. The basis of the rule is that minority shareholders in a company are expected and obliged to respect the decisions of the majority shareholders. A problem arises for a minority shareholder when (i) the directors are responsible for the wrong and refuse to take action against themselves; and (ii) wrongs are committed by majority shareholders or third parties and the aggrieved members do not

[42] *Re Drogheda Steam Packet Company Limited* [1903] IR.
[43] (1843) 2 Hare 461.

have sufficient voting power at general meeting to compel directors to institute proceedings.

Traditionally, it is the view that there are four exceptions to the rule *Foss* v. *Harbottle* although more recently a fifth exception is receiving recognition:[44]

- the majority cannot commit an act which is illegal or *ultra vires* the company;
- where the company purports to act on the strength of a decision by a simple majority in cases where more than a simple majority is required;
- where a member's personal rights are infringed;
- where the majority who are in control commit a fraud upon a minority; and
- where the justice of the case requires a minority to be permitted to institute proceedings.

In circumstances where one or more of the above exceptions apply, a member may be allowed to institute proceedings on behalf of the company to redress a wrong committed against the company. In such cases the minority shareholders may bring a derivative action on the company's behalf. The main question in deciding whether a minority shareholder should be allowed to bring a derivative action is whether a wrong committed against the company would go unredressed unless the action is permitted.

In order to bring a derivative action a member must establish a prima facie case:

- that the company is entitled to the relief; and
- that the action falls within the criteria of the exceptions to the rule in *Foss* v. *Harbottle*.

5.1.1 Ultra vires *and illegal acts*

An individual member may seek to prevent the company from committing an *ultra vires* act by way of injunction proceedings. The member may also bring an action on behalf of the company for a declaration that an act already committed is *ultra vires*,[45] or to have the *ultra vires* act set aside.

5.1.2 Transactions which must be ratified by more than a simple majority

Where a simple majority of members ratify an act which requires the sanction of a special resolution, the rule in *Foss* v. *Harbottle* does not prevent a dissenting member from taking proceedings. Also, where inadequate notice is given of a proposed resolution at a general meeting of the company, any member can bring a derivative action to prevent the company from acting on any resolutions passed.

5.1.3 Fraud on a minority by those in control

This is argued to be the only true exception to the rule in *Foss* v. *Harbottle*. A minority may take a derivative action on behalf of the company where the majority in

---

[44] *The Law of Private Companies*, Thomas B. Courtney.

[45] *Hennessy* v. *National Agricultural and Industrial Development Association* [1947] IR.

control of the company commit a fraud on the minority. This exception only provides relief to the company. The case law on this exception commonly involves appropriation of corporate property by a controlling majority. Other cases involve a directors' breach of their fiduciary duties, negligence and *mala fide* exercise of their powers permitted and indeed even supported in some instances by majority shareholders. The essential requirements for the fraud on the minority exception are control and fraud.

5.1.3.1 Control

The minority must show that those who committed the fraud are in control of the company. In the case where voting control cannot be established the minority shareholder "must account for the fact that the company has not seen fit to bring action on its own behalf. This may be done by showing that the company has refused to allow the action to be brought on its own behalf, or that, by reason of the wrongdoer being in control of the company at the time of bringing the action, it would be idle to apply to the company."[46]

5.1.3.2 Fraud

There has been much case law on what majority shareholders are not permitted to do. They may not transfer to themselves money, property or advantages which belong to the company or in which the other shareholders are entitled to participate or they may "not put something into their pockets at the expense of the minority".[47]

5.1.4 Where justice requires derivative action to be brought

In the Irish case of *Moylan* v. *Irish Whiting Manufacturers Limited*,[48] it was held that "having regard to the provision of Bunracht Na hEireann" (the Irish Constitution), the court was "satisfied that an exception to the rule must be made where the justice of the case demands it".

6. Other "Formal" Rights

6.1 Do minority shareholders have any other specific rights comparable to those mentioned in 2–5 above?

The following are some additional statutory rights conferred on members:

- The High Court may, on the application of any member or holder of debentures of the company, restrain such company from doing any act or thing which the company has not the power to do (ie which is *ultra vires* the company).[49]

---

46 *Fisher* v. *St. John Opera House Company* (1937) 4 DLR 337 at 342.
47 *Menier* v. *Hoopers Telegraph Works Limited* (1874) LR 9 Ch App 350.
48 High Court 14 April 1980, Hamilton J.
49 S. 8(2), Companies Act, 1963.

- Where a company has altered its objects, an application may be made for the alteration to be cancelled: (i) by the holders of not less than 15% in nominal value of the company's issued share capital or any class thereof; or (ii) if the company is not limited by shares not less than 15% of the company's members. An application under this provision will only be successful if it can be shown that the alteration of the objects was unfair as between the members.[50]
- An application may be made within 28 days after the date of a special resolution of a company authorizing the giving of financial assistance for the purchase of its shares, for the cancellation of such special resolution. This application may be made by the holders of not less in aggregate than 10% in nominal value of the company's issued share capital or any class thereof.[51]
- Where special rights attach to shares, such shares may be varied with the consent of a specified proportion of the shareholders of the issued shares of that class or the sanction of a resolution passed at a separate meeting of the holders of those shares. Where the rights are varied, the holder(s) of not less than 10% of the issued shares of that class, being the person(s) who did not consent to or vote in favour of the resolution for the variation may apply to court to have the variation cancelled.[52] Alternatively, dissenting shareholders may be able to claim relief under section 205 of the Companies Act, 1963 on the grounds that the variation is oppressive or in disregard of their interests as members.[53] (This is discussed further under question 8 below.)
- Any provision in a companyís Articles is void in so far as it makes ineffective a demand for a poll: (i) by not less than five members having the right to vote; or (ii) by members representing not less than one-tenth of the total voting rights of all the members having the right to vote; or (iii) by a member or members holding shares in the company conferring a right to vote at the meeting, given that the aggregate sum paid up for such shares is equal to not less than one-tenth of the total sum paid up on all shares conferring that right.[54]
- Every member has the right to apply to the court for rectification of the register of members where the name of any person is entered in error or a default is made in noting the cessation of membership.[55]
- A right to requisition a members meeting[56] (discussed under question 2 above).
- The right to apply to the court for the investigation of a company's affairs (discussed under question 3.2 above).[57]
- A company may, by notice in writing, require a person who has been interested in shares in the company at any time during three years prior to the notice to give details in relation to their interests in the company.[58] A company may also be required to exercise this power on the requisition of the members holding at

---

[50] S. 10(2), Companies Act 1963.
[51] S. 60, Companies Act, 1963.
[52] See S. 78, Companies Act, 1963.
[53] *Re Williams Group, Tullamore Limited* [1985] IR.
[54] S. 137, Companies Act, 1963.
[55] S. 122, Companies Act, 1963.
[56] Ss. 132, 134 and 135, Companies Act, 1963.
[57] S. 7, Companies Act, 1990.
[58] S. 81, Companies Act, 1990.

the date of deposit of the requisition not less than one-tenth of the paid up capital of the company as carries voting rights.[59]

7. Extension of these Rights by Statute or Shareholders' Agreements

7.1 Can the Articles of Association provide for additional rights of the minority shareholders? If not, can such rights be provided for in shareholders' agreements? Are these options commonly used?

A company's constitutional documents and shareholders' agreements may be drafted to provide minority shareholders with rights such as a right to appoint or remove directors or a right of veto on certain company decisions. Their position as minority shareholders is thereby enhanced.

Shareholders' agreements only bind those who are a party to them. The agreement may be expressed to take precedence over the company's Articles of Association. Shareholders' agreements can be used to increase or strengthen the rights and powers (especially of veto) of a minority shareholder. The courts have shown a willingness to enforce and respect shareholders' agreements.[60]

The Articles themselves may also extend the rights given to minority shareholders. The Articles which set out the internal rules and regulations for the management of the company and by which the members agree to be bound may, however, be altered by special resolution without the consent of all the contracting parties (the shareholders). The individual rights conferred on the minority shareholders by the Articles are subject, therefore, to being altered or curtailed by the majority of shareholders by special resolution.

A company cannot by its Articles, shareholders' agreement or otherwise deprive itself of the power to alter its Articles by special resolution.[61]

8. Remedies Where a Shareholders' Resolution or Other Action Impairs the Rights of Minority Shareholders

8.1 What are the requirements for such remedies?

Section 205 of the Companies Act, 1963 provides minority shareholders with a potentially powerful remedy against the company's directors in cases of oppression and disregard of their interests. This is the remedy most frequently resorted to by

---

59 S. 83, Companies Act, 1990.

60 *BLM Group Limited* v. *Harmon, The Times* 8 April 1994.

61 *Allen* v. *Gold Reefs of West Africa* [1900] 1Ch 656 at 673 and *Carvill* v. *Irish Industrial Bank* [1968] IR 325.

shareholders. Section 205(1) provides that any member of a company who complains that the affairs of the company are being conducted or that the powers of the directors of the company are being exercised in a manner oppressive to him or any of the members (including himself), or in disregard of his or their interests as members may apply to the court for an order under this section.

The requirements for this statutory remedy are:

- oppression; or
- disregard of a member's interests (as a member).

In defining "oppression" and "disregard of interests", the courts will regard the particular facts of each case.[62]

The only persons who have *locus standi* to petition the court for relief under section 205 are:

- the members of the company;
- the personal representatives of a member or any trustee thereof, or persons beneficially interested in shares in the company by virtue of the will or intestacy of a member.

It is not required that the petition under section 205 be by minority shareholders only. A petition should, however, be brought by a member.

8.2 When do the courts of your country accept these requirements?

8.2.1 Oppression

To constitute oppression within the meaning of section 205 the conduct complained of must be "burdensome, harsh and wrongful".[63] Such oppressive conduct will be judged by applying objective standards.[64] It has been held in Ireland that a single act can constitute oppression.[65]

Oppression was found to exist by the Irish High Court (and not contested on appeal to the Supreme Court) in the recent leading Irish case of *Irish Press Plc* v. *Ingersoll Irish Publications Ltd.* Here it was held that the conduct of one of the parties to a joint venture, while not undertaken as part of a plan to destroy the business of the joint venture company, was nevertheless a plan against the interests of the other party to the joint venture arrangement and accordingly was deemed to be oppressive.[66]

Conduct does not need to be unlawful to be oppressive.[67] Mere incompetence or mismanagement of a company's affairs will not *per se* amount to oppression within

---

62 *Scottish Co-Operative Wholesale Society Limited* v. *Meyer* [1959] AC 324.

63 In *Greencore Trading Company Limited* [1980] ILRM 94 and *Scottish Co-Operative Wholesale Society Ltd* v. *Meyer* [1959] A.C. 324.

64 In Re *Irish Visiting Motorists Bureau Ltd*, High Court unreported 7 February 1972.

65 *Westwinds Holding Company Ltd*, High Court unreported 21 May 1974.

66 High Court 16 December 1993 and Supreme Court 24 May 1995.

67 Re *Clubman Shirts* [1983] ILRM 323.

the meaning of section 205.[68] However, it is thought that irregularity in the conduct of the company's affairs will be oppressive where it is part of a deliberate scheme. Such circumstances may also provide strong grounds for arguing that a member's interests have been disregarded.

Exclusion from management can amount to oppression in certain circumstances.[69]

Directors' non-consultation with shareholders does not per se amount to oppressive conduct but it may do so.[70]

Acts may be oppressive, even if done honestly and in good faith. It is also apparent that the conduct or exercise of the powers complained of in a section 205 petition must relate to the internal management of the company.[71]

Even in cases where some other relief is also available to a petitioner, for example, a derivative action, a remedy may be sought under section 205.[72]

8.2.2 Disregarding members' interests

It is understood that the reference to "interests" in section 205 enables the court to have regard to the widest possible matters in connection with the petitioner's purely legal rights as a member.[73] This interpretation recognizes that members may have different interests although their rights as members are the same.

Damage suffered in relation to the disregarding of interests must be in the capacity as a member. The disregarding of interests must result from either the conduct of the affairs of the company or the exercise of the powers of the directors.

The alteration of the rights of one class of shareholders, even if brought about in accordance with the appropriate procedures may, in some circumstances, constitute oppression or disregard of the interests of another class of shareholders within the meaning of section 205.[74]

8.3 What remedies are available to the claimant?

Section 205 of the Companies Act, 1963 provides for relief in potentially broad terms in that the court has power to end the matters complained of.

Where oppressive conduct or conduct in disregard of the member's interests is found to exist the court may, with a view to bringing to an end the matters complained of, make such order as it thinks fit. Such orders may include directing or

---

68 *Re Five Minute Car Wash Service Limited* [1966] 1 AER 242, *In Re Clubman Shirts Limited* [1983] ILRM 323.

69 [1979] ILRM 141.

70 Re *Clubman Shirts Limited* [1983] ILRM 323.

71 Unreported, High Court 7 February 1972–Kenny J.

72 *Re Westwinds Holding Company Ltd* (High Court Kenny J. 21 May 1974). *Re Greencore Trading Company Ltd* [1980] ILRM 94.

73 Thomas Courtney, *The Law of Private Companies*, p. 433, and Lyndon MacCann, *Companies Acts, 1963–1990*, p. 203.

74 *Re Williams Group, Tullamore Ltd* [1985] IR.

prohibiting any act, cancelling or varying any transaction, or for regulating the conduct of a company's affairs in the future or for the purchase of the shares of any members of the company or by the company and in the case of purchase by the company for the reduction accordingly of the company's capital, or otherwise.[75]

The court will only grant relief to a petitioner under section 205(3) where its order can bring to an end the matters complained of.[76]

The recent Supreme Court decision in the case of *Irish Press Plc* v. *Ingersoll Irish Publications Limited* held that the High Court has no power to award damages in a petition under section 205 of the Companies Act, 1963. The relief which may be granted under section 205 is that the Court may make an order as it thinks fit with a view to bringing an end to the matters complained of. It is interesting to quote from the judgment of the Supreme Court in the *Irish Press* case. The Court stated that:

> "An award of damages would not satisfy the condition that the order be made with a view to bringing to an end matters complained of, secondly, an award of damages is a purely common law remedy for a tort, breach of statutory duty or breach of contract, and acts of oppression would not come within any of these categories and finally if the Oireachtas [the Irish Parliament] had intended to include the remedy of damages as one of the reliefs which could have been granted, there would have been no difficulty in doing so, it is quite clear that this was not done."

The remedies set out in section 205(3) are not thought to be exhaustive.[77] In addition, the claimant may petition the High Court to have the Company wound up. This the Court can do where, *inter alia*:

- It is of the opinion that it is just and equitable that the company be wound up.[78]
- The Court is satisfied that the company's affairs are being conducted or the powers of the directors are being exercised in a manner oppressive to any member or in disregard of his interests as a member and that despite the existence of an alternative remedy, winding up of the company would be justified in the general circumstances of the case.[79]

The court may dismiss a petition to wind up a company if it is of the opinion that proceedings under section 205 would be more appropriate.

The court's discretion to wind up a company for just and equitable reasons is broad. This remedy is considered to be an appropriate remedy for small private companies founded on a personal relationship involving mutual trust and confidence between the parties.[80]

[75] S. 205(3), Companies Act, 1963.

[76] [1979] ILRM 141. See also *Re Greencore Trading Company* [1980] ILRM94, *Re Clubman Shirts Ltd* [1983] ILRM 323, *Re Westwinds Holding Company Limited* High Court; *Colgan* v. *Colgan* High Court, unreported, 22 July 1993 and *Re OC (Transport) Services Ltd* [1984] BCLC 251; *Irish Press* v. *Ingersoll* High Court, 13 March 1994; *Re Williams Group, Tullamore Limited* [1985]IR 613, *Re Irish Visiting Motorists Bureau*, High Court unreported, 7 February 1972.

[77] See judgment of Blayney J in *Irish Press plc* v. *Ingersoll*; Irish Publications Ltd. Supreme Court 24 May 1995, "the Court is not at large as to what it may do".

[78] S. 213(f) of the Companies Act, 1963.

[79] S. 213(g) of the Companies Act,1963.

[80] *Company Law in the Republic of Ireland, ibid.* Mr. Justice Ronan Keane.

It has been argued that "it would be sufficient to ground a case for an order under this section if the petitioner can show that the other members have not acted in good faith towards him and have in the broadest sense acted inequitably".[81]

It is common for petitions under section 205 on the grounds of oppression to be taken in conjunction with a winding up petition on just and equitable grounds.

9. Specific Protection if the Company is Controlled by Another Company

9.1 What are the rights and remedies of a shareholder of Company A when Company B gains control over it (by acquiring the majority of its shares or otherwise)?

Section 204 of the Companies Act, 1963 enables a transferee (Company B in this instance), to acquire compulsorily the shares of a dissenting minority shareholder in a company which is being taken over (Company A), where not less than 80% in value of the shareholders in the transferring company have agreed to the take over.

Any shareholder who is unwilling to accept the offer and therefore unwilling to see their shareholding acquired in this manner may apply to the High Court for an order setting aside the claimed compulsory purchase. The court may set aside a purported compulsory purchase notice "if it thinks fit".

When applying to the court for such an order, the onus is on the dissenting shareholder to establish that the terms of the take over are not fair.[82] The court will also consider the views of the majority who have accepted the bid.

Section 204 may not be used by the existing majority shareholders of a company as a means of compulsorily acquiring the shares of the minority.[83]

If the transferee company (Company B) does not wish to exercise the powers of compulsory purchase under section 204 the dissenting shareholders must nevertheless still be given the opportunity of selling their shares. The transferee company (Company B) when it acquires four-fifths in value of all the shares must give notice of this fact within one month to any shareholders whose shares are not acquired.[84] Those shareholders receiving the notice may, within three months from the giving of the notice, compel the transferee company to acquire his shares.

81 *Ibid.*

82 *Re Hoare & Co.*, (1974) 150 LTR 134, *McCormick* v. *Cameo Investments Ltd*, [1978] ILRM 191, *Securities Trust Ltd* v. *Associated Properties Ltd*, High Court, McWilliam J. 19 November 1980.

83 *Re Bugle Press* (1960) 3 AER 791.

84 S. 204(4), Companies Act, 1963.

9.2 What are the shareholder's rights and remedies when Company B exerts his control over Company A in a way which damages the interests of the latter?

The minority shareholder has the right to take a derivative action or an action under section 205 or, alternatively, he may apply to the High Court to have the company wound up on just and equitable grounds pursuant to section 213(f) or 213(g) of the Companies Act, 1963.

ITALY

Massimo Audisio

Scamoni e Associati

Milan

PROTECTION OF MINORITY SHAREHOLDERS

***EDITOR* MATTHIAS W. STECHER**

ITALY

Massimo Audisio

1. Majority Requirements for Shareholders' Resolutions

1.1 What are the majority requirements in general?

The internal organization of the Italian corporations (stock and share companies) comprise of several bodies, each of which has a specific authority.

The shareholders' general meeting is responsible for the decisions that affect the existence of the company. However, the day-to-day management of the company is entrusted to the directors, who are appointed by the meeting.

The Civil Code makes a distinction between ordinary and extraordinary meetings according to the ordinary or extraordinary character of the subjects or matters to be deliberated. Article 2364 para. 1[1] provides that the ordinary meeting:

- approves the balance sheet;
- appoints the directors, the (internal) auditors and the chairman of the board of auditors;
- decides on the remuneration of the directors and of the auditors if it is not set out in the Articles of Association.

---

[1] If not indicated otherwise, Articles are those of the Civil Code, *codice civile*.

Moreover, the ordinary meeting decides on the revocation of directors (Article 2383, para. III), the determination of the profit dividend (Article 2483, para. I) and authorization for purchase of equity shares (Article 2357, para. 1).

The ordinary meeting resolves, on first call, by simple majority (that is with a vote in favour of 50% plus one of the shareholders attending the meeting), provided that the shareholders present represent at least half of the company's capital; otherwise the meeting must deliberate on a second call, by simple majority, of whatever is the percentage of capital represented by the shareholders attending the meeting (Article 2368, 2369).

1.2 Which resolutions require a greater majority?

The extraordinary general meeting resolves on modifications of the Articles of Association, the issuing of bonds and the appointment and powers of the liquidators. When it is called to resolve essential matters, such as the changing of the corporate purpose, company transformation or anticipated winding up, transfer of the headquarters abroad, issuing of preference shares or exclusion of the right of option, the extraordinary meeting to make the changes decides if shareholders representing half of the company's capital are in favour, both on first and on second call. Other resolutions of the extraordinary meeting which imply a modification of the Articles of Association are taken on the second call with the effective vote of shareholders representing more than one-third of the company's capital.

1.3 To what extent can they be modified by the Articles of Association?

The Articles of Association (hereinafter also called statute – in Italian *statuto*), as set out by Articles 2368 and 2369, can admit or explicitly require higher majorities but cannot reduce the required majorities. They may not, however, require the unanimous vote of the shareholders or majorities equivalent to unanimity. This prohibition is due to the need to ensure that the company may still function in the presence of a small number of dissenting shareholders who hold a negligible amount of the overall share capital. For the same reason the statute cannot require the presence, or a vote in favour, of the majority of the capital even at the ordinary meeting on second call.

2. Influence on the Decision-Making Process

2.1 Do minority shareholders have the right to call a shareholders' meeting?

2.2 Do they have the right to put matters on the agenda?

Article 236 states that the meeting has to be called by the directors by a notice indicating the day, hour and place of the meeting as well as the agenda.

Directors hold the power (and have the duty) to call the meeting whenever they deem necessary, appropriate or when they deem it necessary to obtain from the meeting opinions or directives. In certain cases stated in the Civil Code they are obliged to call the meeting.

In addition to the duty of the directors to call the meeting, Article 2367 gives minority shareholders who represent at least one-fifth of the company's capital the power of demanding that the directors convene the meeting, provided that this request contains the matters to be listed on the agenda. Experience shows that it is quite difficult to reach the minimum of one-fifth, especially for large companies with widespread capital.

When the minimum percentage is reached, the directors have to call the meeting immediately. Nevertheless, directors have the right not to call the meeting when the purpose of such a request is to discuss items contrary to law, impossible or outside the competence of the meeting. Moreover, some innovative recent court decisions assign to the directors the power to decide on the request and to reject it with good reason, if the calling of the meeting seems to the directors futile or inopportune. In the light of the most recent court decisions the provision of Article 2367 establishing that "directors have to call the meeting without delay" should be construed to mean that directors have to consider the request, but are not necessarily obliged to call the meeting.

In any event, the minority cannot require the calling of the meeting for subjects delegated to the directors, such as the approval of the balance sheet or all other cases in which the meeting has to decide on the proposals of the directors completed by a report that requires discussion.

Even when the directors deem the calling requested by the minority legitimate and convenient, they do not have to fully respect the agenda proposed by the minority but may change it if it appears too lengthy; they can also include requests from other groups in the same agenda.

3. Rights of Information, Independent Auditing and Supervision

3.1 To what extent do the (minority) shareholders have a right to be informed on company matters?

As mentioned above, the management and administration of share and stock companies is entrusted to its directors. After appointment by the shareholders' meeting, they directly manage the company without any interference from the company's meetings.

The director's conduct is controlled by the board of auditors (internal body control) that pursuant to Article 2403 ensures that everything is done in compliance with the law and with the Articles of Association. The board of auditors is a completely impartial control body and, even though it is appointed by the meeting, it may be considered independent from the meeting majority. This character of the board of auditors is confirmed by the strict regulations on ineligibility for holding office of auditor and by those regulations that require special moral and professional qualities for appointment as auditor.

Under the legislation, the board of auditors becomes the minority shareholders' "weapon", since it guarantees correct management by the directors even though minority shareholders are excluded from the control of the company. In practice, however, this legislative intention is often distorted and the control and guarantee function of the board of auditors has diminished. There may be a degree of complicity in the relationships between the board of directors and the board of auditors, notwithstanding the rights of minority shareholders.

The guaranteed function of the board of auditors in respect of the position and rights of company minorities is confirmed by Article 2489, which extends the right to information and control of every partner in stock companies where there is no board of auditors and establishes that in these cases each partner has the right to receive from the directors news on the development of the company's businesses (started and about to be started) and to inspect the corporate books. In practice, the right to consult the corporate books does not have great relevance because it is not extended to accountancy checking, which is not expressly referred to in Article 2489.

Article 2489 gives to minority shareholders of companies without a board of auditors the right to receive news on the development of the business of the company. The corresponding article of the Civil Code for stock companies with a board of auditors give the shareholders the right to be informed on company matters but not on the company's management. As a matter of fact, Article 2422, para. 1, by granting every single partner the right to inspect the corporate books, permits each shareholder to have a direct knowledge of the identity of the co-shareholders and therefore of the amount of their shareholdings. The same article gives the shareholder the opportunity to consult the book of meeting minutes.

Access to these corporate books is mainly of instrumental value for the shareholder. For example, it allows the shareholder who does not hold the capital share necessary to demand, for example, the calling of the meeting, to communicate and make agreements with other shareholders.

The shareholders, after examining the minutes book, will then have at their disposal information which may be necessary for an impugnment of the resolution of the meeting.

The right of inspection of the corporate books is specifically protected by legislation which grants the shareholder, in cases of illegitimate refusal by the director, the possibility of obtaining a court order against the company.

As described above, the board of auditors is the internal control body that should check and guarantee the respect of the law in company operations; but the effectiveness of this function is greatly reduced because the board of auditors is elected by the same majority of shares which controls the meeting and elects the board of directors.

3.2 Do they have the right to demand independent auditing or to initiate the supervision of company matters by an independent institution?

Article 2489 of the Civil Code grants to the shareholders of companies without a board of auditors who represent at least one-third of the capital the right to request at their own expense, on a yearly basis, that the company's management be checked; that is, the auditing and the control of the balance sheet and of the accountancy function. Thus the lack of a control body is counterbalanced by an individual power of inspection given to every single shareholder and, consequently, the directors have a duty to give the interested party the requested information without any limitation.

The Civil Code adds to the indirect protection carried out by the board of directors other forms of minorities' self-protection against a wrong committed by the directors. A less stringent form of self-protection is provided by Article 2408 and consists of the right of each shareholder to urge the board of auditors to control specific facts known by the shareholder and deemed reprehensible. Paragraph 1 of Article 2408 sets out that "every shareholder can denounce the facts that he considers reprehensible to the board of auditors; the board then has to take into account this denunciation in the report to the meeting". This provision also presumes a certain independence of the board from the meeting majority.

Obviously, the more the board of auditors "colludes" with the board of directors and the meeting majority, the less importance and relevance will be given to the reprehensible facts denounced by the minority shareholders. However, if the denunciation of these facts comes from a shareholder or from several shareholders that represent at least one-twentieth of the company's capital, then the board of auditors shall, pursuant to Article 2408, para. II, "investigate without delay and submit conclusions and eventual proposals to the meeting, calling the meeting immediately if the denunciation seems legitimate and if it is necessary to take urgent steps". This latter obligation of the board of auditors is also set forth by a criminal provision, by Article 2632, no. 2 of the Civil Code.

A form of self-protection which is certainly more effective and, therefore, more frequently used, is set out by Article 2409, which gives minority shareholders representing at least one-tenth of the company's capital the power to denounce certain facts to the court if they have a well-grounded suspicion of serious irregularities in the fulfilment of the duties of the directors and of the auditors. The applicability of this kind of direct protection is reserved for small to medium-sized stock companies since the capital share necessary for initiating a procedure under Article 2409 is as high as to allow, in large companies, the control of the meeting.

Admittance to the otherwise rigorous procedure is tempered by the last paragraph of the same article that also grants the right of action to the Public Prosecutor, so that, in practice, the shareholder who does not have the required minimum shareholding can turn to the Public Prosecutor and convince him on the grounds of his reasoning to lodge a petition.

In any event, the minority indicated above or the Public Prosecutor can base a petition only on misconduct concerning compliance with the rules of law or of the articles which govern the working of directors and of auditors, and may not question the activities of directors solely on the grounds of unreasonableness or inconvenience.

Should the court, after hearing the board of directors and the auditors, be convinced of the relevance of the petition, it will order the inspection of the company records at the expense of the shareholders that have requested it. The court, after the brief investigation, may also decide, pursuant to Article 2409, para. III, on the measures to be taken (seizures to the charge of the directors, a prosecution injunction against the carrying out of certain acts) as well as calling the meeting and fixing the agenda for the consequent resolutions (dismissal of the managers and related actions against them). In extreme cases the court may also dismiss the directors, appoint an administrator and decide his terms of reference.

Therefore minority shareholders will use the means provided by Article 2409 when the directors fail to call a requested meeting (ex Article 2367) or when the directors are pursuing purposes other than those provided for by the corporate objectives. Neither of these cases will necessarily cause past or future economic damage to the company.

Whatever the measures adopted by the court may be, the meeting holds full powers which, if the court appoints an administrator, have to be compatible with the measures of the court. In this case the meeting may decide upon either the transformation of the company or, in order to stop the procedure under Article 2409, its anticipated winding up and the appointment of the liquidators.

The administrator appointed by the court will be in charge for a period of time to be fixed by the same court. During this period he will call the meeting for the appointment of new directors or new auditors and, if necessary, propose to the meeting the winding up of the company.

The court can therefore only order measures that have been requested by the petitioners and can neither discuss the directors nor appoint a judicial director *ex officio* unless the claiming shareholders or the Public Prosecutor file a specific petition.

4. Capital Increases and Distributions

4.1 To what extent do (minority) shareholders have the right to participate in capital increases?

A solution to the minority shareholders' problem of taking part in capital increases resolved by the meeting is found in Article 2441 of the Civil Code which acknowledges the right of the old shareholders, and therefore also the minority shareholders, to the new shares. This so-called "defined option", which is a pre-emptive right, enables shareholders to maintain the proportion of their shareholdings. Thus, this right protects the interest of shareholders so that their vote rights and participation in profits is the same after the capital increase.

This pre-emptive right on newly issued shares is not absolute and is not applicable to every capital increase. Articles 2441, in fact, excludes this right where the capital increase is made with contributions in kind; and where the extraordinary meeting increases the capital and offers the company's employees a maximum of 25% of the new-issue shares. Moreover, the pre-emptive right is denied when the interests of the company demand this exclusion and when there is a vote in favour of at least half of the company's capital.

Therefore, the exclusion of the option right of the old shareholders shall be preceded by a duly documented and reasoned meeting resolution which has to demonstrate a real interest of the company in the exclusion of the option right and the absence of an intention to pursue a conflicting interest.

The need for the exclusion or limitation of the option right shall be demonstrated by the directors with a proper report which contains the reasons for the exclusion or the limitation arising from effective and real company interests.

It is quite obvious that the expression "interest of the company", being so general, allows, in practice, considerable abuse by those who run the company. They may be tempted to eliminate the old minority shareholders' pre-emptive right by a discretionary interpretation of the concept of "company interest".

4.2 Do minority shareholders have the right to demand dividends or other distributions?

The shareholder has no individual right to the distribution of profits. Only on the basis of a resolution stating the distribution, may the shareholder claim his rights against the company. This principle does not apply to the savings shares for which a minimum dividend of 5% is established by law (Article 15, Law 216/74).

This rule is confirmed by the fact that the carrying forward of the profits, and therefore the investment of the profits in the company's productive activity, needs no justification and the law does not even require the general meeting to allocate a specific purpose to profits, according to the principle that the management of the company is entrusted to directors and not to shareholders.

It is, however, possible to insert clauses limiting to the power of the meeting in its decisions for or against profit sharing. In any case, the statute may not provide that the whole profit must necessarily be distributed, nor that it may not be distributed. In fact, both of these clauses would be considered null and void since they infringe Article 2433, which provides that the general meeting may take decisions on the distribution of the profit according to the needs of the moment.

A clause providing for the distribution of a minimum percentage of profit would be valid, and in this case the general meeting would, pursuant to Article 2422, decide either to carry forward the remaining profit (as reserve) or to distribute it to shareholders.

Another practical problem is whether statutory clauses providing for the distribution of the whole profit unless the meeting resolves otherwise are lawful or not. Many theories answer this question in the affirmative, noting that the preference given to the shareholders' vote is perfectly in harmony with Article 2247 and that in this specific case it gives the shareholder the right to the credit related to the profit.

A recent legal provision, included in DPR 10.2.1986 no.30, has introduced Article 2433 bis, which anticipates a possible interim dividend distribution to shareholders, generally in mid-year. This power, which is quite often used in practice, exists only under special conditions. First of all, the company's balance sheet must be certified by a third party; this must be registered in the Articles of Association, and the balance sheet of the previous year's accounting period must have already been certified and approved. Moreover, the interim dividend in the middle of the year may be distributed only if there are no losses in the previous accounting periods and only after verifying that the accounting report drawn up by the directors states that the company is in a position to allow the distribution of interim dividends in any case. Only under these conditions may directors deliberate, during the accounting period, the distribution of interim dividends, the total amount of which may never exceed the lower of the amounts of the profit achieved in the previous accounting period and the reserves available.

5. Derivative Actions

5.1 Can (minority) shareholders enforce rights that the company has against other shareholders, directors, or third parties?

As a general rule, all and every right of a company can be enforced only by the company itself, which means by the directors who represent the company. Bearing in mind this principle one can easily say that there is no possibility for the shareholders to enforce the rights of the company.

It may happen that a director acting (or refusing to act) on behalf of the company causes damage to the company itself or to the shareholders directly. In such a case Article 2393 of the Civil Code expressly allows the company to initiate a judicial action for damages against the director. Minority shareholders do not have the power to start the action of liability against the directors since this power can be exercised only if the shareholders' meeting decides to take legal action against the directors.

Article 2395 of the Civil Code gives to every shareholder the right to claim compensation for damages caused to him "directly" by the directors. This means that the shareholder shall not start an action under Article 2395 where he has suffered only an indirect damage such as, for example, the decrease of the value of his shareholding. For example, the shareholder may act directly against a director if the latter has transferred profits to his own advantage in a period prior to the distribution resolution or if he has collected from the shareholders the money necessary for a capital increase and, instead of delivering the related registered shares, has registered them in his name.

On the other hand, it is possible that any unlawful action by the directors may lead to a liability towards the company and towards the shareholder at the same time. This happens when by unlawful action the director causes detriment to both the company assets and those of the shareholders. In these cases the company may request the director to pay compensation for damages suffered, after the related meeting resolution, while the shareholder may act independently for the damage that he has suffered by promoting an action of responsibility, as stated by Article 2395 of the Civil Code.

The responsibility of a director will always exist when the latter, not acting within his powers as a representative of the company, has caused harm to shareholders.

The single shareholder who has acted directly against directors ex Article 2395 may, in cases of insolvency of the same, claim compensation from the company which is considered jointly and severally responsible according to Article 2049 concerning the liability of the company in case of unlawful actions committed by assistants or employees.

It is clear that the action for damages provided by Article 2395 does not derive from the company contract since the contract exists only between the company and the shareholder and not between the shareholder and the management body of the company (the directors).

The Civil Code does not provide rules similar to those above for the board of auditors. The reason is that it is difficult to conceive any infringement by the board of auditors which could cause direct damage to shareholders. Therefore, a part of the doctrine, and some court decisions, believe that the liability action set out by Article 2395 of the Civil Code cannot be exercised against the auditors. Nevertheless, an opinion to the contrary prevails, but rather for reasons of substantial justice than proper juridical arguments. It is said that Article 2395 already implies a responsibility of auditors as well, even though it is not mentioned by Article 2400, which concerns responsibilities of the board of auditors.

In practice, it is said that an auditor can, for instance, damage the interests of the shareholder, by drawing up a report or a false balance sheet which is submitted by the directors to a prospective shareholder to convince him to underwrite a capital increase, thus hiding the difficulties of the company. But it is also evident that it would be quite difficult to prove the connection between the work of the auditor and the damage suffered by the shareholder.

The same difficulties also exist concerning the action of responsibility against an auditing company, which, like the board of auditors, carries out an auditing function which to some extent, theoretically, could damage the assets of the single shareholder.

6. Other "Formal" Rights

6.1 Do minority shareholders have any other specific rights comparable to those mentioned in 2–5 above?

Apart from the rights mentioned under points (2) and (5), minority shareholders do not have other specific rights.

7. Extension of these Rights by Statute or Shareholders' Agreement

7.1 Can the Articles of Association provide for additional rights of the minority shareholders? If not, can such rights be provided for in a shareholders' agreement? Are these options commonly used?

A shareholders' agreement is a contract by which the stipulating shareholders undertake to exercise the rights granted to them by the Articles of Association in a predetermined way.

The most important example of shareholders' agreements are:

- "voting trusts" by which all the shareholders who take part in the agreement undertake to agree with one another, before every meeting, on the vote and its content, or to vote expressing the will of their majority, and
- "block trusts" by which all the shareholders or a part of them undertake not to sell their shares.

Such agreements affect the rights of the shareholder – including the minority – who, by making agreements with other shareholders, limit their right to vote but, on the other hand, allow them to play a part in taking the more relevant company decisions.

With the stipulation of a "voting trust", a minority shareholder, in agreement with the other shareholders of the trust, can also decide beforehand on the content of the vote related to specific arguments, should these become the subject matter of a meeting resolution. This voting trust is useful when none of the shareholders is, on his own, able to influence the decisions of the shareholders' meeting.

The voting trusts, like all internal company agreements, are effective only among the parties of the agreement; in fact, they only bind the shareholders who have signed them and they are ineffective regarding third parties and with respect to the company. This means that if some shareholders who are part of the trust and who, for example, represent together the majority of the company's capital, decide to vote differently from the way agreed in the shareholders' agreement, the minority shareholder, who fulfils the contract, does not have the right to impugn the resolution of the meeting, which will remain perfectly valid and effective. In such a case he will only have the right to act against the unfulfilling shareholders (members of the voting trust) and to claim compensation for damages caused or the payment of the penalty if it has been agreed.

Besides the limits described above, shareholders' agreements are also subject to specific validity limits that are summarized by the principle according to which the shareholders' agreement shall not be prejudicial to "the primary interest of the company which is guaranteed by imperative rules". This principle has been applied to voting trusts where the agreement by which several shareholders before every meeting undertake to agree that the content of the vote has been considered valid. On the other hand, the engagement to vote in conformity with the decision of the majority of those who agreed within the trust has been considered null since this could create false majorities in the meeting and allow minorities, which are in a majority within the trust, to dominate it.

The courts deem as "primary interest" the one due to which the resolutions of the meeting must correspond to the will of the majority of the capital. For this reason, an agreement under which some shareholders grant an irrevocable proxy to another, giving him the power and freedom to decide and vote also on their behalf on any subject of the agenda, has been considered null and void.

As mentioned above, should a shareholders' agreement be declared null this would not affect the validity of the meeting resolution if it were taken with the majorities required by law. The annulment of the shareholders' agreement is relevant only with regard to the shareholders who have infringed the shareholders' agreement, who will no longer be compelled to compensate for damage eventually suffered by the contracting parties.

By logical inference, the flexible structure of the shareholders' agreement is extensively compensated by limits as to its powers and to its validity such as to hinder the effective enlargement and extension of the rights of the minority shareholders in the joint-stock companies.

8. Remedies Where a Shareholders' Resolution or Other Action Impairs the Rights of Minority Shareholders

8.1 What are the requirements for such remedies?

During the life of the company it may happen that a meeting resolution is prejudicial to, in a more or less extensive way, the positions and to the rights of the minority shareholder.

8.2 When do the courts of your country accept these requirements?

The meeting majority could, for example, with a statutory modification, exclude in a definitive way the distribution of the profits to the shareholders or, contrary to Article 2437, para. III, exclude or render more burdensome the exercise of the withdrawal of the shareholder or even exclude the shareholders' right of option for future capital increases.

The minority shareholder who believes he has been damaged by the resolution of the meeting can act for the annulment of the resolution only in the cases in which the content of the resolution:

- has caused damage to the shareholder, and
- has not been taken in conformity with the provisions of the law or of the statute (Article 2377 para. II).

Therefore, the fundamental requirement for the impugning of the meeting resolution by the shareholder is that the purpose of the resolution is in conflict with the law and the statute, the demonstration of damage suffered by the minority shareholder not being sufficient. In brief, a resolution which completely excludes the distribution of the profits to the shareholders, with contextual alteration of the Articles of Association, besides causing undeniable damage to the minority shareholder, is certainly in conflict with the law because it infringes the provisions of Article 2433 that give to the meeting the power of deciding on the distribution of the profit, according to the exigencies of the moment.

Such a resolution will then be voidable as it was "not taken in conformity with the law or the statute" (Article 2377 para. II).

8.3 What remedies are available to the claimant?

By way of a petition, the absent or dissenting minority shareholders can contest the meeting resolutions. These resolutions can be annulled within three months from the date of the resolution. After the expiry of this term no action can be taken based on the invalidity of the decision. The impugning does not immediately suspend the execution of the resolution but a suspension can be granted during the lawsuit by the investigating magistrate if there are "serious reasons" to do so.

The annulment of the resolution cannot take place if the same resolution is substituted by another taken in conformity with the law and statute or if, apart from any substitution, it is revoked by the meeting.

It is important to note that, in the case of the impugned resolution, the rights that the annulled resolution had assigned to third parties or to shareholders are cancelled by substitution or revocation.

A particular type of meeting resolution, subject to annulment action, is that inspired by an external interest of the majority. In fact, it may happen that the majority uses its right to vote in its own interest, which is distinct from that laid down in the deed of partnership, with a consequent and unavoidable prejudice to the minority shareholding. This would be the case if a capital increase had as its only purpose the reduction of the participation of an undesired minority shareholder. In such a case, the judge called to decide on the validity of the resolution does not enter into the merits nor does he ascertain whether or not the capital increase is opportune or convenient for the company. Instead, the judge will consider that the right of vote has been exercised by the majority to accomplish their own particular interests, which had nothing to do with the interests of the company.

The resolution inspired by a majority's interest lying outside of the company could therefore be annulled, being in conflict with the law and statute, ignoring any damage suffered by the company or by the single shareholder.

9. Specific Protection if the Company is Controlled by Another Company

9.1 What are the rights and remedies of a shareholder of Company A when Company B gains control over it (by acquiring the majority of its shares or otherwise)?

Italian law does not provide any specific protection in these cases.

9.2 What are the shareholder's rights and remedies when Company B exerts its control over Company A in a way which damages the interests of the latter?

Italian law does not provide any specific protection in these cases.

LUXEMBOURG

Pierre Schleimer

Zeyen Beghin Feider Loeff Claeys Verbeke
Luxembourg

PROTECTION OF MINORITY SHAREHOLDERS

***EDITOR* MATTHIAS W. STECHER**

LUXEMBOURG

Pierre Schleimer

Introduction

Six types of commercial company are recognized under the Luxembourg legal system: partnerships, limited liability partnerships, public limited liability companies (SA), private limited liability companies (Sàrl), limited partnerships with share capital, and cooperative societies. Each type of company is primarily governed by the Act of 10 August 1915 on commercial companies, as amended (the law), and unless otherwise provided, is also subject to the rules encompassed by the Luxembourg Civil Code which is modelled along Napoleonic French lines.

On corporate matters, legislative and regulatory materials are effectively supplemented by judicial case law. In this context it should be noted that where no legal literature or case law exists in Luxembourg on a specific point, the courts (and legal practitioners) turn to solutions evolved from Belgian law. Thus, Luxembourg law is largely comparable to Belgian law, and attendant references are accepted. On certain issues involving the broad principles of company law, French case law is also consulted, but on a secondary basis.

In Luxembourg, the SA and Sàrl are the most common used form of company. For the purposes of this report, and to avoid unnecessary complexity, we will primarily confine our study to these two main types of commercial companies.[1]

1. Majority Requirements for Shareholders' Resolutions

1.1 What are the majority requirements in general?

For an SA, the law establishes the principle whereby shareholders have complete freedom in choosing how the ordinary general meeting should proceed. Their choice is reflected in the company's Articles of Association.

If no such provisions are created, the law requires that decisions be made in accordance with the ordinary rules applicable to deliberative assemblies,[2] that is by a majority of votes duly cast at the assembly (50% of the votes plus one), not counting abstentions.[3] Where the votes are tied, the proposal under consideration is rejected.[4] In addition, where no provision exists in the Articles of Association, proceedings are not subject to any quorum requirement.[5] Consequently, resolutions may be passed purely on the strength of one shareholder.

For a Sàrl, decisions are not valid unless adopted by members representing more than 50% of the share capital.[6,7] If this majority is not reached, a further meeting must be held, and decisions will be subject to a majority of votes cast regardless of the proportion of capital represented.

1.2 Which resolutions require a greater majority?

For a SA, a qualified majority is mainly required for amending the company's Articles of Association.[8]

---

1 The rules governing limited partnerships with share capital are to a large extent similar to the provisions governing the SA.

2 In the Grand Duchy of Luxembourg, it would appear that, in principle, reference must be made to the rules of the Lower House, the Chamber of Deputies.

3 It is important to note that all shares must represent the same proportion of share capital and that each share must only attach one vote (subject to shares which do not attach voting rights). In addition, neither the board nor the Articles of Association can impose a minimum share requirement enabling shareholders to participate in the general meeting.

4 Cf. Art. 46, Chamber of Deputies Rules.

5 J. Delvaux, *Le droit des sociétés au Grand-Duché de Luxembourg*, Centre Universitaire de Luxembourg, edn 12/95, p. 153

6 Approved legal works interpret this provision as merely establishing a quorum requirement, with voting accordingly subject to a simple majority: cf. L. Metzler, *Le régime juridique et fiscal des sociétés à responsabilité limitée dans le Grand-Duché de Luxembourg*, Luxembourg, 1933, p. 113.

7 As applicable to the SA, the shares must represent the same proportion of share capital and must only carry an entitlement to one vote per share.

8 Any decision to wind up the company is treated in the same way.

In the absence of more stringent provisions in the Articles of Association, the law requires a quorum equivalent to 50% of the capital on initial calling. If the requirement is not met, a further meeting can be convened irrespective of the proportion of capital represented. In both cases, resolutions require at least two-thirds of the votes cast by the shareholders attending or represented.

Where several classes of shares exist and decisions reached by the general meeting could potentially affect their respective rights, the above quorum and majority requirements will apply to each share category.

However, any change in the nationality of the company or increase in shareholders' liabilities can only be decided with the unanimous agreement of the shareholders.[9,10]

In the event of a 75% loss in the company's share capital, a decision must be taken on the winding up of the company which must be supported by only a quarter of the votes cast. This voting is subject to the same quorum requirements as those applicable to decisions to amend the articles of association.

Any decision to change the nationality of a Sàrl must receive the unanimous approval of the members.

Unless more stringent provisions are made in the Articles of Association, any other amendments to the Articles must be resolved by a majority of members representing at least 75% of the share capital.[11]

It should be noted that under no circumstances can a majority require an individual member to increase his share of the capital.

1.3 To what extent can they be modified by the Articles of Association?

Regarding the rules governing the proceedings of ordinary general meetings, the shareholders, or founders, of an SA have total freedom in drafting the Articles of Association provided the general principle of establishing equality among shareholders is respected.[12]

---

9 Where appropriate, this also applies to debenture holders which does seem a little strange in respect of the second circumstance (ie any increase in *shareholders'* liabilities). In addition, it should be noted that in principle, any changes affecting the objects or form of the company require the consent of the debenture holders.

10 We hold the view that here, the use of the term "unanimity" must be interpreted as a requirement for the unanimous consent of the general meeting, *acting with 100% of those attending*: cf. Council of State Opinion, 23 April 1987, *Documents parlementaires*, no. 2897, 4, p. 6; N. Schaeffer, "Les minorités dans les sociétés de capitaux luxembourgeois", *Feuille de Liaison de la Conférence St-Yves*, no. 47, 1980, p. 23.

11 The interpretation of this provision appears to be that the majority of shareholders *in terms of number* (irrespective of how many shares they hold) encompassing at least 75% of the share capital must vote in favour of any proposal amending the company's Articles of Association in order for it to be adopted: cf. Metzler, *op. cit.*, p. 122.

12 Note: The creation of preference shares without voting rights is possible within the confines of the law. In several cases, however, shareholders' voting rights are reinstated (ie in substance, whenever their rights are at risk).

Concerning extraordinary general meetings, legal literature considers that the Articles of Association can only make provisions for more stringent quorum and voting requirements which, accordingly, provide greater protection for minority shareholders.[13]

For ordinary resolutions, the Articles of Association cannot provide for the meeting of an Sàrl to act on initial calling in such a way as to undermine the voting requirements prescribed by law. Apparently, however, more stringent quorum and majority requirements which better protect minority shareholders are allowed in so far as the law makes no restrictions. Moreover, the Memorandum and Articles of Association may do away with the need to proceed to a second meeting by not requiring any specified quorum in accordance with the provisions of law.

Qualified majority rules are only subject to more stringent formulations if laid down in the Articles of Association in accordance with approved legal literature.[14]

2. Influence on the Decision-Making Process

2.1 Do minority shareholders have the right to call a shareholders' meeting?

The law states that shareholders of a SA may require a general meeting to be held provided they represent at least one-fifth of the share capital This portion of the share capital may include, where applicable, shares not carrying voting rights.[15] Case law allows the Articles of Association to provide for a lesser percentage of share capital, but never a greater percentage than stipulated by law.[16] This right of shareholders to seek a general meeting is derived from the *ordre public*.[17]

The actual convening of the meeting, however, must be left to the board of directors or the auditor(s). Any refusal to act accordingly may lead to civil proceedings[18] (preliminary relief) and criminal sanctions.

Special rules apply to annual general meetings in so far as precise times and dates must be laid down in the Articles of Association. The meetings must be held in the municipality accommodating the company's registered office. In the event that the board of directors fails to convene the meeting on the specified date, any shareholder, regardless of the amount of equity held, may file a motion in the courts to force the board to hold the meeting.[19]

Different rules apply for a Sàrl. Here, it is primarily for the managers or secondarily, the supervisory board or, in its absence, members representing 50% of the

---

13 J. Delvaux, *op. cit.*, p. 154.
14 L. Metzler, *op. cit.*, p. 122.
15 cf. J. Delvaux, *op. cit.*, p. 149.
16 Supreme Court of Appeal (*cassation*), 7 July 1950, *Pasicrisie Luxembourgeoise*, XV, p. 39.
17 Luxembourg District Court (summary proceedings), 29 October 1984, *Roland* v. *Fisa*.
18 N. Schaeffer, *op. cit.*, p. 23 and continuations.
19 *Ibid.* p. 24.

share capital to call the meeting. In no event can a minority of shareholders call a meeting.

2.2 Do they have the right to put matters on the agenda?

In principle, the agenda is drafted by whichever governing body convenes the general meeting. Consequently, even if the items for the agenda of a meeting called at the instigation of one-fifth of the shareholders of a SA are determined by those shareholders, it will be for the board of directors or auditors to draft the formal particulars.[20,21]

In addition, pursuant to legal literature, a general meeting is, in principle, only allowed to consider items included on the agenda as specified in the attendant summons. Exceptions lie where an unforeseen problem arises requiring an urgent solution or in respect to any extension of an item implicitly included on the agenda.[22] These two exceptions, however, are not regulated by law. Thus, there are no formal provisions allowing minority shareholders to have a specific item added to the agenda.

Given that only those entitled to convene a general meeting for an Sàrl can lay down the agenda, minority members are not vested with any right or entitlement to require items to be included on the meeting agenda.

3. Rights of Information, Independent Auditing and Supervision[23]

3.1 To what extent do the (minority) shareholders have the right to be informed on company matters?

Shareholders of an SA have an individual right to the following information:

- the right to be informed of any general meeting to be held by a sufficiently detailed summons to attend;
- the right to inspect the balance sheet, profit and loss account, the list of shares and securities constituting the company's portfolio and auditors' report[24] (the

---

20 J. Delvaux, *op. cit.*, p. 151.

21 They must, however, be careful not to misrepresent any agenda drawn up by minority shareholders: cf. N. Schaeffer, *op. cit.*, p. 25.

22 J. Delvaux, *op. cit.*, p. 151.

23 We would emphasize here that listed companies are in principle subject to the same common law system as any other SA, with the addition, however, of certain information requirements of a general nature (such as prospectus particulars and the regular publication of management reports) which do not specifically affect minority shareholders.

24 Or, where appropriate, certification by the company auditor and not a full report where the company is required to use this type of professional service: cf. J. Delvaux, *op. cit.*, p. 100.

namely by precluding oppressive agreements, or "leonine conventions". However there are certain limitations.

Majority shareholders, in principle, can decide to allocate profits to the reserves unless such allocation is viewed as unjustified and, consequently, as an abuse of the law subject to the attendant rules. Hence, minority shareholders have no formal right to require the award of dividends. Moreover, legal literature accepts that the company's Articles of Association may, in the last instance, stipulate that all profits be allocated to the reserves, leaving minority shareholders powerless to oppose such a provision.[29]

In addition, preference shares, cumulative type shares, as well as preference shares in line with nominal, or par, redemption values, and/or liquidation surplus are allowed under Luxembourg law. These types of shares could potentially be used as a way of divesting minority shareholders of their rights without, however, giving rise to any breach of the *affectio societatis* principle or Article 1855 of the Civil Code which precludes "leonine" conventions. in which case, under the law, the clauses in question would be deemed not to have ever been written.[30]

These rules also apply with the necessary adaptations to a Sàrl.

5. Derivative Actions

5.1 Can (minority) shareholders enforce rights that the company has against other shareholders, directors, or third parties?

Neither the law nor legal literature currently recognizes any right of individual shareholders or even of a group of minority shareholders to initiate legal action on behalf of the SA.

In principle, only the board of directors representing the company has the right to proceed against other shareholders (eg if they do not pay their contributions) or against third parties (eg to seek compensation for damage caused to company assets).

According to legal authority, only through the general meeting can action be taken against the directors (*actio mandati*).[31] Individual shareholders or a group of shareholders can only take direct action against the directors in so far as they can show that tortious or quasi-tortious action on the part of the directors has caused them loss or detriment which is independent and distinct from that inflicted on the company.[32] Such action, however, can no longer be regarded as *actio mandati*.

---

29 J. Delvaux, *op. cit.*, p. 96.

30 J. Delvaux, *op. cit.*, p. 96.

31 P. Thielen and J. Delvaux, "La responsabilité civile des administrateurs de sociétés anonymes en droit luxembourgeois – Situation actuelle et tendance future", *Bulletin Droit et Banque*, no. 4. Although this issue would previously appear to have given rise to some controversy: L. Metzler, *op. cit.*, p. 101. Against, but in our opinion, wrongly: N. Schaeffer, *op. cit.*, p. 28.

32 J. Delvaux, *op. cit.*, p. 142: according to this author, for the purposes of a company action, the individuality of shareholders would in some measure be affected by the legal status of the company.

It should be noted that under common law, indirect action can in principle be taken in the event of any failure or default (as opposed to refusal) on the part of the body responsible. However, although it is clear that such a course of action is recognized in respect of third party creditors (exercising, in this case, the rights of the company itself on behalf of the company), it does not in principle apply to minority shareholders in so far as legal literature is reluctant to regard minority shareholders as creditors of the company (which would be a requirement for such an action).[33]

These same observations apply in the case of a Sàrl.[34]

6. Other "Formal" Rights

6.1 Do minority shareholders have any other specific rights comparable to those mentioned in paragraphs 2–5 above?[35]

The law stipulates that shareholders of an SA representing at least one-fifth of the share capital can require any general meeting to be adjourned for four weeks. This type of adjournment does not need to be substantiated and will cause any decision or resolution taken to be revoked. The right to adjourn, however, can only be exercised once in respect of the meeting concerned. Consequently, it is not a conclusive mechanism for countering the wishes of the majority shareholders but, where appropriate, does give minority shareholders the time needed to bring relevant summary legal proceedings to avert any damage which could arise from the decision in question.

Earlier reference has been made to the procedure applicable in the event that the board of directors reports a reduction in share capital of more than 75%. To avoid incurring personal liability, the directors must call an extraordinary general meeting to consider winding up the company. Under such circumstances, a minority of one quarter of the votes cast at the meeting will be sufficient to instigate the winding up of the company. The quorum is determined in the same manner as for amendments to the company's Articles of Association.

It should be added that there is also a mandatory requirement that the annual general meeting be held in the community where the company's registered office is

---

33 There is, however, an apparent distinction between the situation in which the shareholder exercises his rights as shareholder (in German, the *Mitgliedsrechte*) excluding him from taking indirect action, and the situation in which the shareholder pursues his distinct rights as creditor (the *Gläubigerrechte*), thereby in theory giving him this facility to proceed: cf. L. Metzler, *op. cit.*, p. 101.

34 L. Metzler, *op. cit.*, p. 101 *et seq.*

35 It is interesting to note that the Luxembourg authorities have at some point in time and contrary to the trend in neighbouring countries, legislated in favour of greater company deregulation and in so doing, reduced the rights of minority shareholders. Hence, it used to be the case that at general meetings of an SA with an ordinary agenda, no shareholder could take part in the voting representing any number of shares which exceeded one-fifth of the shares issued or two-fifths of the shares represented at the general meeting. Similarly, a qualified majority of 75% of votes cast was needed to amend the objects or form of an SA. These rules have since been rescinded.

located. This provision prevents minority shareholders from *de facto* exclusion by the meeting being held in an "exotic" location.

Regarding the Sàrl, it is worth mentioning that shareholders holding at least one quarter of the share capital can oppose any disposal of shares to third parties.

7. Extension of These Rights by Statute or Shareholders' Agreement

7.1 Can the Articles of Association provide for additional rights of the minority shareholders? If not, can such rights be provided for in shareholders' agreements? Are these options commonly used?

The right to extend the protection of minority shareholders by stipulating provisions in a company's Articles of Association is well recognised by legal literature in so far as the arrangement in question does not conflict with *ordre public* rules (eg the capacity to revoke directors *ad nutum* or the preclusion of leonine conventions). For example, it is possible to provide for the right of a minority coalition to propose directors,[36] for a higher majority for "delicate" decisions, for approval clauses[37] or for share transfer restrictions.[38]

Invoking clauses which are only encompassed by a shareholders' agreement is more doubtful when given that (i) their legal force is confined to the contracting parties and, consequently, does not necessarily extend to all present and future shareholders,[39] and (ii) they have no binding effect on the way in which the governing bodies of the company operate as provided in the Articles of Association. In addition, of course, they are still subject to the same public policy restrictions as the and must not conflict with the interests of the company.[40]

It has to be said that the use of shareholders' agreements of a purely contractual nature is far more common than creating relevant provision in the Articles of Association. Undoubtedly, in most cases, these agreements are used for reasons of dis-

---

36 But not to make direct appointments; in principle, only the general meeting has the power to appoint directors.

37 L. Metzler, *op. cit.*, p. 78

38 J. Delvaux, *op. cit.*, p. 112; such restrictions, however, cannot make shares totally untransferable which would be contrary to Luxembourg *ordre public*.

39 The parties to a shareholders' agreement not encompassed by the company's Articles of Association often attempt to remedy this by stipulating that in the event of equity being transferred to a third party, the transferor will be responsible for ensuring that the transferee becomes party to the agreement. It is also common practice, particularly in order to add extra weight to approval and pre-emption clauses, to require that the shares in question be pledged as security to prevent the owner from disposing of them in breach of his contractual liabilities.

40 In the absence of attendant decisions promulgated in Luxembourg, legal literature refers to adjudications made in Belgium, at least to those awarded prior to the legislative changes made there; cf. J. Delvaux, *op. cit.*, p. 97. Reference is more especially made to an article on shareholders' agreements under Belgian law written by P. Van Ommeslaghe "Les conventions d'actionnaires en droit belge", *Rev. prat. soc.*, 1989, no. 6532.

cretion and flexibility, even though any compulsory implementation of this type of arrangement is at risk.

Providing additional protection in favour of groups of minority shareholders, whether in the Articles of Association or otherwise, is quite common in the Grand Duchy, particularly among international joint ventures and groupings which use a Luxembourg company structure to promote mutual business activities. Hence, where three or more partners join forces, provisions which go beyond the (excessively) liberal legal framework are mostly necessary.

8. Remedies Where a Shareholders' Resolution or Other Action Impairs the Rights of Minority Shareholders[41]

8.1 What remedies are available to the claimant?

An initial distinction must be made between two key types of actions: main actions (specifically, actions to quash prejudicial decisions, liability actions and actions seeking the winding-up of a company on just grounds) and summary actions which are to be heard by the court which has summary jurisdiction, the *Tribunal des référés*.

8.1.1 Main actions

Regarding main actions, a further distinction can be made between "immediate" actions, that is actions to quash the decision in question (whether emanating from a general meeting or administrative body),[42] and two types of "indirect" actions: (i) liability proceedings against directors (guilty of making a prejudicial decision) which can also be accompanied by criminal action, notably for abusing company assets, or against other shareholders (either on a tortious or contractual basis, if a contractual relationship exists between the parties), and (ii) proceedings to wind up the company on just grounds (due to serious disagreement among the shareholders, or more generally, the absence of *affectio societatis*).

8.1.2 Summary actions

In summary proceedings, the courts are restricted to ordering interim protective measures and provisional restitution. To ensure effective proceedings, these orders may be accompanied by penalty payments and fines.

---

41 The rules referred to are generally praetorian in origin, with the law making little or only vague stipulations on the conditions for such action.

42 Case law accepts that any misuse of majority on the part of a company's administrative body may be subject to judicial penalty: Luxembourg District Court, 21 January 1988, *Bulletin du Cercle François Laurent*, III, 1991, p. 32.

The following types of measure have been previously imposed:[43]

- postponement of a general meeting;
- suspension of voting rights;
- a block on shares;
- suspending the operation of a general meeting;
- appointment of a receiver;
- appointment of a legal consultant;
- appointment of a provisional administrator.

8.2 What are the requirements for such remedies?

8.2.1 Main proceedings[44]

Shareholders bringing an action to quash a decision which undermines their rights must first demonstrate an interest in the proceeding. In main revocation proceedings (eg abuse of majority,[45] breach of a substantial provision of the Articles of Association),[46] there is no express requirement in this regard. The shareholders, who can choose to proceed individually, must simply establish that the decision in question is prejudicial to them. Any failure to comply with formalities involving, for example, the calling or agenda of a meeting, will, in principle, invalidate a meeting only in so far as it has a potential influence on the decision taken.[47,48]

Liability actions against board members are less straightforward in that they involve actions *ut singuli*, which require a minority shareholder to demonstrate his

---

43 For further details on these decisions, see N. Edon on intervention by the summary judge in company life, "L'intervention du juge des référés dans la vie des sociétés", *Livre Jubilaire de la Conférence St-Yves*, 1986, p. 185, and on the summary appointment of provisional directors and receivers, E. Penning, *Bulletin du Cercle François Laurent*, II, 1991, and by the same author, "Les procédures rapides en matière civile, commerciale et de droit du travail", *Bulletin du Cercle François Laurent*, II, 1993.

44 The conditions and procedures for appropriate criminal proceedings are not considered here (eg for falsification or the misuse of company assets) which are governed by specific provisions. It should be noted, however, that criminal action (with or without a private prosecution) is often the only way in which minority shareholders can effectively implement their rights.

45 Case law regards as an abuse of majority any decision taken which is not in the interests of the company and which is purely intended to favour majority members to the detriment of minority members: Luxembourg District Court, 13 October 1989, no. 319/89.

46 Or, where appropriate, a provision of a shareholders' agreement. The effectiveness of proceedings seeking the compulsory fulfilment of a purely contractual obligation is, however, doubtful in this context once a valid decision has been adopted by the governing bodies of the company in accordance with the articles of association and legal rules applicable. Even presupposing that the shareholders' agreement is valid, all that injured shareholders can invariably do is to seek compensation in line with the prejudice suffered from their contracting parties. It could be conceivable that, if the majority shareholders failed to act in fulfilment of their contractual liabilities, the court could order them to comply, by performance in kind, with their obligations; we do not, however, know of any corresponding court decisions.

47 Luxembourg District Court, 29 October 1993, case list no. 41316

48 For information on the Sàrl, see L. Metzler, *op. cit.*, p. 113 *et seq.*

individual interest in proceeding, that is that he specifically has suffered an individual prejudice. This action is based on common civil liability law. The prejudice suffered by the company is not in itself sufficient to justify action being taken by an individual shareholder against a director.

The same observations apply, with appropriate adaptations, to liability proceedings against other shareholders.

Finally, proceedings to wind up the company on "just grounds" (by way of indirect penalty following a decision which is prejudicial to the minority shareholders), will not be successful unless the applicant can prove that the submissions made encompass a series of factors such as preclusion of any joint action or placement of the company's existence at risk.[49,50]

8.2.2 Summary proceedings

A distinction must be made between two basic situations: the situation in which the company has governing bodies capable of operation and the situation where it does not.

In the second situation (which seldom involves any abuse of majority), the essential criterion justifying court intervention is an urgent need to remedy a situation threatening the company's existence.[51]

In the first, and far more common situation, the court can only intervene (i) if it can be demonstrated that by not intervening, irreparable consequences would ensue (ie. intervention by the court is required to avert imminent damage) or (ii) if the applicant can establish that a clearly illicit disturbance exists which must be remedied by recourse to the court. An underlying aspect of urgency applies in both cases.[52]

Regardless of which situation is involved, it appears that the conditions requiring intervention by the court are invariably appraised in relation to the interests of the company *per se*, and not by reference to any possible existing or future prejudice suffered by individual (minority) shareholders even though, of course, in identifying the real foundation for court intervention, attention must be focused on the dangers to which the rights of minority shareholders are exposed if things were to be left as they are. There are, however, no express formal criteria in this regard.

---

49 Luxembourg Court of Appeal, 29 September 1993, case list no. 14197; Luxembourg District Court, 14 May 1993, case list no. 42183; Luxembourg District Court, 13 Dec. 1991, case list no. 40049; Luxembourg District Court, 8 November 1990, case list no. 39521

50 It should be noted that the law allows the public prosecutor to seek to wind up companies involved in activities which contravene criminal law or which are in serious breach of the company law provisions. It is, however, doubtful as to whether an abuse of majority falls under this category of action; cf. Luxembourg District Court, 29 November 1990, case list no. 39884.

51 Here, the role of the judge is to protect the right of the company to exist and operate properly; Luxembourg District Court (summary proceedings), 28 July 1986, no. 832/86; Luxembourg District Court (summary proceedings), 31 August 1993, *D.* v. *Petraco Inc. SAH.*

52 Luxembourg Court of Appeal, 18 December 1990, case list no. 12638.

8.3 When do the courts of your country accept these requirements?

8.3.1 Main actions

As a general rule, actions seeking revocation due to a failure to comply with specified formalities can only be sought by the injured party provided that there has been no attendant waiver on his part, for example having attended the meeting in question without protest. In summation, non-compliance with a procedural formality will only invalidate the meeting insofar as it has any potential bearing on the decision-making process. The judge can revoke a decision on the ground that the excluded shareholders were in a position to put forward serious major arguments.[53] In certain instances, it seems such influence can be presumed where the gravity of the procedural breach is extreme. This presumption would apply where the agenda was insufficiently detailed, the quorum and majority requirements were not satisfied, or the shareholders did not have free access to the meeting.[54]

When turning to actions seeking revocation due to a breach of substantial rules, the applicants must be able to demonstrate that either the decision in question is fraudulent or that it was taken due to interests other than those of the company. A decision which is taken at a meeting favouring the principal shareholder or which puts the interests of a group of majority shareholders before the general interests of the company could be revoked either for being in breach of the principle requiring shareholders to be treated on an equal footing or in order to protect the company's interests.[55]

Regarding liability proceedings taken against board members or other shareholders, we refer to point 8.1.1 above. The common law of civil liability applies to such matters.

Finally, concerning proceedings to wind up the company on "just grounds", the court hearing the main application has complete discretion in appraising this aspect.[56] The judge must consider whether the submissions made encompass a series of factors such as the preclusion of any joint action or placement of the company's existence at risk. Mere disagreement between majority and minority shareholders is therefore not enough to justify any such winding up action.[57]

---

53 Luxembourg District Court, 29 October 1993, no. 41316; this judgment rejected both a "stringent interpretation", systematically invalidating any general meeting not properly called, and an "arithmetical interpretation", which would only invalidate the meeting if the votes cast in support of the decision in question were insufficient in themselves to form a majority; in this instance, the court opted for a "discretionary interpretation" which weighed up all the circumstances surrounding the case in point.

54 J. Delvaux, *op. cit.*, p. 156

55 *Ibid.* Luxembourg District Court, 13 October 1989, referred to earlier.

56 Luxembourg Court of Appeal, 29 September 1993, case list no. 14197

57 Luxembourg District Court, 13 December 1991, case list no. 40049

8.3.2 Summary actions

Regarding intervention by a summary judge in internal company life, it is generally accepted that this kind of intervention must be regarded as exceptional and reserved only for acutely serious cases. Such is particularly the case in instances where the company is normally operated by the majority shareholders.[58] In such cases, it must be established that the very existence of the company is at risk and in serious danger of collapse or that the applicants are victims of what is clearly unlawful interference (providing the summary judge can give this some form of legal semblance).

9. Specific Protection if the Company is Controlled by Another Company

9.1 What are the rights and remedies of a shareholder of Company A when Company B gains control over it (by acquiring the majority of its shares or otherwise)?

Luxembourg law currently makes no provision for any specific remedy to deal with this type of problem. Provided that the general rules of company law are observed on acquiring control (specifically, preferential subscription rights or pre-emption clauses laid down in the company's Articles of Association), minority shareholders have no legal recourse to oppose the takeover or any preventive safeguards to protect their rights.

9.2 What are the shareholder's rights and remedies when Company B exerts its control over Company A in a way which damages the interests of the latter?

At the present time, it appears that Luxembourg law continues to adopt the conventional criterion residing in the interests of the sole company to the exclusion of the interests of the group. Given the current absence of express legal provisions and, to our knowledge, no established case law in this regard, it has to be concluded that

[58] Hence, at the Luxembourg District Court a summary judge held that "joint stock companies are totally subject to government by the majority shareholders; providing the company continues to be governed accordingly without default or abuse, opposition by the minority shareholders, who must submit, does not allow the authority of the majority shareholders to be substituted for the authority of the court" (Luxembourg District Court (summary proceedings), 28 July 1986, no. 832/86).

the governing bodies of a company cannot take decisions which go against the pure interests of the company they represent although such decisions may be beneficial to the group as a whole.[59]

Hence, this restriction applies *a fortiori* where after acquiring control of another, a company adopts measures which are prejudicial to the interests of the minority shareholders (eg by stripping the company of its assets).

Concerning the rights and means of redress of minority shareholders in such instances, reference should be made to the various remedies available under common law as outlined earlier in point (8).

[59] In line with French and Belgian case law and legal literature, queries should, however, be raised over certain company decisions regarded as legitimate when, while taking into account the interests of the group, the interests of the minority shareholders (or creditors) are given due consideration.

NETHERLANDS

Anita de Jong, Paul W. J. Coenen

Caron & Stevens/Baker & McKenzie
Amsterdam

PROTECTION OF MINORITY SHAREHOLDERS

***EDITOR* MATTHIAS W. STECHER**

THE NETHERLANDS

Anita de Jong, Paul W. J. Coenen

This country report provides answers to questions referring to the common types of corporations in the Netherlands, namely, the *besloten vennootschap* (the "private limited liability company") and the *naamloze vennootschap* (the "public limited liability company").

1. Majority Requirements for Shareholders' Resolutions

1.1 What are the majority requirements in general?

Shareholders' resolutions are passed by an absolute or simple majority of the votes cast (ie more than 50%), unless the law or the articles of association prescribe a larger majority.[1] The validity of resolutions generally does not depend on the proportion of the capital represented at the meeting.[2] However, the law sometimes requires a quorum.

With regard to subjects which have not been proposed for discussion in the notice convening the meeting or which have not been proposed in a timely manner,

[1] Art. 2:120(1) of the Netherlands Civil Code for the public company and Art. 2:230(1) for the private company.

[2] Arts. 2:120(2), 2:230(2) Civil Code.

valid resolutions can only be passed if the entire issued capital is represented at the meeting and if it adopts the resolution unanimously.[3]

(The above requirement also applies if the notice convening the meeting is not given (in a timely fashion) or if the shareholders' meeting is held at another place than that required by law or under the Articles of Association (the "Articles").)[4]

1.2 Which resolutions require a greater majority?

A resolution of the general meeting of shareholders to convert either a public company or a private company into another legal entity which is not a private or public company requires a majority of at least nine-tenths of the votes cast.[5]

A resolution of the general meeting of shareholders regarding a legal merger requires a majority of at least two-thirds if less than half of the issued capital is represented at the meeting.[6]

In a public limited liability company, a two-thirds majority is required for a resolution to restrict or exclude preferential subscription rights on shares to be issued or to grant rights to take shares (options or warrants) when shares are issued or to delegate this authority to another company organ to reduce capital unless more than half of the capital is represented.[7]

Finally, the Articles may require a qualified majority for nearly all subjects, with the exception of resolutions to suspend or remove managing or supervisory directors. In such a case, a two-thirds majority is the maximum.[8]

1.3 To what extent can they be modified by the Articles of Association?

Even though the Articles may exclude any amendment of majority requirements, such an amendment will nevertheless be possible if it is unanimously adopted in a meeting at which the entire issued capital is represented.[9]

The Articles may also provide that the general meeting of shareholders will appoint managing directors upon nomination of at least two persons for each vacant position. The general meeting of shareholders may render such a nomination non-binding through a resolution adopted by two-thirds of the votes cast, representing more than half of the issued capital.[10]

The Articles may also impose a quorum requirement for other resolutions,[11] although a limit is placed on the quorum which may be required by the Articles for

---

3 Arts. 2:114(2) and 2:224(2).
4 Arts. 2:115/225 and 116/226 Civil Code.
5 Art. 2:18(2) and (3) Civil Code.
6 Art. 2:330(1) Civil Code.
7 Cf. Arts. 2:96a (7,8), 2:99 (5,6) Civil Code.
8 Cf Arts. 2:134(2), 2:244(2), 2:144(2), 2:254(2) Civil Code.
9 Arts. 2: 221(1), 2:231(1) Civil Code.
10 Arts. 2:133(2), 2:243(2) Civil Code.
11 Arts. 2:120(2), 2:230(2) Civil Code.

the suspension or removal of managing and supervisory directors of public and private limited liability companies.

If a quorum requirement pursuant to the Articles is not complied with, it is generally possible to convene a new meeting where such quorum requirement does not apply, unless the Articles provide otherwise.[12]

Finally, the number of votes to be cast by a single shareholder may be restricted under certain circumstances by the Articles.[13]

2. Influence on the Decision-Making Process

2.1 Do minority shareholders have the right to call a shareholders' meeting?

Netherlands law does not grant to the shareholders a general authority to call a shareholders' meeting.

Articles 2:109 and 2:219 Civil Code stipulate that the board of managing directors and the supervisory board shall have the power to call a general meeting of shareholders. The Articles may additionally vest this authority in others, for example, the meeting of holders of "preference" shares, each managing director individually, or individual shareholders.

There are, however, exceptions. One or more shareholders who represent at least 10% of the issued capital may (or such lesser proportion as is permitted under the Articles) may, if they have a reasonable interest, request the board of managing directors and the supervisory board to convene a shareholders' meeting, stating the items for discussion.[14] If the board of managing directors, or the supervisory board have failed to do so, one or more of these applicants may be authorized by the President of the District Court to convene a shareholders' meeting.[15]

Furthermore, *each* shareholder may be authorized by the President of the District Court to call an *obligatory* shareholders' meeting prescribed by the law (see Article 2:108/218 Civil Code and Article 108a Civil Code) or the Articles. If the board of managing directors, the supervisory board (or any other organ having this power according to the Articles) have failed to do so.[16]

2.2 Do they have the right to put matters on the agenda?

Calling a meeting of shareholders involves drawing up an agenda.[17] The observations in 2.1 above also apply to this case. Unless the Articles of Association state differently, shareholders do not have a right *per se* to put matters on the agenda.

---

[12] Arts: 2:120(3), 2:230(3) Civil Code.
[13] Art. 2:118(4) and (5), 2:228(4) and (5) Civil Code. Also see 7.1.1 below.
[14] See Art. 2:110(1) and (2) and Arts. 88(4) and 89(4), 220(1) and (2) Civil Code.
[15] Art. 2:111, 2:221 Civil Code.
[16] Art. 2:112, 2:222 Civil Code.
[17] Art. 2:114, 2:224(1) Civil Code.

3. Rights of Information, Independent Auditing and Supervision

3.1 To what extent do the (minority) shareholders have a right to be informed on company matters?

The general meeting of shareholders is entitled to all required information unless there is a sound commercial reason for withholding the same (eg if it may damage the competitive position of the company).[18] Moreover, the right to information is limited in that it must be exercised according to the principles of reasonableness and fairness.[19] Further, the right to require information may only be exercised during a shareholders' meeting.

There is controversy as to whether the board of managing directors or the supervisory board are obliged to provide individual shareholders or a commission of shareholders with the information they request,[20] or rather the shareholders' meeting as a whole. There is little case law on this subject. A District Court[21] has ruled that in principle only the general meeting of shareholders as a whole has the right to require information.

Under Articles 2:101 and 2:210 Civil Code, the management of the company must draw up annual accounts (balance sheet, profit and loss account plus explanatory notes) within five months of the end of the fiscal year (unless the general meeting of shareholders extends this term by no more than six months on the grounds of special circumstances) and must file these with the office of the company for inspection by the shareholders. The holders of shares, or (registered) depositary receipts of shares issued with the company's co-operation, may examine the records there and obtain a copy without payment.[22]

3.2 Do they have the right to demand independent auditing or to initiate the supervision of company matters by an independent institution?

The general meeting of shareholders (not individual shareholders) appoint the auditors.[23] One or more shareholders or depositary receipt holders and, in principle, usufructuaries and pledgees of shares in the company, individually or jointly representing at least one-tenth of the issued capital, or entitled to an amount of shares up to a nominal value of NLG500,000 (or any lower amount as provided by the Articles of Association) may assert an inquiry right.[24] This means that they may re-

18 Art. 2:107(2), 217(2) Civil Code.
19 Cf. Art. 2:8 Civil Code.
20 Positively: Van der Grinten, *Handboek voor de Naamloze en Besloten Vennootschap* (1989), no. 203(1); negatively: P van Schilfgaarde, *Van de BV en de NV* (1992), pp. 166 and 341.
21 Summary proceedings of 15 June 1988, KG 1988, 276.
22 See Arts. 2:102 and 2:212 Civil Code.
23 Art. 2:393(2) Civil Code.
24 Art. 2:346 Civil Code.

quest, in writing, that the Enterprise Chamber of the Court of Appeals in Amsterdam appoint one or more persons to conduct an inquiry into the policies and the course of affairs of a legal entity (either entirely, or with regard to part of a certain time period).[25]

The Enterprise Chamber can only honour such request if it finds well-founded reasons for questioning an otherwise correct policy (eg an impasse in the decision-making process, a conflict between the managing directors and the company, or a failure to provide information or correct information.

The following sanctions may be imposed by the Enterprise Chamber:

- suspension or nullification of a resolution of the managing directors, the supervisory board members, the general meeting or of any other constituent or corporate body of a legal person;
- suspension or dismissal of one or more managing directors or supervisory board members;
- temporary appointment of one or more managing directors or supervisory board members;
- temporary deviation from such provisions in the Articles as shall be specified by the Enterprise Division;
- temporary transfer of shares to a nominee;
- the winding up of the legal person.[26]

4. Capital Increases and Distributions

4.1 To what extent do (minority) shareholders have the right to participate in capital increases?

Every shareholder has a preferential subscription right proportional to his total shareholding in respect to the issuance of ordinary shares. For private limited liability companies, the Articles may limit or even exclude this preference right.[27] The general meeting of shareholders may restrict or exclude the preferential subscription right for each issue, unless the Articles provide otherwise.

There are several exceptions to the above rule:[28]

- Shareholders do not have preferential subscription rights with respect to shares issued to employees of the company or a group company.
- Moreover, holders of preferred shares have no preferential subscription rights when new shares are issued.[29] This may be altered by the Articles.
- Holders of ordinary shares do not have preferential subscription rights in respect of preferred shares, again, unless the Articles provide otherwise.

[25] Art. 2:345 Civil Code.
[26] Art. 2:356 Civil Code.
[27] Arts. 2:96(1), 2:206(1) Civil Code.
[28] Arts. 2:96 (1)–(3), 2:206(1)–(3) Civil Code.
[29] Arts. 2:96a (2), 2:206a(2) Civil Code.

- Shareholders do not have preferential subscription rights with respect to issues of shares on which payment is made in kind.

The exceptions explained above also apply in the event that options on shares or convertible bonds (warrants) are issued.[30]

4.2 Do minority shareholders have the right to demand dividends or other distributions?

Shareholders are entitled to a dividend, but the Articles may stipulate that the profits will be used for another purpose.[31] There is much leeway in this matter, except that profits may never be appropriated under the Articles to the effect that any shareholder is excluded from sharing in the profits. In practice, the Articles usually state that the profits will be made available to the general meeting of shareholders (who may reserve profits rather than distribute them).

If a minority shareholder disagrees with the appropriation of the profits, he may try to demonstrate that the relevant resolution is in breach of Articles 2:15(1) and 2:8 Civil Code (see 8.2 below).

A resolution to appropriate the profits may be in breach of reasonableness and fairness "if in adopting the profits, the company has followed a course of action which, under the given circumstances, could not have been followed by any reasonably acting company in respect to those entitled to the profits".[32] A breach of reasonableness and fairness may also follow from the abuse of power by a majority shareholder.[33]

However, the court will only conduct a "marginal" (limited) review in such proceedings. If the court honours the claim, it may give instructions on the amount of the dividend.[34] In the event of a dissolution of the company, the shareholders may be entitled to the balance, if any, after liquidation up to the nominal amount of their shares.[35]

5. Derivative Actions

5.1 Can (minority) shareholders enforce rights that the company has against other shareholders, directors, or third parties?

In a ruling dated 2 December 1994,[36] the Supreme Court explicitly decided that only the company shall be entitled to claim any damages from a third party. The

---

30 Arts. 2:96a(8), 2:206a(6) Civil Code.
31 Arts. 2:105(1), 2:216(1) Civil Code.
32 Cf. HR, 21 May 1943, NJ 1994 3, 484 (second *Koedoe* ruling).
33 Cf. District Court of Dordrecht, 1 February 1978, NJ 1983, 393.
34 District Court of Zutphen, 17 January 1991, TVVS 1991, 160 and Court of Appeal Arnhem, 26 May 1992, NJ 1993, 182.
35 Cf. Art. 2:23b Civil Code.
36 RvdW 1994, 265.

Supreme Court acknowledged that the loss of property, as long as not compensated, entails a reduction in the value of the company's shares.

A shareholder may only in very exceptional circumstances assert rights which the company has against other shareholders, managing directors or third parties, namely, when they have committed a wrongful act against the shareholder.

6. Other "Formal" Rights

6.1 Do minority shareholders have any other specific rights comparable to those mentioned in 2–5 above?

6.1.1 Other formal rights of minority shareholders

6.1.1.1 Suspension and removal of supervisory directors[37]
For both the private and the public limited company, installing a supervisory board as defined in Articles 2:140 and 2:250 of the Civil Code is optional. The supervisory directors not yet appointed in the deed of incorporation are appointed by the general meeting (unless a large structure regime applies, in which case they are appointed by cooption).[38] The authority to suspend or remove supervisory directors lies with the organ authorized to make the appointment.[39]

The Articles may provide that one or more supervisory directors (up to one-third of their number) be appointed by others than the general meeting (with regard to large structure companies the Articles may provide that one or more supervisory directors may be appointed by government authorities).[40] There is complete freedom to state in the Articles who shall have appointing authority. Such authority often vests in a category of shareholders, for example, the holders of priority shares. It may be envisaged that minority shareholders thus exert direct control over the composition of the supervisory board and indirect control[41] over any suspension of managing directors.

6.1.1.2 Dispute rules
According to the dispute rules in Article 2:336 *et seq.* Civil Code, one or more shareholders who jointly or individually hold at least one-third of the issued capital may claim in court that another shareholder transfer his shares to the company, on

---

37 For the suspension and removal of managing directors see 1.3 above.
38 Arts. 2:158 and 2:268 Civil Code.
39 Arts. 2:144 and 2:254 Civil Code.
40 Arts. 2:158(12) and 2:268(12) Civil Code). Cf. Art. 2:253 (143) Civil Code.
41 By means of Arts. 2:147 (1) and 2:257 (1) Civil Code.

the grounds that his conduct inflicts such damage on the company that continuing his shareholdership can no longer be reasonably tolerated.[42]

6.1.2 Minority shareholders' buy-out rules

In this context, the so-called buy-out arrangement for minority shareholders shall be discussed even though this is not exactly a formal right of minority shareholders. In some circumstances, a majority shareholder may find it inconvenient to be unable to exercise his rights without being confronted with minority shareholders every time.

In the absence of an offer or transfer obligation no shareholder can be obligated to transfer his shares. An offer or transfer obligation may be agreed to by shareholders' agreement, while a transfer obligation may also exist under the Articles of Association.

Article 2:201a Civil Code contains a provision on the buy-out of minority shareholders.[43] A shareholder who provides at least 95% of the company's issued capital for his own account may claim from the other shareholders jointly that they transfer their shares to the claimant. Hence, the claimant cannot act selectively. The same applies if two or more group companies jointly provide this amount of issued capital and jointly claim that shares be transferred to them.[44]

The Enterprise Chamber of the Court of Appeal in Amsterdam[45] will deny the claim against all the defendants (the minority shareholders) if such claim does not meet the following requirements:

- the claimant must provide at least 95% of the issued capital for his own account to the company;
- the defendant may not suffer any serious financial damage because of the transfer;[46]
- the claim may not be on priority shares;
- the claimant must not have renounced his right to file a claim against the defendant.

With respect to the price of the shares to be transferred, the Court may order that one to three experts will report on the value of the shares. The Court may also determine the price itself.

Where depositary receipts of shares have been issued, it is mandatory, according to case law, to also summon the beneficial owners.[47,48]

---

42 Art. 2:341 Civil Code.

43 This provision was added to the Act on the buy-out of small minority interests in public and private limited liability companies (Stb. 1988, 85) which entered into force on 1 May 1988.

44 Art. 2:201a(1) Civil Code.

45 Art. 2:201a(2) Civil Code.

46 A situation may be envisaged where a company has undertaken not to compete with a minority shareholder as long as he remains a shareholder. Upon a requisite transfer, that shareholder could be placed at a disadvantage.

47 Enterprise Chamber of the Court of Appeal of Amsterdam, 15 November 1990, NJ 1991, 176.

48 The buy-out programme rules bear some resemblance to the dispute rules addressed in 6.1.1.2 above. One important difference is that the buyer only has to argue that he provided 95% or more of the capital. Unlike the dispute rules, the conduct of the minority shareholders is irrelevant.

7. Extension of These Rights by Statute or Shareholders' Agreements

7.1 Can the Articles of Association provide for additional rights of the minority shareholders? If not, can such rights be provided for in shareholders' agreements? Are these options commonly used?

7.1.1 Enhanced minority shareholders' right under the Articles of Association

7.1.1.1 Priority shares

Articles 2:92 and 2:201 Civil Code provide that all shares carry equal rights and obligations proportional to their value, unless the Articles of Association provide otherwise. This means that the Articles may attach special voting rights to shares. Shares having these rights are "priority shares" (*prioriteitsaandelen*).

The holders of priority shares may have additional rights, such as a veto right in regard to the amendment of the articles or dissolution of the company. The priority shareholders of private limited companies may be further authorized to decide on the issue of shares. It should be noted, however, that the shareholders of public limited companies may only delegate this right for a maximum period of five years.

Not all powers may be granted to priority shareholders. Mandatory law may dictate that powers vest in certain company organs and may not be transferred to priority shareholders. These powers may only be submitted for approval by the priority shareholders, thereby granting them a veto right.[49]

7.1.1.2 Letter shares

The Articles commonly denote certain classes of shares by a letter (A,B,C, etc.), indicating that these classes carry special rights. When this is done, classes of shares denoted by a letter are effectively just different classes of priority shares.[50]

Under the Ministry of Justice's departmental guidelines of 1986[51] certain resolutions of the board of managing directors may be proposed for approval to a company organ, for example, a meeting of a certain class of shareholders. In practice, this gives a veto right to the company organ. The 1986 departmental guidelines allow the Articles to provide that:

- a company organ may determine the nature of the resolutions to be submitted for approval, provided that the Articles prescribe that the company organ in its resolution clearly describes the relevant board of managing directors' resolutions.

---

[49] See Arts. 2:92 and 2:201 Civil Code.

[50] Cf. Arts. 2:92 and 2:201 Civil Code.

[51] Guidelines regarding the enactment by the Ministry of Justice of Arts. 68, 179, 125, 235, 72 and 183 of Book 2 of the Netherlands Civil Code, as determined by the State Secretary of Justice by decision of 18 November 1985, Stc. 1985, 227 (guidelines for the appraisal of formations and amendment of articles of public and private limited liability companies).

- approval is required for board resolutions involving a larger sum than determined by a company organ.
- the board of managing directors must act according to the directions of a company organ regarding general financial, social, economic and personnel policies.

Letter shares also make it possible to differentiate dividend policies for each class of shareholders. To achieve this, the articles will state that different dividend reserves will be created and only shares carrying the same letter as the dividend reserve will be entitled to that reserve.

Letters are sometimes used to impose a certain regime of ownership passage on certain shares. For example, if a private limited company is formed by three persons, A, B and C, each may want to provide that his family members have a right of first refusal when the ownership of shares originally held is transferred.

7.1.1.3 Right to make a binding nomination of supervisory directors[52]
Supervisory directors not yet appointed by the deed of incorporation are appointed by the general meeting.[53] The Articles may provide[54] that the appointment of supervisory directors by the general meeting must be made upon a binding nomination by another organ (eg the board of managing directors), other persons (holders of priority shares) or a third party (the state, or another institution).[55] In this case as well, the nomination must state at least two names per vacancy. Again, the general meeting may retain control in that it may render the nomination non-binding by a resolution adopted by two-thirds of the votes cast, jointly representing more than half of the issued capital.[56]

7.1.2 Pooling agreements

A pooling agreement is an agreement between one or more shareholders to vote in a specified way in certain cases. From a substantive law perspective, such an agreement affects the voting right vested in every shareholder under Articles 2:117 and 2:227 Civil Code. The question is to what extent such pooling agreements regulating the exertion of power within the company are allowed.

As early as 1944, the Supreme Court, in a ruling regarding NV Wennex,[57] held that pooling agreements are, in principle, not contrary to law or common decency. The Supreme Court adopted the position that the individual shareholder's voting right is his own right and serves this shareholder's (own) interest in the company.

---

52 For the right to make binding nomination of managing directors, see 1.2 and 1.3 above.

53 Arts. 2:142 and 2:252 Civil Code; cf. a different arrangement for companies under a "large structure regime", Art. 2:252 9158 of the Netherlands Civil Code.

54 Based on Arts. 2:144(2) jo 134(2) and 254(2) jo 244(2) Civil Code.

55 Cf. Art. 2:253 (143) of the Netherlands Civil Code. The Articles may provide that one or more supervisory directors, though not more than three, be appointed by others than the general meeting. Note that this provision does not apply to companies under a large structure regime.

56 Arts. 2:133(2) and 2:243 Civil Code.

57 Supreme Court 30 June 1994, NJ, 1944, 465.

This leaves him the option to bind that vote contractually to others as long as this does not deprive the shareholder of every possibility to weigh independently his interests.

Individual (minority) shareholders may thus freely attempt to bind other shareholders to vote in a specified way. This may, *inter alia*, occur in "preliminary meeting agreements" in which a certain group of shareholders undertake to hold a "preliminary meeting" prior to every general meeting and, subsequently, vote at the general meeting as they decided at the preliminary meeting.[58]

8. Remedies Where a Shareholders' Resolution or Other Action Impairs the Rights of Minority Shareholders

8.1 What are the requirements for such remedies?

8.1.1 Void and voidable resolutions

In so far as resolutions are adopted by authorized company organs–with due observance of the limits set by law and the Articles (particularly with respect to the required majority) – they are considered valid.

According to the basic rule of Article 2:14 (1) Civil Code, a resolution of a legal entity in which the contents or purport are contrary to the law or the Articles is void (*ex tunc* effect). In such a case, the court has no discretionary power. If the required prior act of or notification to another organ which has made the resolution has not taken place, the other organ can ratify the resolution.[59]

In other cases, resolutions may not be void *per se* but only voidable (with *ex nunc* effect). Under Article 2:15 (1) Civil Code, resolutions are voidable in cases of:

- a breach of the legal provisions or provisions in the Articles with respect to the adoption of resolutions;
- a breach of the reasonableness and fairness principles as required by Article 2:8 Civil Code;
- a breach of certain rules and regulations;
- a vitiated consent.[60]

A claim for the avoidance of a resolution can be filed against the legal entity by anyone who has a reasonable interest in compliance with the non-observed obligation. This includes, in principle, (minority) shareholders, managing directors, supervisory directors and, for instance, holders of profit-sharing certificates who may

---

58 See also Van der Heijden, *Handboek voor de naamloze en besloten vennootschap*, Zwolle 1992, No.217.1, who argues that any material transfer of a voting right is improper.

59 Art. 2:14 (2) Civil Code.

60 Based on mistake of a fact, duress, threat, deceit, undue influence.

be put at a considerable disadvantage. Furthermore, it may include holders of depositary receipts if the administrative office, as shareholder, fails to take action. It may also include the Works Council under certain circumstances. The circle of interested parties may be broadly defined; however, the more remotely a party is involved in the orderly conduct of the company's business, the more clearly it will need to demonstrate that it has a reasonable interest in the avoidance of the resolution. Shareholders may be assumed to have an interest in the orderly conduct of the company's business. Even so, a reasonable interest will still be a requirement to claim avoidance of a resolution.

A reasonable interest will generally only be deemed to exist where non-observance of a standard relevant to the claimant causes him damage. In the event of a dispute, the claimant will have to substantiate it. As a rule, it may be assumed that no reasonable interest is present if avoidance of the resolution will not bring the effect desired by the claimant any closer to realization.[61]

There is no provision in the law on any conspiracy between certain shareholders or other interested parties and the board of managing directors. Where an "indirect conflict of interest" is concerned, Articles 2:47, 2:146 or 2:256 Civil Code may be applied. The claim may also be filed by legal entities; however, this requires a resolution of the board of managing directors of those entities.

8.1.2 Claim to take over shares

A shareholder who is so injured by his co-shareholder(s) that he can no longer be reasonably required to keep his shares may claim that his shares be taken over by the other shareholders.[62]

Unlike a claim for the transfer of shares, it is not required in a claim for shares to be taken over[63] that the claimant have supplied at least one-third of the issued capital, nor is there the additional requirement that the company's interest must be injured. Such a claim may be filed even if the company's interest is injured and shareholders other than the claimant may also be injured as a consequence of the relevant acts. If the shareholder against whom the claim is filed also acted wrongfully in respect to the claimant, the claimant may claim damages in addition to a claim for a share take-over.

The claim for a share take-over cannot be filed on the grounds of unacceptable acts undertaken by the company. If difficulties ensue from the acts of the company, this constitutes improper management for which an inquiry procedure may be commenced.

Pursuant to Article 2:343(2) Civil Code, a shareholder against whom a claim to take over shares is filed may start proceedings against another shareholder if the first-mentioned shareholder believes that the claim should also or exclusively be filed against that shareholder. If the court finds that the claim is founded, it will set a price for the shares and determine how many shares each of the defendants will

---

[61] Cf. Supreme Court of 6 June 1969, NJ 1969, 317 and Supreme Court of 19 May 1989, NJ, 1989, 652.

[62] Art. 2:343 Civil Code.

[63] Art. 2:336 Civil Code.

have to transfer for simultaneous payment of the price.[64] The claimant cannot withdraw at a later stage.

If the Articles contain an offer system in respect to the transfer of shares, these rules shall have preference in that they will need to be observed to the extent possible. The shares will then be offered by the company, acting as representative of the claimant.

8.2 When do the courts of your country accept these requirements?

A resolution can be avoided if it is in breach of statutory provisions or provisions in the Articles laying down the adoption of resolutions,[65] or if it is in breach of the reasonableness and fairness principles.

Breach of the reasonableness and fairness principles as required by Article 2:18 Civil Code includes both "abuse of power" and "abuse of majority power". This principle is rather vague and must be further elaborated by case law, subject to marginal examination only. Account must be taken of generally recognized legal principles, the prevailing legal opinion in the Netherlands, and social and personal interests. Often, conflicting interests will need to be weighed in the decision-making process. In essence, the test for reasonableness and fairness must be limited to the question of whether the organ involved could have reasonably reached its decision. This principle leaves such a margin that it is not easily transgressed.

The fact that a resolution can, in principle, be reversed on the grounds of vitiated consent (*wilsgebre*) follows from Article 3:44 and Article 59 Civil Code and the reference in Article 2:15(1) Civil Code to "any other legal provision regarding the possibility of reversal". Familiar examples of vitiated consent are threat (*bedreiging*), absence of informed consent (*dwaling*), deceit (*bedrog*) and undue influence (*misbruik van omstandigheden*). Special arrangements to assess resolutions have been laid down in various legal provisions.[66]

A claim on the basis of Article 2:343 Civil Code can only be filed against one or more shareholders who, because of their conduct, cause such damage to the rights and interests of the claimant that he cannot reasonably be expected to continue his shareholdership.[67]

8.3 What remedies are available to the claimant?

The available remedies have already been explained under 8.1 above. The reversal of a resolution has *ex nunc* effect. A claim to take over shares leads to the compulsory take-over and transfer of shares.

---

[64] Art. 2:343(3) Civil Code.

[65] Cf. in particular the procedural rules regarding the general meeting, such as the convening notice requirements of Art. 2:218(108) *et seq*. Civil Code.

[66] Compare Arts. 2:209, 2:100, 2:356, 2:257 Civil Code and 1002 Code of Civil Procedure.

[67] Compare decisions of the Court of Appeal of Amsterdam, 24 February 1994, NJ 1995, 354; Court of Appeal of Amsterdam, 9 December 1993, NJ 1994, 296; Netherlands Supreme Court, 8 December 1993, NJ 1994, 273; and the Court of Appeal of Amsterdam, 22 October 1992, NJ 1993, 411.

9. Specific Protection if the Company is Controlled by Another Company

9.1 What are the rights and remedies of a shareholder of Company A when company B gains control over it (by acquiring the majority of its shares or otherwise)?

No specific protection exist in this case. The rights of minority shareholders are limited to those explained under 8 above. The minority shareholder must, therefore, attempt to protect his interests by including provisions in the Articles of Incorporation to the greatest extent possible, especially in the stage prior to a possible (hostile) takeover of the company by a third party.

This can be achieved by the so-called blocking arrangement through the right of first refusal or approval,[68] or by oligarchic (protective) constructions by which control over the company is conferred upon a small group within the company. Even though these means of protection can be introduced only with the consent of a majority of the shareholders, they shall be explained hereinafter.

9.1.1 Transferability restrictions

Shares in a private limited company are not freely transferable. Legislators have laid down this rule in Article 2:195 Civil Code, stating that the Articles of Association must set forth a restriction on the transfer of shares to others than a closed circle of persons. In regard to the public limited company, the Articles may contain a restriction on transferability, provided that transfer does not become completely impossible.

9.1.1.1 Approval system

In drafting transferability restriction rules, the private limited company may choose from two systems. The first system is based on approval, which must be obtained from a company organ for every transfer.[69] The approval will be deemed granted if, at the time that the refusal of the request is notified, the applicant is not advised of one or more prospective buyer(s) willing to take over the shares for a certain cash payment.

9.1.1.2 Offer system (right of first refusal)

The second system provides that a shareholder who wants to dispose of one or more shares must first offer these to his co-shareholders.[70] The system may provide that if the co-shareholders do not accept the offer, it must be made to other prospective buyers designated by a company organ. If there are no prospective buyers who,

---

[68] In case of a transfer of shares see 9.1.1.2 and 9.1.1.3 below.

[69] Art. 2:105(3) Civil Code.

[70] Art. 2:195(4) Civil Code.

jointly or individually, want to buy the package of shares as a whole for a cash payment, the offerer shall be free to transfer the shares to a third party designated by him within three months.

9.1.1.3 Practice
Under the departmental guidelines of 1986, different transfer restriction systems may be combined and different transfer restriction systems may apply depending on the classes of shares or the shareholder. It is permissible to have a system in which transfer is only freely permitted to a group of relatives as defined in Article 2:195(1) Civil Code or to certain shareholders. The company organ which must grant the approval may not be obligated or prohibited by the Articles to grant approval to certain persons or groups. The approval system may not obligate the offerer to transfer his shares to designated prospective buyers.

9.1.1.4 The public limited company
Transferability restrictions in the Articles of a public limited company generally have the structure as defined in Article 2:195 Civil Code.

9.1.2 Oligarchical clauses

In the ordinary structure of a company, the general meeting of shareholders has important powers.

An oligarchy within the company can effectively be realized by legal (protective) structures. The devices used to such effect fall into two groups. The first group of devices aims at restricting the power of the general meeting of shareholders. Thus, the Articles of Association will contain provisions which restrict the powers of the general meeting. Another group of devices deprive the suppliers of capital from shareholders' rights by placing control at meetings with others than the ordinary shareholders. The rationale underlying the first group is that the company should not be dependent on the (accidental) majority of the votes at a shareholder's meeting. The majority at that meeting may pursue objectives which are incompatible with the continuity, independence and development of the company.

The five protective structures from the second group of devices include priority shares (see 7.1.1.1 above), voting restrictions (see 1.3 above), as well as the following three structures:

9.1.2.1 Issuing preferred shares in a "friendly corporation"
In public limited companies, the power to issue or place shares to increase capital is often allotted to the board of managing directors or the supervisory board (see 1.2 and 1.3 above), in order to have a weapon against a possible assault (ie a public bid on shares of a public limited company without the consent of the board of managing directors of that company). The idea is that by placing a sufficient block of shares with a "friendly corporation", an assault can be frustrated. As the shares placed with the friendly company will not be offered, the assailant will not succeed in acquiring a majority. After the danger has receded, the shares will be purchased back to the extent this is permitted.

To make the weapon more effective, the Articles may provide that part of the authorized capital consist of preferred shares.

9.1.2.2 Depositary receipts of shares

Rather than issuing shares directly to the interested suppliers of capital, shares may be issued to an interposed "administrative office". Depositary receipts are issued for these shares. The administrative office (most often a foundation, but sometimes another private or public limited company) is the actual shareholder and holds the voting rights. In turn, the administrative office will issue depositary receipts to the capital suppliers (which may be registered or to bearer). Depositary receipts may be convertible, non-convertible, or partly convertible.

Even though, in some respects, the position of a depositary receipt holder is the same as that of a shareholder (cf. regarding the right to attend general meetings and take the floor and the right to obtain a copy of the annual accounts without payment),[71] a depositary receipt holder is not entitled to vote at a general meeting.

By means of the administrative conditions, the rights of depositary receipt holders may be restricted in comparison to those of the (majority) shareholders.

Depositary receipts in private limited liability companies and public limited companies not listed on the stock exchange are often issued with a view to placing the voting rights in the general meeting with certain persons, often the managing directors or the supervisory directors. In these cases, it is primarily a measure to place control with an oligarchy. In public limited liability companies listed on the stock exchange, the issue of depositary receipts is clearly intended to create a protective structure to ward off hostile take-overs by public bid on issued shares or any private or systematic purchase of shares listed on the stock exchange.

To some extent, the administrative office's position is comparable to that of a trustee under Anglo-American law. However, unlike the trustee, the administrative office is a "full" owner.

9.1.2.3 Holding structure

In this structure, the shares of the operating company are transferred to a public limited holding company, which in turn issues the shares to the public. In this way, the shareholders have only indirect control over the operating company. The control vested by law in the shareholders is exercised by the holding company's board of managing directors. It should be noted that this structure in itself does not grant a great deal of protection. Freely transferable shares of a holding company may equally fall victim to a hostile take-over.

9.2 What are the shareholder's rights and remedies when Company B exerts its control over Company A in a way which damages the interest of the latter?

No specific protection exist in this case. The rights of minority shareholders are limited to those explained under 8 above.

---

[71] Arts. 2:102 and 2:212 Civil Code.

PORTUGAL

Miguel de Avillez Pereira

Avillez Pereira & Associados
Lisbon

PROTECTION OF MINORITY SHAREHOLDERS

***EDITOR* MATTHIAS W. STECHER**

PORTUGAL

Miguel de Avillez Pereira

Introduction

Portuguese law provides for various types of corporations, two of which are the most commonly used, namely the private company limited by shares (*sociedade anónima*, hereinafter SA) and the private company limited by quotas (*sociedade por quotas*, hereinafter Lda). Both the SA and the Lda are governed by the Companies Code[1] (*Código das Sociedades Comerciais*, hereinafter CSC) and the by-laws, and both must meet the same formalities to be set up. Even though the legal regime of the SA applies subsidiarily to the Lda, there are some differences with respect to the protection of the stockholders. The basic features of each of the said corporations are preliminarily noted, so that reference may simply be made to one or other when appropriate.

---

[1] The Companies Corporation Code was enacted on 2 September 1986, through Decree Law no. 262/86. Decree Laws 184/87, of 21 April, 280/87, of 8 July, 229-B/88, of 4 July, 238/91, of 2 July, 225/92, of 21 October, 20/93, of 26 January and 323/95, of 9 December have introduced new provisions or alterations to the Code. The general provisions are set out in Arts. 1 to 174. Provisions applicable to the Lda in particular are included in Arts. 197 to 270 and those applicable to the SA in Arts. 271 to 464

Basic Characteristics of the SA

An SA must be incorporated by at least five shareholders and must have an initial minimum share capital of PTE5,000,000. The shares must have a minimum value of PTE1,000, with the shareholders being liable up to the amount of their respective share participation. The shares may be nominative or bearer and ordinary or preferential.[2]

The governing bodies of an SA are the general meeting (*Assembleia Geral*), formed by all the shareholders or by the shareholders which fulfil the requirements stipulated in the by-laws for participation in the general meeting, the board of directors (*Conselho de Administração*) formed by an uneven number of members, and an Audit Board (*Conselho Fiscal*) composed of three or five members.[3]

Basic Characteristics of an Lda

The incorporation of an Lda requires at least two quota holders and a minimum quota capital of PTE400,000. The value of the quota may not be lower than PTE20,000. Only the assets of the company will be used to fulfil the financial obligations.[4]

The governing bodies of an Lda are the general meeting, formed by all quota holders and one or more managers (*Gerentes*). If certain turnover, asset and staff limits are exceeded, then the company must have an Auditor.[5]

1. Majority Requirements for Shareholders' Resolutions

1.1 What are the majority requirements in general?

The general rule is that share and quota holders' resolutions are adopted by a simple majority of the votes cast in the general meeting, regardless of the percentage of share capital or quota capital represented therein, unless otherwise provided by the Articles of Association.[6]

Each share or quota corresponds to one vote, unless otherwise provided by the Articles of Association.

---

2 CSC Arts. 271, 276, 299, 302, 241, 345.
3 CSC Chapters V and VI–Sections I and II of Title III.
4 CSC Arts. 197, 198, 201, 219.
5 CSC Chapters V and VI of Title IV.
6 CSC Arts. 248, 250, 379, 384, 383, 386.

It should be noted that share and quota holders are entitled to unanimously adopt written resolutions without the necessity of formalities, including the requirement of form in general meetings.[7]

1.2 Which resolutions require a greater majority?

With respect to the Lda, resolutions on various matters, such as alterations of the Articles of Association, merger or split of the company, change of the company into a new type of company and dissolution of the company, require the votes of at least 75% of the quota capital, unless the Articles of Association require a greater majority.

In the SA, the shareholders may only adopt a resolution for modification of the Articles of Association, merger or split of the company, change of the company into a new type of company or dissolution of the company, in a general meeting gathering at first call. Holders of shares corresponding to at least one-third of the share capital must be present or represented. Regardless of whether the general meeting gathers at first call or at second call, resolutions on such matters may only be adopted by two-thirds of the votes cast therein. However, in the case of a general meeting gathering at second call, the same resolutions may be adopted by a simple majority, if holders of shares corresponding to at least one-half of the share capital are present or represented.[8]

1.3 To what extent can they be modified by the Articles of Association?

The Articles of Association of both the Lda and SA may require a greater majority or even unanimity of the votes to adopt resolutions. The Articles of Associations may not, however, reduce the majorities stipulated by law.

In an SA, the Articles of Association may even provide that only the holders of a certain amount of shares may participate in the general meeting.[9]

---

7 CSC Art. 54, no. 1: "In any type of corporation, the partners may adopt unanimous written resolutions as well as meet in General Assembly, without observing the prior formalities, as long as they are all present and they all express their will to gather the assembly to decide upon a certain matter."

8 Regarding the Lda, CSC Arts. 217, 250, no. 3, 86, 265, 270; regarding the SA, CSC Arts. 86, 386, 383, 464.

9 CSC Art. 379: "1–The shareholders that are entitled to at least one vote, in accordance with the law or the articles of association, have the right to participate in the General Meetings and therein to discuss and vote. 2–The shareholders without the right to vote ... may attend the general meetings ... if the articles of association do not provide the contrary ... 5–Whenever the articles of association demand the holding of a certain amount of shares for the grant of voting rights ..." However, the same Article continues "5–Whenever the articles of association demand the holding of a certain amount of shares for the grant of voting rights, the shareholders which hold a lower amount of shares may join in order to achieve the required amount or a higher amount and may be represented in the General Meeting by one among them."

2. Influence on the Decision-Making Process

2.1 Do minority shareholders have the right to call a shareholders' meeting?

Any of the managers of an LDA have the authority to call the general meeting.. Notice of such meeting shall be given by a registered letter sent at least 15 days prior to the date of the meeting.

The general meeting of an SA is called by its chairman, at least 30 days prior to the meeting.[10]

The rights granted to minority shareholders of an SA concerning the call of general meetings apply to all quota holders.[11]

The general meeting must be called if one or more holders of at least 5% of the share capital so request. The request to call the general meeting must be made in writing, setting forth the reasons to convene and the matters to be discussed. The request is to be addressed to the chairman of the general meeting. If the chairman does not agree to call the General meeting, such decision must be in writing and founded. The minority shareholders may then seek a judicial order for the convening of the general meeting at the expense of the company.

2.2 Do they have the right to put matters on the agenda?

Any quota holder or holders of at least 5% of the share capital may request to put matters on the agenda of a general meeting which will be or has already been called. The said request shall be addressed to the chairman of the general meeting within five days of the date on which the meeting was called. Shareholders must be notified of requests five days prior to the shareholders' assembly. In case the request to put matters on the agenda is refused, the minority shareholders may seek a court order to call a new general meeting for deliberation of the said issues.[12]

3. Rights of Information, Independent Auditing and Supervision

3.1 To what extent do the (minority) shareholders have a right to be informed on company matters?

The managers of the Lda shall provide to any quota holder correct, true and complete information upon request of the latter, as well as permission for access to any

---

10 Regarding the Lda, CSC, Art. 248, no. 3 ; regarding the SA, CSC Art. 377.

11 CSC Art. 248, no. 2: "The rights granted to minority shareholders of private companies limited by shares concerning the call of General Meetings and the indication of matters to be submitted to it may be exercised by any quota holder." CSC Article 375, no. 2 (specifically addressed to the SA): "The General Meeting must be called when required by one or more shareholders which hold shares corresponding to at least 5% of the capital stock."

12 CSC Art. 378, no. 1 applying specifically to the SA, however, applies as well to the Lda according to CSC Art. 248, no. 2.

documents and books of the company. The information shall be in writing if so requested. The information requested may be related to acts already completed, or acts to be executed and may involve responsibility of the quota holder concerned. The examination of the documents and books must be done on the company's premises, the quota holder having the right to make copies if necessary. What has been said above in relation to documents and books applies as well to the company's assets. Unless otherwise provided by the Articles of Association, the information requested may only be denied by the managers if they suspect that the information is intended to be used to prejudice the company or that such providing of information would represent an infringement of third parties' right of confidentiality. The quota holder may, in any case, seek a judicial order to provide the information resolved by the general meeting. In addition, the refusal to provide the information so requested by the quota holders may be challenged through a request for a judicial examination of company matters.[13]

The exercise of the right for information within the general meeting is governed by the same rules applicable to the SA and will, therefore, be treated jointly below.

Any holder or representative of a holder of shares corresponding to at least 1% of the share capital of an SA has the right to examine, on the company's premises, various documents related to the company. The shareholder or shareholder representative may be assisted by an auditor or other expert. Also, prior to or during the general meeting, any shareholder may request information concerning matters which are related to the company or companies controlled by the former, specifically, information regarding the matters included in the agenda. The unfounded refusal to provide said information may constitute a ground for the annulment of resolutions adopted in the general meeting. The holders of 10% of the share capital may at any time demand information concerning company matters, which may not be refused if such information is intended to be used for liability claims against the members of the Board of Directors or Audit Board. The possibility of judicial examination of the company's matters is also available in the case of an SA.[14]

3.2 Do they have the right to demand independent auditing or to initiate the supervision of company matters by an independent institution?

Shareholders or quota holders may carry out independent auditing of the company or may supervise company matters under the same conditions as those explained above for the exercise of the right to information.

Whenever a shareholder is illegally denied information[15] or the information provided is incomplete or unclear, such shareholder may request a judicial examina-

[13] CSC Arts. 21, 58, no. 1(c), 274, 290, 292, 518 and 519 and Civil Code Art. 576.

[14] CSC Arts. 21, 58, no. 1(c), 290, 291, 292, 450, 518, 519.

[15] According to CSC Art. 292, no. 6, the judicial inquest may be requested without prior request to the company for information in case it may be assumed that the relevant information will not be provided to the shareholder.

tion of the company, in which case the court will have the power to order that the desired information be produced. Likewise, a shareholder who is given information which appears to be false may also request a judicial examination. In both cases, the court may find grounds to dismiss a member of the company's governing bodies who is responsible for the relevant decision, and, where appropriate, the court shall appoint a director to carry on the business until the appointment of a new director is made by the company. The court also has the power to start legal proceedings on behalf of the company against the person liable for the relevant decision, and to determine the winding up of the company.

4. Capital Increases and Distributions

4.1 To what extent do (minority) shareholders have the right to participate in capital increases?

Any (minority) quota or shareholder has a preferential right to participate in capital increases in the amount proportional to their quota or share participation. Such a right may only be restricted or denied by a resolution of the general meeting adopted by the holders of at least three-quarters of the quota capital or two-thirds of the share capital, and such restriction must be required by a justified interest of the company. If the quota or shareholder does not agree with the restriction or denial to participate in the capital increase they may seek the annulment of the resolution.[16]

4.2 Do minority shareholders have the right to demand dividends or other distributions?

Unless otherwise provided by the Articles of Association or by a resolution of the general meeting which must be adopted by a three-fourth majority of the holders of the quota or share capital, (minority) quota or shareholders have the right to demand the distribution of half of the profits after the retention in the company of funds sufficient to cover the legal reserve for the quota or share capital and the losses which have been carried forward to the following year. The right of the quota or shareholders to their share in the distribution of dividends will accrue within 30 days of the date of the resolution regarding the distribution of dividends.[17]

---

[16] As said, such preferential right is recognized for any shareholder. In relation to the Lda, Art. 266 and also Arts. 267 and 268, regarding the transmission of the preferential right. In relation to the SA, Arts. 458–462, concerning a capital increase through the issuance of new shares and Art. 367 concerning a capital increase resulting from the conversion of bonds into shares.

[17] CSC Arts. 217, 218, 295 and 296 regarding the Lda; CSC Articles 294–7, 32 and 33 with relation to the SA.

5. Derivative Actions

5.1 Can (minority) shareholders enforce rights that the company has against other shareholders, directors, or third parties?

Any quota or shareholder(s) holding at least 5% of the quota or share capital may initiate a legal action against the managers or directors of the company in order to compensate the company for damages and losses which have been caused as a result of actions taken by said managers or directors, if the company itself has failed to do so. The same quota or shareholders may, in addition, claim compensation for damages directly suffered as a result of the same actions. With respect to the rights of the company against quota or shareholders or third parties, only the company may legitimately initiate legal proceedings.[18]

6. Other "Formal" Rights

6.1 Do minority shareholders have any other specific rights comparable to those mentioned in 2–5 above?

Portuguese law provides various rights intended to specifically protect minority capital holders, of which the following are the most relevant.

The general rule is that one vote corresponds to each quota or share. The law provides, however, for the possibility that the Articles of Association of an SA or the general meeting may stipulate not to count the votes above a certain number when cast by one shareholder alone or on behalf of another shareholder. For example, it can be provided that for a certain number of shares only one vote will correspond, or a limit can be put on votes which may be cast by one single shareholder.[19]

With respect to an Lda, the Articles of Association may increase the number of the votes corresponding to quotas below 20% of the quota capital.[20]

Subject to certain conditions, the holders of at least 10% of the share capital have the right to appoint one member of the board of directors. In addition, the

---

[18] CSC Arts. 77, 79, 80, 81, 82, 72.

[19] CSC Art. 384 stipulates : "1–To each share shall correspond one vote, unless otherwise provided by the Articles of Association. 2–The Articles of Association may: a) Determine that one vote shall correspond to a certain amount of shares, as long as this limitation applies to all the shares of the company and a sole vote corresponds at least to PTE 100.000 of capital stock. b) Establish that the votes above a certain number are not to be counted when issued by one shareholder alone or on behalf of another shareholder as well. 3–The limitation of votes which is provided in number 2, item b), may be imposed on all shares or simply to one or more types of shares, but not to determined shareholders, and it is not valid in case the shareholder is the State or any similar legal entity ...". Article 386, no. 5 further clarifies that: "In case the law or the Articles of Association require greater majorities, determined in relation to the company's capital stock, ... the limitations of vote that are permitted by Article 384, no. 2, line b) are not to be taken into account."

[20] CSC Art. 250, no. 2.

holders of at least 10% of the share capital may petition the court to appoint a member to the Audit Board, if the said shareholders have voted against the appointment of the members to the Audit Board in the general meeting.[21]

Any quota holder may petition the competent court to reduce the wages of its managers if these are seriously disproportional to the job to be carried out or to the situation of the company.

Any quota or shareholder may petition the court to order the company to submit its annual accounts.

7. Extensions of These Rights by Statute or Shareholders' Agreements

7.1 Can the Articles of Association provide for additional rights of the minority shareholders? If not, can such rights be provided for in shareholders' agreements? Are these options commonly used?

Any additional rights that are intended to increase the influence of minority quota or shareholders, including the number of votes or the appointment of members to the bodies in the company, may be provided by the Articles of Association. Similarly, quota or shareholders may enter into an agreement which provides additional rights for minority quota or shareholders. However, shareholders agreements may not concern the behaviour of any member of the company's bodies, nor, in relation to the voting rights, may they require that any of the parties to the agreement always vote in accordance with the company's or any of its bodies' instructions or proposals. It is also forbidden to provide that a shareholder shall use his voting rights in consideration of special advantages. Provisions for additional rights of minority holders in the Articles of Association are rarely used. Shareholders' agreements are most commonly used in large SAs in order to create a sort of task force of shareholders, who together hold a share participation of 10% to 20%. In such agreements, often the parties are bound to vote in the same way or not to sell shares, or each party is given a preferential right in case of a sale of shares. However, although shareholders' agreements legally bind the parties to the agreement, their infringement does not invalidate the company's act or resolution nor an act of its shareholders before the company. Therefore, if a party to a shareholders' agreement does not respect its provisions, the other parties may only seek compensation for damages.

---

[21] CSC Art. 392 contains special rules regarding the appointment of members of the Board of Directors with the purpose of granting to minority shareholders the possibility of appointing at least one director . The said provision avails two systems: the system of appointment through lists (nos. 1–5) and the system of appointment by the minority (6 to 7). However, in general, the adoption of such systems is not mandatory and, therefore, is seldom used.

8. Remedies where a Shareholders' Resolution or Other Action Impairs the Rights of Minority Shareholders

8.1 What are the requirements for such remedies?

To suspend the effects of a resolution or of an action which impairs their rights, the minority holders must demonstrate:

- that such resolution or action is illegal (ie an infringement of the law or of the Articles of Association); and
- that the resolution or action is likely to cause considerable damage to them.[22]

It should be noted that, within the proceedings for interim measures, circumstantial evidence is sufficient and the actual existence of damages is not necessary for the injuction to be held. It is sufficient that damages may occur.

To obtain the annulment of an illegal resolution, the following requirements are necessary:

- the annulment must be held against the company;
- the holder has not voted in favour of the resolution (if the resolution was adopted in a secret ballot, the holder must have his contrary vote registered in the minutes at the relevant meeting, or by a Notary Public);
- the resolution must be illegal, that is, against the rights of a quota or shareholder as provided by law or by the Articles of Association.[23]

A special ground on which such annulment may be founded is provided by Portuguese law, namely, the adoption of a resolution by which a quota or shareholder causes damage to another holder, if indeed there was an intention of the former to damage the latter.

---

22 The judicial proceedings concerning the suspension of resolutions are regulated in Arts. 396 and 397 of the Civil Procedure Code. According to Abílio Neto in *Código de Processo Civil Anotado*, 12th edn, November 1995, the suspension of a resolution depends on two requirements: the illegality of the resolution, namely that the resolution violates the law or the Articles of Association, and the probability that its execution causes a considerable damage (Article 396, no. 1). In relation to the first requirement, Courts take the view that it is simply a demand of probability while in relation to the second, the Courts generally demand certainty or a strong probability (see Alberto dos Reis, *Código de Processo Civil Anotado*, 1st volume, p. 677 and Decision of the Supreme Court of 27 February 1962 published in *Boletim do Ministèrio da Justiça* no. 114, p. 500, also Dec.SC of 27 May 1954, BMJ, no. 42, p. 400). Even if these two requirements are fulfilled, the Court may deny the suspension if it finds, at its own discretion, that the damages which may be caused by the suspension are greater than those that may result from the resolution.

23 CSC Art. 59 concerning the annulment of resolutions. According to Armando Braga in *Código das Sociedades Comerciais Anotado e Comentado*, Lisbon 1991, p.147, the holder which subsequently approved the resolution, whether expressly or not, may not also request its annulment due to the good faith principles and to the general prohibition of abuse of rights in its modality of *venire contra factum proprium*.

It is not required for the annulment of such a resolution that it was adopted due to the vote of the quota or shareholder who was willing to damage the other quota or shareholder. In fact, if it is proved that even without the vote of that quota or shareholder the decision would had been taken, the court cannot annul the resolution.[24]

If a resolution of the general meeting, or of a decision or resolution of a director or manager, even though it is within their competence, causes damages to any quota or shareholder, indemnity from the company is available by proving:

- the existence of damages;
- that the damages were caused by an action or resolution of one of the bodies of the company within its competence, or that they were caused by a resolution of the general meeting within its powers;
- that there was violation of the law or of the Articles of Association;
- that there was culpability.[25]

If the resolution or decision was adopted beyond the powers or competence of the relevant body or person, compensation can only be sought from the responsible body or person.[26]

When the damages are due to a resolution, a decision or an action of a director, manager, or of the general meeting, to obtain compensation in relation thereto, the quota or shareholder has to prove before the court:

- the existence of damages;
- that the damages were caused by an act or a resolution of the referred bodies;
- that there was a violation of their legal or corporate duties or obligations;
- that there was culpability, if the decision or resolution is of one or more holders. If the responsible party is a manager or a director, culpability is presumed. Therefore, to avoid damages, the defendant has to prove that he did not act with culpability, by demonstrating, at least, that he took all the necessary precautions when adopting the decision.[27]

Any request for indemnity may only be accepted if brought by the legitimate holder (see 8.3 below). The illegality of the action, decision or resolution must have caused damages. If the claim concerns a director's or manager's responsibility arising from a resolution of the body of which they are members, the manager or director may argue that he did not participate in the meeting or that he did not vote in favour of the resolution. The law permits the manager or director to register his contrary vote in the minutes or before a notary public. In any case, the defendant may also present other evidence to show his contrary vote.[28]

In various circumstances, which depend on the type of company (see 8.3 below), a quota or shareholder may leave the company. For each cause the law pro-

---

24 CSC Art. 58, no. 1(c).

25 Arts. 500 and 483 and following of the Civil Code and CSC Art. 79, 72, nos. 2–5, 73, 74, nos. 1, 80 and 81.

26 Art. 500 of the Civil Code *a contrario* and Art. 483 and following of the same Code.

27 CSC Art. 79 No. 2 and Art. 72, in particular no. 1.

28 CSC Art. 79 No. 2 and Art. 72 Nos. 2 and 3.

vides a time frame within which the quota or shareholder may inform the company of his intention to leave the company. The company may acquire the quota or shares, pay a price for them and then cancel the shares, or arrange a quota or shareholder or third party to buy the shares.

8.2 When do the courts of your country accept these requirements?

In relation to the suspension of a resolution or action, the court will generally accept the request in case the resolution or action is deemed illegal and there is a high likelihood that its execution will cause considerable damages to the shareholder. In principle, the requirement of a serious risk of damages would imply that the resolution or action has not been already completed. However, the courts have recently held that a resolution which has lasting effects can be suspended, in particular a resolution which excludes a shareholder or extinguishes the shares of a shareholder.[29]

Even in situations where the legal requirements for suspending a resolution are met, the court may decide to refuse its suspension if the damage to the company following from such a suspension is expected to be higher than the possible damage that the execution of the resolution would cause the shareholder.

The law stipulates the cases in which a resolution is null and void, namely:

- adoption of a resolution by a general meeting that was not called, unless all the shareholders were present or duly represented;
- adoption of a resolution through written votes when not all shareholders with the right to vote were called to exercise such right;
- adoption of a resolution relating to a matter beyond the competence of the general meeting;
- adoption of a resolution contrary to compulsory legislation.

In addition to these cases, the courts generally tend to hold null and void resolutions that infringe the so-called essential rights of the shareholder, including but not limited to the right to vote or the right for information.[30] Moreover, all infringements of the law or the Articles of Association may be annulled but only if legal action is brought within a 30-day time limit.

---

[29] There are not many decisions regarding this controversy: the Decisions of the Supreme Court of 26 January 1932, in *Colecão Oficial* no. 31, p. 35, of 22 April 1949, in *Revista dos Tribunais,* year 67, p.231, of 25 November 1949, in *A Vida Jurdiciária*, 12th year, no. 233, p. 47, of 11 May 1956, in the same journal, no. 57, p.398 and of January 1961 in *Revista dos Tribunais*, 79th year, p. 101, have supported that a resolution already completed may not be suspended, while the same Court decisions of 20 March 1962, in the same journal, 80th year, p. 183, of 13 April 1962, in p. 212, of 12 November 1987, in *Boletim do Ministério da Justiça*, no. 371, p. 378 have defended the contrary.

[30] "A resolution of an SA in which the General Meeting has decided upon the transmission of shares belonging to certain shareholders which were not present, nor have been called to the meeting is null", Decision of the Supreme Court of 23 March 1988, in Boletim do Ministério da Justiça, no. 375, p. 403; "Because it limits the shareholder's right for information, the resolution which determines that the company may extend for one month the term to provide information requested

8.3 What remedies are available to the claimant?

Basically the claimant may:

- request an interim measure;
- seek the judicial annulment of a resolution or decision;
- seek indemnity for suffered damages;
- seek indemnity for damages to the company; or
- have his shares bought out, thereby leaving the company.

If the company adopts a resolution contrary to the law or the Articles of Association, the quota or shareholder may request from the court an interim measure to suspend the resolution.

Any quota or shareholder can also lodge a legal action against the company, asking the court to annul a resolution adopted.

If a quota or shareholder is damaged by a resolution or an action, it can claim damages before the competent court. The judicial proceeding may be brought against the company, against its managers or directors, or against the other quota or shareholders. Compensation can be sought from the company if the holder's damages were due to an action of the other quota or shareholders, due to directors or managers within their competence or powers, or if the damages were caused by a resolution of the general meeting or of the board of directors within the competence of these bodies. If this is not the case, indemnity may only be demanded from the responsible managers, directors or quota or shareholders. In principle, compensation can only be requested from the other quota or shareholders if the latter voted for a resolution or took a decision which caused damages. In the following special circumstances, however, a quota or shareholder may be sued together with the responsible director or manager, that is:

- if the responsible manager was chosen by a holder or group of quota or shareholders who entered into an agreement for the right to choose a manager with their votes, according to the Articles of Association, without interference from the other quota or shareholders, as long as there was culpability in the choice;
- if the responsible manager or director was chosen with their votes which represented more than half of the votes presented or represented at the relevant general meeting, and it is proved that there was culpability in the choice;
- if the responsible manager could be dismissed by the votes of a quota or shareholder or a group of quota or shareholders which entered into a quota or shareholders' agreement, and they influenced the responsible manager or director to take the illegal decision or resolution which caused the damages, under the said agreement.[31]

---

cont.
by its shareholders to participate in a General Meeting is null ... ", Dec. S.C. of 13 April 1994, in *Colectânea de Jurisprudência,* 1994, no. 2, p. 27.

[31] CSC Art. 83 and Art. 500 of the Civil Code; CSC Arts. 105, 120, 137, which apply to both the Lda and the SA; CSC Art. 240 concerning the Lda.

In some special cases the holder can also have his shares bought out, thereby allowing him to leave the company. Such cases include a merger, a change in the type of the company or other situations provided by the Articles of Association. If the company is an Lda, the right to leave the company and the right to have the respective quota bought out is automatically provided by the law, not only in the latter situations, but also in the case of:

- capital increases opened to third parties;
- a change of the company's purpose;
- an extension of the company's previous duration;
- a transfer of the company's main office to a foreign country;
- the liquidated company's return to business.

9. Specific Protection if the Company is Controlled by Another Company

9.1 What are the rights and remedies of a shareholder of Company A when Company B gains control over it (by acquiring the majority of its shares or otherwise)?

Portuguese law provides that a company which holds at least 90% of the shares in another company must inform the latter company. The same applies to a company holding the said percentage together with another company in which the former holds at least 10% of its share capital, or together with a company which holds at least 10% of the former's share capital. In such a case, within six months following the communication, the dominant company can make an offer to acquire the shares held by the minority shareholders.

If the offer is not reasonable, any minority shareholder may ask the court to fix the adequate value of his shares and to order the company to buy the shares for this value. If an offer is not made, any shareholder can demand that the company present an offer. According to law, the holder must give the company at least 30 days to present its offer. If the offer is not made, the shareholder may also ask the competent court to fix an adequate value for his shares and to order the company to buy those shares for that value.[32]

If a company, through a contract, submits its management to the bodies of another company, its quota or shareholders are entitled to sell their shares. The subordination contract must fix the value of acquisition offered for the shares and must determine the time limit within which the quota or share holders may demand the offered value from the dominant company for the sale of their shares. If a quota or

[32] CSC Art. 490. According to CSC Art. 541 the provisions of Art. 490 do not apply if the 90% were acquired before 1 November 1986, the date in which DL 262/86 entered into force – see its Art. 2.

share holder finds the contract to be illegal or the offered value unsatisfactory, he has 19 days to oppose the contract before the competent court. If the issue in question is the value of the offer, the court may fix an adequate value and order the dominant company to buy the shares for that value.

Having the right to sell his shares, any quota or share holder can also decide not to sell them and, instead, ask for a profit guarantee. In fact, by the subordination contract, the main company assumes the obligation of paying to the quota or shareholders the difference between the real profit obtained and the greater of the following values:

- the average of the profits obtained by the quota or shareholder during the last three years before the execution of the subordination contract (calculated in relation to the capital stock);
- the profit which would have been realized due to the holding of the quotas or the shares of the dominant company, in this case, if such company, in the subordination contract, offered to the quota or shareholders the purchase of their shares against its own shares. The quota or shareholder shall benefit from this guarantee during the period of validity of the contract and for a period of five years following its termination.[33]

9.2 What are the shareholder's rights and remedies when Company B exerts its control over Company A in a way which damages the interests of the latter?

If a company has entered a subordination contract which submits its management to another company, the dominant company is legally responsible for all obligations of the subordinated company.[34]

Portuguese law recognizes the right of the subordinate company to be compensated by the dominant company for the annual losses incurred for whatever reason, during the duration of the subordination contract, so long as such deficits are not compensated with the subordinated company's reserves provided during the same period. In principle this compensation can only be demanded after the subordination contract is terminated. However, if the company is declared bankrupt, the said compensation can be demanded immediately.[35]

The dominant company has the right to give instructions to the subordinated company as of the date on which the subordination contract enters into force. The dominant company may even instruct the subordinated company contrary to the interests of the latter, but in benefit of the dominant company or of a company in its group, unless otherwise provided by the contract of subordination. However, the dominant company is forbidden to require the transmission of the assets of the sub-

---

33 The subordination contract and its legal regime is regulated by CSC Arts. 493 – 508.
34 CSC Art. 501.
35 CSC Arts. 502 and 504.

terests of the latter, but in benefit of the dominant company or of a company in its group, unless otherwise provided by the contract of subordination. However, the dominant company is forbidden to require the transmission of the assets of the subordinated company to it or to another company of its group without fair compensation. If the rules indicated above are not observed, any quota or share holder may use the remedies indicated in question 8.3 above.[36]

[36] CSC Art. 503 – The dominant company's right to give mandatory instructions to the subordinated company, although it may permit following a group strategy with the undeniable advantages associated therewith, permits, at the same time, the inadequate management of the subordinated company with the notorious negative effects concerning its creditors' guarantees. This explains the provision of Art. 501 regarding the dominant company's responsibility for the obligations of the subordinated company (see Brito Correia, "Grupos de sociedades", in *Novas Perspectivas do Direito Comercial*, 1988, p. 395 and Castro Silva, "Das relações inter-societárias", in *Revista do Notariado*, 1986, p. 529).

SPAIN

Coloma Armero Montes

Bufete Armero

Madrid

PROTECTION OF MINORITY SHAREHOLDERS

***EDITOR* MATTHIAS W. STECHER**

SPAIN

Coloma Armero Montes

1. Majority Requirements for Shareholders' Resolutions

1.1 What are the majority requirements in general?

Sociedad anónima (SA) As a general rule, shareholders' resolutions are adopted in a general meeting by a simple majority vote of the shareholders attending the meeting.[1]

Spanish legislation establishes the following minimum requirements for the valid constitution of a general meeting:

- The first time a general meeting is convened, attendance of shareholders present in person or by proxy who represent at least 25% of the voting share capital is required.[2]
- The second time a general meeting is convened there is no quorum requirement.[3]

---

1 Art. 93. *Ley de Sociedades Anónimas* (LSA) of 22 December 1989.
2 Art. 102 LSA *ibid.*
3 Art. 102 LSA.

Sociedad de responsabilidad limitada (SL) As a general rule, shareholders' resolutions are adopted at a general meeting by a simple majority of votes cast provided that these represent at least one-third of the share capital. There are no minimum requirements for the shareholders quorum to hold meetings. However, the one-third voting share requirement implies that there is a requirement of one-third of the share capital for a valid quorum.[4]

1.2 Which resolutions require a greater majority?

1.2.1 SA

1.2.1.1 Additional attendance quorum for general meetings

Any modification of the by-laws, and in particular the passing of a resolution on

- issue of bonds;
- increase of share capital;
- reduction of share capital;
- transformation of the company;
- merger of the company;
- restructuring of the company; or
- exclusion of the right to preferential subscription of shares in a capital increase,

requires, in the first general meeting, a quorum of shareholders who represent at least 50% of the voting share capital. If the meeting is reconvened at a later date only 25% of the voting share capital must be represented.[5]

1.2.1.2 Increased majority of votes

The general requirement for a simple majority is increased in the case of a general meeting being convened for a second time (when the meeting is attended by shareholders representing less than 50% of the voting share capital). In case of the above-mentioned modifications or resolutions, it will be necessary to obtain the approval of two-thirds of the share capital present or represented at the meeting.[6]

1.2.1.3 Other majorities

When the company's capital is divided into more than one class of shares and there is a proposed change in the by-laws which is prejudicial to one class of shares, then, in addition to the majority vote of the total share capital represented at the general meeting, approval by a majority of the affected class of shares is also required.[7] When several classes of shares are affected it is necessary to obtain separate approval from each class.

When there is a reduction of share capital with the aim of redeeming shares, and the measure does not affect all shareholders equally, ie not all shareholders can par-

---

4 Art. 53 *Ley de Sociedades De Responsabilidad Limitada* (LSRL) Ley 2/1995 of 23 March 1995.

5 Art. 103 LSA.

6 *Ibid.*

7 Art. 148 LSA.

ticipate, it will be necessary to obtain the consent of a majority of the shareholders thereby affected.[8]

An alteration of the by-laws which will impose new obligations on certain shareholders will require the consent of each of the shareholders affected.[9]

Under Spanish law there is the concept of "accessory contributions", contributions by the shareholder to the company which can be monetary or non-monetary (ie the transfer of real estate or services rendered to the company). Such contributions do not form part of the share capital of the company. Approval of all shareholders who are affected by the creation, alteration, or early termination of an obligation to make such accessory contributions is required.[10]

A resolution increasing the share capital by raising the nominal value of the shares requires the consent of all shareholders.[11]

1.2.2 SL

1.2.2.1 Increased majority of votes

A majority of the votes cast at a meeting in which participants represent at least one-half of the share capital will be necessary in the following circumstances:[12]

- increase in share capital;
- reductions in share capital;
- any other alteration to the company's by-laws which does not require a specific majority.

A majority of votes cast in a meeting at which at least two-thirds of the share capital is represented will be necessary in the following circumstances:[13]

- transformation, merger or division of the company;
- removal of the existing shareholders' preferential rights in the event of an increase in the share capital;
- granting an administrator (a company director) express authority to engage in some activity, whether on his own account or on behalf of another, which competes with the company's activities;
- the exclusion of shareholders.

1.2.2.2 Other majorities

If the members unanimously agree, a redemption of shares which reduces the share capital can be made on a basis other than according to the proportion of the members' holdings.[14]

---

8 Art. 164 LSA.
9 Art. 145 LSA.
10 *Ibid.*
11 Art. 152 LSA.
12 Art. 53 LSA.
13 *Ibid.*
14 Art. 81 LSRL.

1.3 To what extent can they be modified by the Articles of Association?

SA The by-laws can restrict the right to attend a general meeting and can increase the quorum or voting majority with the following limitations:

- with respect to the right to attend a general meeting: The by-laws can require the ownership of a minimum number of shares (although not more than 0.1% of the existing share capital) for attendance of a shareholder at a general meeting.[15]
- with respect to the quorum of a general meeting: The quorum necessary in a meeting which is recovened at a later date must always be lower than the one established by law or the by-laws for the first time the meeting is convened.[16]
- with respect to the majority of votes: It is not possible to include a provision in the by-laws which, directly or indirectly, requires a unanimous vote to adopt certain types of resolutions. Nor is it possible to include a requirement which would (directly or indirectly) alter the proportionality between the nominal value of the shares and the right to vote.[17]
- the by-laws can limit the maximum number of votes which can be exercised by a shareholder or group of companies.[18]
- with respect to resolutions, it is not possible for the by-laws to alter the general majority requirements if an action shall be initiated against the administrators for breach of duty.[19]

SL The company's by-laws can require a higher percentage of votes to pass a resolution, as long as this does not require unanimity.[20] The by-laws can also require a specific quorum of shareholders for a vote in favour of a resolution. There are two exceptions to this rule: For the removal of administrators,[21] it is not possible to change the voting majority above two-thirds of the share capital. For decisions relating to an action against administrators for breach of duty,[22] the voting majority may not be changed to more than a simple majority.

Unlike an SA, the by-laws cannot restrict a shareholder's right to attend a general meeting.

2. Influence on the Decision-Making Process

2.1 Do minority shareholders have the right to call a shareholders' meeting?

SA and SL Any shareholder, regardless of his shareholding, can request that judicial authorities convene an ordinary general meeting (if the administrators have not

[15] Art. 105 LSA.
[16] Art. 98 LSA.
[17] Art. 50 LSA.
[18] Art. 105 LSA.
[19] Art. 134 LSA.
[20] Art. 53 LSA.
[21] Art. 68 LSRL.
[22] Art. 69 LSRL.

done so within the first six months of the company's accounting year), to approve the accounts of the previous accounting year, pass a resolution as to how to apply the profits or losses and to censure the management.

Also, minority shareholders representing at least 5% of the share capital can seek to convene an extraordinary general meeting. The general meeting must be convened by the administrators not later than 30 days after receipt of such a request from the shareholders. If the administrators fail to convene the meeting, shareholders representing at least 5% of the share capital can request the judicial authorities to convene the meeting.[23]

2.2 Do they have the right to put matters on the agenda?

SA and SL Shareholders have the right to include any matter on the agenda when they have requested that a general meeting be convened, as the request to either the Administrators or the judge must indicate what matters are to be considered at the meeting.[24]

3. Rights of Information, Independent Auditing and Supervision

3.1 To what extent do the (minority) shareholders have a right to be informed on company matters?

SA From the date on which an annual general meeting is convened, any shareholder is entitled to obtain without charge a copy of the annual accounts to be approved at the meeting, the director's report and, if appropriate, the auditor's report on the accounts. The notice convening the meeting must state this right to information.[25]

When a proposal is offered to modify the by-laws at a general meeting, the shareholders have the right to examine the entire proposed text, any reports produced by its promoters relating to the modification, and free delivery of a copy of such document.[26]

Also, any shareholder can request in writing, prior to a general meeting or orally at the meeting, information concerning any issue on the agenda. A shareholder can ask for any type of information if such information relates to an issue detailed in the agenda of the meeting. The law does not extend the right to information on other issues although in practice it is often possible to seek additional information in a question and answer session at the end of the meeting. The company is obliged to supply this information unless it believes that dissemination of such information could prejudice the company's interests. This limitation does not apply if a request

---

[23] Arts. 100 and 101 LSA; Art. 45 LSRL.
[24] Art. 100 LSA and Art. 45 LSRL.
[25] Art. 212 LSA.
[26] Art. 144 LSA.

for information is supported by shareholders who represent at least 25% of the share capital.[27]

In relation to quoted companies, the rules regulating the stock market impose numerous obligations on the publication and dissemination of information.

SL The law is the same as that for an SA In addition, (unless the by-laws provide otherwise) shareholders representing at least 5% of the share capital can, during the period between the date the general meeting was announced and the general meeting, inspect at the company's registered office the documentation used to prepare the annual accounts.[28]

3.2 Do they have the right to demand independent auditing or to initiate the supervision of company matters by an independent institution?

SA Companies that are obliged to audit their annual accounts: The shareholders may request that the Mercantile Registry for the company's registered office appoint an auditor if the general meeting has not done so before the end of the accounting year, if those who were appointed did not accept the appointment, or if they cannot fulfill their duties.[29]

Companies that are not obliged to audit their annual accounts: Shareholders who represent at least 5% of the share capital can ask the Mercantile Registry to name an auditor to review the accounts for a particular accounting year within three months from the end of that accounting year.[30]

SL Shareholders have the same rights as those of an SA. In addition, when inspecting (at the company's registered office) the documents used in preparation of the accounts, shareholders representing over 5% of the share capital can bring with them an accounting expert to review these documents.[31]

4. Capital Increases and Distributions

4.1 To what extent do (minority) shareholders have the right to participate in capital increases?

SA In the case of a capital increase which involves the issue of new shares, the existing shareholders and the holders of convertible bonds have a preferential right to subscribe for a number of shares proportional to the nominal value of their existing holding or, in the case of convertible bondholders, in proportion to their holding,

---

27 Art. 112 LSA.
28 Art. 86 LSRL.
29 Art. 205.1 LSA.
30 Art. 205.2 LSA.
31 Art. 86 LSRL.

were they to convert the bonds at that particular time. This preferential right is transferable on the same conditions that apply to the respective shares.[32]

There is no preferential right when the increase in capital is due to conversion of bonds into shares or due to the merger of company or with part of another divided company.

It is not possible for the by-laws to exclude preferential rights. However, an individual shareholder may waive such right. Also, a general meeting which approves a capital increase can expressly exclude this right, in whole or part, in relation to that particular capital increase, but only when this is in the company's interests.[33]

Such a resolution must be passed with the majority necessary for an alteration of the company's by-laws.

SL The law is the same as that for shareholders of an SA but it does not give preferential rights to bondholders as an SL cannot issue bonds.[34]

A resolution approving the exclusion of the right to a preferential subscription for shares requires the approval of two-thirds of the voting share capital.

4.2 Do minority shareholders have the right to demand dividends or other distributions?

SA Upon liquidation of the company, a shareholder has, at the minimum, the right to participate in a distribution of company profits and of the remaining assets.[35] However, a shareholder only has the right to receive a dividend when a majority of the company at the general meeting agrees to the distribution of a dividend. Therefore, there is nothing which prevents the general meeting from deciding not to distribute profits obtained during one or more accounting years.

The holders of shares which do not confer voting rights have, in addition to the right to receive the ordinary dividend, the right to receive a minimum dividend of 5% of the nominal value of their non-voting shares. This right does not require the approval of the company at the general meeting.[36]

SL As in an SA, shareholders have the right to receive a dividend once approved by the company at the general meeting, as described above.

5. Derivative Actions

5.1 Can (minority) shareholders enforce rights that the company has against other shareholders, directors, or third parties?

SA and SL Shareholders representing at least 5% of the share capital can bring a derivative action against the administrators for breach of duty in the following cases:[37]

---

32 Art. 158 LSA.
33 Art. 159 LSA.
34 Art. 75 LSRL.
35 Art. 48 LSA.
36 Art. 91 LSA.
37 Art. 134 LSA.

- when the administrators have not taken the necessary steps to convene a general meeting within 30 days of a request by shareholders who represent at least 5% of the share capital, and the purpose of the meeting is to debate matters relating to administrators' duties.
- when the company has agreed to bring such an action and a month has elapsed from the date of the resolution without any action having been initiated.
- when the general meeting resolved not to pursue the administrator for breach of duty.

The law does not expressly permit shareholders to enforce the company's rights against other shareholders or third parties.

6. Other "Formal" Rights

6.1 Do minority shareholders have any other specific rights comparable to those mentioned in 2–5 above?

SA Minority shareholders (with specified holdings) have the following additional rights. Shareholders representing at least 1% of the share capital can require the administrators to ensure the presence of a notary at the general meeting in order for the minutes of that meeting to be notarized.[38]

Shareholders representing at least 5% of the share capital can:

- prevent the general meeting from settling or waiving an action against the administrators for breach of duty.[39]
- request the suspension of the board resolution which shareholders are seeking to have judicially annulled.[40]
- seek a judicial order annulling an agreement by the board or other management body.[41]

Shareholders representing at least 20% of the share capital can seek government intervention to ensure the continuity of the company.[42]

Shareholders representing at least 25% of the share capital present at a general meeting can postpone that meeting.[43]

Shareholders who voluntarily unite have the right to appoint members to the board. The number they are entitled to appoint shall be proportional to the sum of their joint holding to the total share capital.[44]

---

38 Art. 114 L.S.A.
39 Art. 134 LSA.
40 Art. 120 LSA.
41 Art. 143 LSA.
42 Art. 265 LSA.
43 Art. 109 LSA.
44 Art. 137 LSA.

SL The law is the same as for an SA but the support of shareholders representing at least 5% of the share capital is required.[45]

7. Extension of These Rights by Statute or Shareholders' Agreements

7.1 Can the Articles of Association provide for additional rights of the minority shareholders? If not, can such rights be provided for in shareholders' agreements? Are these options commonly used?

SA and SL The by-laws can incorporate specific provisions which grant additional rights to minority shareholders provided that they do not exceed the limitations regulated by law.[46]

The minority's existing legal rights cannot be limited. It is not possible to impose conditions on existing voting requirements which would hinder the exercise of such rights. For instance, in addition to requiring the approval of 25% of the voting capital to pass a resolution to postpone a general meeting it is not possible to require that a specified number of shareholders vote in favour of that resolution thus preventing a single shareholder with a 25% holding from passing that resolution.

The SA Companies Act provides for the proportional appointment of board members. These provisions cannot be altered by the by-laws if the preconditions stipulated by law are fulfilled. However, they can be indirectly modified by various mechanisms, such as the appointment of a sole administrator.

The SL Companies Act does not expressly provide for proportional representation on the board. However, there is nothing to prevent the establishment of the same system.

Shareholders' agreements are not commonly used in Spain. The most common type of agreement are voting agreements but such agreements are not binding on the company or third parties.

8. Remedies Where a Shareholders' Resolution or Other Action Impairs the Rights of Minority Shareholders

8.1 What are the requirements for such remedies?

SA and SL Spanish law provides for two types of remedies in connection with resolutions or actions that impair the rights of minority shareholders. One type requires legal action through the courts and the other concerns a shareholders' right to leave the company, that is, to terminate his status as a shareholder of the com-

---

45 Art. 55 LSRL.

46 Art. 70 LSRL. The law on SLs remits to the provisions of the LSA.

pany in certain cases (referred to by the law as a separation). In such a case, no legal action before the courts is necessary, and the company is obligated to purchase the shares in question.

8.1.1 Judicial proceedings

Shareholders' resolutions can be legally challenged in any of the following cases:[47]

- the resolution is contrary to the law.
- the resolution contravenes provisions in the by-laws.
- the resolution harms the interests of the company and at the same time benefits one or more shareholders or third parties.

Resolutions contrary to law are void. All shareholders, the administrators and any third party with a legitimate interest have the right to legally challenge such a resolution.

Resolutions which are contrary to the by-laws or which harm the interests of the company are voidable. The resolution may be challenged by all shareholders who attended the general meeting but who opposed the resolution, shareholders who were absent from the general meeting, shareholders who were unlawfully deprived of the right to vote on that resolution, or the administrators.

The procedure and grounds for challenging board and other management resolutions[48] are the same as those established for shareholders' resolutions. Any administrator and any shareholder representing at least 5% of the share capital has the right to challenge board or management resolutions.

If a shareholder believes that a shareholders' or board resolution (even though not contrary to the law or by-laws) harms his interests he can seek to challenge the resolution by claiming that the company has also been harmed through the resolution.

In relation to the above the shareholder must prove the following:[49]

- that the resolution is contrary to the company's interests. All shareholders will be deemed to have a common interest.
- that the resolution benefits one or more shareholders or a third party. This benefit need not be economic but may include any political, social or professional advantage.
- that there is a causal connection between the harm suffered by the company and the benefit gained by the shareholder(s) or the third party.

Moreover, shareholders representing 5% of the share capital who have been harmed indirectly by administrators' misconduct (and such conduct directly harms the company) can seek the holding of a general meeting. Such meeting would then attempt a resolution to bring a derivative action against the administrators for breach of duty.

Shareholders may also commence a legal action for damages concerning acts by the administrators which directly harm their interests.

---

47 Art. 10 LSA and Art. 12 LSRL.
48 Art. 115 LSA and Art. 56 LSRL.
49 Art. 143 LSA and Art. 70 LSRL.

8.1.2 "Separation"

In certain circumstances a shareholder can demand that his shares be repurchased by the company without any requirement for judicial action. Examples of such circumstances include the following.

In an SA, shareholders without a vote and those who have not voted in favour of resolutions approving a change in the company's objectives or transferring its registered office abroad, if an international convention permits, have the right to leave the company.[50]

If the shareholder wishes to leave the company, the company's auditors will provide a valuation of the shareholder's holding and within two months of the auditor's report the company shall reimburse the shareholder the value of his holding. The company will then proceed with a corresponding reduction in its share capital.[51] It is not required that the company have sufficient profits to achieve this.

The company's by-laws can specify additional circumstances which permit a shareholder to leave the company and have his shares bought in.

For an SL, the law is the same as for an SA. A shareholder may, however, request the buying-out of his shares if the shareholder has not voted in favour of a resolution which[52]

- alters the system for transferring shares,
- extends or reactivates the company,
- changes the company into a *sociedad anónima* or other type of Spanish company, or
- creates, alters or terminates early any shareholder's obligation to make contributions other than share capital contributions.

8.2 When do the courts of your country accept these requirements?

8.2.1 Judicial proceedings

The Spanish courts have accepted legal challenges to resolutions in the following cases, and have declared void those resolutions which are:

- contrary to public policy (these resolutions cannot be corrected so as to render them valid and there is no limitation period); or
- contrary to the law. The courts have included in this category: resolutions which have been passed at a general meeting which has not been validly constituted in accordance with the requirements established by law;[53] and resolutions passed without the required majorities.[54]

---

50 STS (Supreme Court), 11 November 1983 and 12 July 1983.
51 STS, 7 July 1983.
52 STS, 23 July 1984.
53 STS 51, 17 May 1979.
54 STS, 52 11 November 1983.

Voidable are:

- resolutions contrary to the by-laws, and
- resolutions which harm the company's interests while benefiting one or more shareholders or third parties.

Examples of cases which the Supreme Court has considered to be within this category are a resolution awarding the chairman of the Board an annual remuneration of an amount greater than the company's annual profits,[55] and a resolution approving a balance sheet for which the administrators had failed to ensure adequate accounting.[56]

8.3 What remedies are available to the claimant?

When a judge declares a resolution to be contrary to law it will be void *ab initio*. When a judge declares a resolution to be contrary to the by-laws or harmful to the company it will be voidable. In both cases there will be a right to claim damages against either the company or the board, as the case may be.

Provisional remedies may also be available, for example:

- the suspension of a resolution which is under review can be sought by shareholders who represent 5% of the share capital.[57]
- a warning that a particular resolution or agreement is under review can be lodged at the Mercantile Registry for the locality at the company's registered office.[58]
- substitution of a shareholders' resolution which is being legally challenged for another resolution which has been validly adopted. In such a case, the legal challenge will not be admitted by the court.[59]
- the judge may grant the parties a reasonable period of time in which to remedy, if possible, the cause of the challenge.[60]

9. Specific Protection if the Company is Controlled by Another Company

9.1 What are the rights and remedies of a shareholder of company A when Company B gains control over it (by acquiring the majority of its shares or otherwise)?

SA and SL There are no rights or remedies other than in the following circumstances:

---

55 Art. 120 LSA.
56 Art. 121 LSA.
57 Art. 115 LSA.
58 *Ibid.*
59 Art. 149 LSA and Art. 147 LSA.
60 Art. 95 LSRL.

- company A is not a listed company or an SL. There is a provision in the by-laws that limits the free transfer of shares, thereby granting the shareholders of company A a right of put and/or call.
- company A is a listed company. Company B will be obliged to make a public offering of acquisition of the shares in Company A. On acquiring a holding of 25% or more in Company A, Company B is required to make a public offer of acquisition and acquire an additional 10% of the share capital of Company A. On acquisition of a 50% holding in Company A, Company B is required to make a public offer of acquisition and acquire a 75% holding of the share capital of Company A.[61]

The public offer of acquisition must be authorized by the *Comision Nacional del Mercado de Valores* "CNMV" (Spanish Securities Exchange Commission). Once authorization has been obtained the offeror is obliged to make a general public announcement of the offer.[62]

The obligation to make a public offer of acquisition provides protection to minority shareholders who are able to sell or exchange their shares on the same terms as the majority shareholders.

There is also an obligation to provide information to shareholders of a quoted company when, as a result of the acquisition of shares in that company, the holding of the purchaser or its group exceeds 5% or any multiple of 5% of the capital of the company.[63]

9.2 What are the shareholder's rights and remedies when Company B exerts its control over Company A in a way which damages the interests of the latter?

SL The shareholders of Company A have the right to seek a judicial decree against any shareholders' or board resolution which benefits a shareholder (in this case Company B) but which harms Company A's interests.

Shareholders can also, if they represent 5% of the share capital, take steps to bring a derivative action for breach of duty against the administrators.

[61] Art. 14 *Real Decreto* (Royal Decree) 1197/1991.
[62] Art. 24 *Ley del Mercado de Valores*.
[63] *Ibid.*

SWEDEN

Hans Ramberg

PROTECTION OF MINORITY SHAREHOLDERS

EDITOR MATTHIAS W. STECHER

SWEDEN

Hans Ramberg

Introduction

This report is based on the Swedish Companies Act of 1975 (1975:1385 – "the Act") which is applicable to both private and public companies. Extensive amendments, among them the introduction of the separate categories of public and private companies (before that, there was only one category of limited companies), were passed during 1993 and 1994 as Sweden adapted its legisation to conform to the rules of the European Union (as one of the parties in the Agreement on the European Economic Area and as a prospective member of the EU, which it now is).

References to the Act in the footnotes do not imply a literal translation of the relevant section in the Act but is merely a reference to where the matter in question is principally dealt with.

1. Majority Requirements for Shareholders' Resolutions

1.1 What are the majority requirements in general?

Generally, a resolution of a shareholders' meeting is passed by an absolute majority of the votes cast and, in the case of parity of the votes, the chairman of the meeting shall have a casting vote.

board of directors) request such a meeting to be convened for a specified objective. Notice convening a shareholders′ meeting shall be issued within 14 days from the day such a request was received by the company.[9]

It is recommended that the request of the shareholders be sent by registered mail to avoid any disagreement concerning if and when such a request has been sent to and received by the company.

If a shareholders' meeting, which is to be held according to the Companies Act, the Articles of Association, or a resolution adopted at a previous shareholder's meeting, is not properly convened for whatever reason (eg the company has no board of directors) any shareholder (or a director, managing director, or an auditor) may apply to the County Administration which shall promptly convene the shareholders' meeting at the company′s expense.

2.2 Do they have the right to put matters on the agenda?

Any shareholder has the right to put matters on the agenda if a request in writing for this purpose is submitted to the board of directors early enough to include the matter in the notice convening the shareholders' meeting.[10]

3. Rights of Information, Independent Auditing and Supervision

3.1 To what extent do the (minority) shareholders have a right to be informed on company matters?

Any shareholder has the right to raise questions at a shareholders' meeting. The board of directors and the managing director shall, upon request of a shareholder, furnish the shareholders' meeting with such information as may be necessary for a proper assessment of the company′s annual report and its financial position or any other matter on the agenda. However, the disclosure of information depends on whether the board of directors considers this to be possible without any material prejudice to the company.[11]

If the board of directors believes that the company will be caused material prejudice, the requested information shall be submitted to the auditors within two weeks of the shareholder's request. The auditors shall, within a month after the shareholder's meeting, submit their comments in writing to the board of directors stating whether they have received the requested information and if the information, in their opinion, warrants an amendment of the audit report. The comments of the auditors shall be made available to the shareholders at the office of the company and a copy thereof shall be sent to the shareholder who requested the information.[12]

[9] Chapter 9, ss. 6 and 8.
[10] Chapter 9, s. 7.
[11] Chapter 9, s. 12, subs. 1.
[12] Chapter 9, s. 12, subs. 1.

If requested information is not available at the shareholders' meeting the information shall be made available in writing within two weeks thereafter at the office of the company and a copy thereof shall be sent to the shareholder who requested the information.[13]

In companies with no more than 10 shareholders, each shareholder is entitled to inspect books, accounts and other documents concerning the activities of the company to the extent required for the shareholder to form an opinion concerning the financial position of the company or a certain issue to be dealt with at a shareholder's meeting. The board of directors and the managing director shall, upon request of the shareholder, assist with the investigation for the above-mentioned purposes and furnish necessary copies, provided this can be accomplished without excessive costs or burden.[14]

3.2 Do they have the right to demand independent auditing or to initiate the supervision of company matters by an independent institution?

The auditors have a duty to consider whether the interests of minority shareholders have been observed and, if not, to comment upon this in the auditors¥report.

The degree of rigour applied by the auditors may vary considerably and therefore the minority shareholders have the following rights.

The County Administration shall, at the request of a shareholder and after inquiring to the board of directors, appoint an extra auditor if such a proposal has been approved by owners of one-tenth of all shares or of one-third of all shares represented at the shareholders' meeting. The appointment of such an auditor is for the period leading up to and including the annual shareholders' meeting to be held in the next financial year.[15]

Such an auditor shall participate in the audit together with the ordinary auditors and has equal duties, rights and obligations.

Owners of one-tenth of all shares may request at a shareholders' meeting in which the appointment of auditors is to be voted on that an authorized public accountant shall be elected auditor, even if this is not required in the Articles of Association.[16]

The county administration shall, at the request of a shareholder and after inquiring to the board of directors, appoint one or more special examiners if such a proposal was approved by owners of one-tenth of all shares or of one-third of all shares represented at the shareholders' meeting, for the period leading up to and including the annual shareholders' meeting to be held in the next financial year.[17]

The scope of the special examination may be the administration and accounts of the company for a previous accounting period, a certain measure, or circumstances relating to the company.

[13] Chapter 9, s. 12, subs. 2.
[14] Chapter 9, s. 12, subs. 4.
[15] Chapter 10, s. 1, subs. 4.
[16] Chapter 10, s. 3, subs. 5.
[17] Chapter 10, s. 14.

The special examination is ended when the examiner delivers his opinion on the matters submitted to him in the shareholders' meeting.

4. Capital Increases and Distributions

4.1 To what extent do (minority) shareholders have the right to participate in capital increases?

The principal rule is that all shareholders have a preferential right to sign for new shares, convertible debt instruments and debt instruments with warrants attached in relation to the number of shares they already own.[18,19]

The preferential right is unconditional when it is a bonus issue. This makes sense since a bonus issue in reality transfers part of the value of the old shares to the new ones.

When it is a non-cash issue the shareholders have no preferential right since the capital in kind normally can be contributed only by a third party or certain shareholders. A non-cash issue with the purpose of by-passing the preferential right so as to shift the power in the company is not allowed. If such a resolution is adopted it may be set aside or amended by a court.

A resolution to alter the fundamental preferential right of the shareholders to subscribe for new shares, convertible debt instruments and debt instruments with warrants attached requires a qualified majority.

4.2 Do minority shareholders have the right to demand dividends or other distributions?

In general, shareholders may not demand dividends of distributable profits since a resolution on this issue must be put on the agenda for the annual shareholders' meeting. However, shareholders representing not less than one-tenth of all shares may request that the shareholders' meeting must declare a dividend of at least half of the distributable net profit. The shareholders' meeting is never bound to pass a resolution on a dividend exceeding 5% of the equity even if the minority pass a request for dividends.[20]

5. Derivative Actions

5.1 Can (minority) shareholders enforce rights that the company has against other shareholders, directors or third parties?

An action for damages on behalf of the company against other shareholders may be instituted by the owners of at least one-tenth of all shares if a shareholder has

[18] Chapter 4, ss. 2, 14 and 15.

[19] Chapter 5, ss. 2, 8 and 9.

[20] Chapter 12, s. 3.

caused the company damage by participating in a deliberate or grossly negligent violation of the Act or the Articles of Association. The shareholder must have caused the damage acting qua shareholder, otherwise general rules and regulations on damages are applicable. In such case an action for damages may not be instituted by any shareholder.[21]

An action on behalf of the company must be instituted within two years from the time the decision or the measure was made upon which the action is based, unless based on criminal activity. A shareholder who has caused damage may also be ordered by the court to purchase the shares of a shareholder who has suffered damage whenever the court finds this appropriate in view of the risk of continued abuse and other circumstances in general.

The same rule applies if a director or managing director has deliberately or negligently caused the company, a shareholder, or others damage.[22] An action on behalf of the company against a director or a managing director for damage caused by a decision or measure taken during a financial year must be instituted within one year from the shareholders' meeting where the annual report and the audit report for the financial year were presented. If the director or the managing director has been granted a discharge from liability or a resolution not to institute any action for damages has been adopted, an action may still be instituted if essential information was omitted in the annual report or the audit report. An action must, however, be instituted at the latest, unless based on criminal activities, within three years after the end of the financial year when the decision or measure on which the action is based was made.

Generally, only the board of directors and the managing director (to a certain degree) represent and sign for the company. In addition, there are different kinds of authorized representatives. A shareholder has no independent right to represent and sign for the company without proxy. Therefore minority shareholders cannot themselves enforce rights the company has against third parties – *Actio pro socio* – with one exception. An action for damages in favour of the company may be instituted by owners of at least one-tenth of all shares. Those who instituted the action are liable for all costs from the action but they are entitled to reimbursement from the company to the extent that the costs are covered by the amount accruing to the company through the action.[23]

A similar rule applies if an auditor, his assistants or, if appointed as auditor, an accounting firm, is liable to pay compensation for damage caused to the company deliberately or negligently.

An action must be instituted, unless based on criminal activities, within three years from the time that the audit report was submitted to the shareholders' meeting or such an opinion as required by the Act was given.

---

[21] Chapter 15, ss. 3 , 5, and 6

[22] Chapter 15, s. 1, 5 and 6

[23] Chapter 8, s. 11; chapter 15, ss. 2, 5 and 6

6. Other "Formal" Rights

6.1 Do minority shareholders have any other specific rights comparable to those mentioned in 2–5 above?

In the Act, a general clause prohibits any resolution of the shareholders' meeting which is likely to give an undue advantage to a shareholder or a third party, or which is detrimental to the company or other shareholders. Although the wording is clear, exercising this clause is, for obvious reasons, extremely difficult. The clause is applicable against decisions and measures which are formally not contrary to the fundamental principle of equal rights of the shareholders but nevertheless give undue advantage to one shareholder or third party at the expense of other shareholders.[24]

Upon request by owners of at least one-tenth of all shares the court may order a compulsory liquidation or a redemption of the shares of the claimant if a shareholder or shareholders have abused his or their influence in the company by participating in infringement of the Act or the Articles of Association. The court shall take into consideration the length of the abuse and other circumstances, as well as the interest of employees and creditors when choosing between liquidation or redemption.

7. Extension of These Rights by Statute or Shareholders' Agreements

7.1 Can the Articles of Association provide for additional rights of the minority shareholders? If not, can such rights be provided for in the shareholders' agreements? Are these options commonly used?

7.1.1 Additional rights in the Articles of Association

There are many opportunities to provide for additional rights for any shareholder in the Articles. Such additional rights could include, for example, that directors shall be appointed in an alternative way than by election at the shareholders' meeting, an increase of the majority requirements for adoption of resolutions at the shareholders' meeting, a reduction or strengthening of the voting roles in the board of directors, giving the minority in general or certain shareholders a veto right in respect to certain resolutions, etc.

---

[24] Chapter 9, s. 16

Several of the most distinguished authors in this area (Birke, Kedner-Roos and Nial) have interpreted the Act in such a way that the rights of minority shareholders may be exercised by a smaller group than one-tenth of all shares if so provided for in the Articles.

Even if and when possible it is not necessarily advisable to modify the Articles to suit a present structure of shareholders. Such adjusted Articles may give rise to difficulties if the balance of power in the company changes, a shareholder wants to sell his shares, or the objectives of the company alter.

7.1.2 Additional rights in a shareholders' agreement

In a shareholders' agreement, the parties may regulate their rights inter se more extensively than in the Articles. Consequently, it is more common to regulate additional rights for the minority shareholders in a shareholders' agreement than in the Articles. This is especially true in smaller and medium-sized companies. The Articles in different companies are, therefore, to a high degree standardized or at least very similar.

The enforceability of a shareholders' agreement in different situations is at issue and uncertain. An agreement on voting or restrictions on the sale of shares are legally binding between the parties but have little or no legal effect on the company or a third party. For example, if a party votes at the shareholders' meeting in breach of the voting agreement the resolution, if adopted, may not be annulled or amended by the court on the grounds of a breach of the voting agreement.

The shareholders' agreement must not have provisions which are contrary to compulsory rules and regulations in the Act, for example, the rights of minority shareholders. Such provisions are null and void. At the minimum, the agreement should not be contrary to the Articles. Furthermore, the agreement should not have provisions which are contrary to compulsory provisions in Swedish labour law.

If either party commits a breach of the shareholders' agreement, the other party has the option of a claim for damages or compensation, termination of the agreement, or enforcement of the agreement. A combination of the above is also possible.

Claims for damages are difficult since the claimant must furnish proof of his damage. A more effective solution is an agreed penalty – especially if the parties furnish each other with securities for the penalty.

In most cases, a shareholders' agreement constitutes a simple partnership. Termination of the agreement must therefore be terminated according to the rules in the Partnerships Act (1980: 1102). A breach of contract must be material to entitle a premature termination.

The enforcement of a shareholders' agreement by legal action is feasible, but time-consuming and expensive.

A shareholders' agreement is judged by the Agreement Act (1905: 218). A provision or the entire agreement itself may be annulled or amended by a court if a provision is unfair in consideration of the agreement itself, the circumstances when the agreement was entered into, or with regard to the circumstances in general.

8. Remedies Where a Shareholders' Resolution or Other Action Impairs the Rights of Minority Shareholders

8.1 What are the requirements for such remedies?

Remedies may be available if:

- a resolution has not been properly adopted or is contrary to the Act or the Articles of Association;
- a resolution gives an undue advantage to a shareholder or a third party to the detriment of the company or other shareholders;
- a shareholder intentionally abuses his influence in the company by assisting in a violation of the Act or the Articles of Association;
- a shareholder inflicts damage on the company, shareholders or others by taking part in or contributing to a deliberate or grossly negligent violation of the Act or the Articles of Association.

8.2 When do the courts of your country accept these requirements?

There are no Supreme Court cases from which general conclusions can be drawn. However, it is normally difficult to provide sufficient proof of deliberate or negligent actions and consequential loss, parties are therefore reluctant to institute legal proceedings in these matters. Therefore, such disputes are normally settled out of court when they arise.

However, if a legal action is instituted, the claimant normally has the burden of proof. After having heard the parties the court will evaluate if the claimant has given enough proof of its claim and, whether proven or not, will give a legal evaluation as to whether the disputed matter constitutes a violation of the Act or the Articles of Association.

Being without guidance from Supreme Court cases, it is not possible to compile reliable statements of courts ruling on a suit that is based upon a resolution or other action in which it is alleged that the rights of the minority shareholders have been infringed.

8.3 What remedies are available to the claimant?

A shareholder, the board of directors, a director, the managing director or a person who has improperly not been duly registered as a shareholder may bring legal action for annulment or amendment of a resolution which has not been properly adopted or is otherwise contrary to the Act or the Articles of Association. Actions shall be instituted within three months from the date of the resolution. An action may, however, be instituted later if:[25]

[25] Chapter 9, s. 17

- the resolution, even if approved by all shareholders, is a violation of law;
- the resolution was subject to approval from all or certain shareholders and such approval was not given; or
- notice convening the shareholders' meeting was not duly given.

If a resolution is annulled or amended by a court the ruling has *ex tunc* effect, that is for example, the resolution is null and void. If the resolution has been put into effect it shall be reversed if possible; a shareholder who has in good faith received a dividend is entitled to keep the dividend even if the resolution is declared null and void, or a third party who in good faith has entered an agreement with the company based on a resolution which is subsequently declared null and void is entitled to enforce this agreement.

The court may, upon petition, issue a provisional stop order on the resolution pending the final ruling. The claimant is normally obliged to provide security for potential damages inflicted by the stop order.[26]

If a shareholder or shareholders have intentionally abused their influence in the company, then, upon request of owners of at least one-tenth of all shares, the court may declare that the company go into liquidation. The duration of the abuse shall be taken in account. Upon the request of the company, the court may instead order the company to redeem the claimant's shares in the company.[27]

If a shareholder is liable to pay damages to a another shareholder, the court may, in view of the risk of continued abuse, order the offending shareholder to buy the shares of the suffering shareholder.[28]

9. Specific Protection if a Company is Controlled by Another Company

9.1 What are the rights and remedies of a shareholder of Company A if Company B gains control over it (by acquiring the majority of its shares or otherwise)?

The rights and remedies of a shareholder are exactly the same regardless that the company is controlled by another company.

However, if a parent company,[29] itself or together with subsidiaries, owns more than nine-tenths of all shares with more than nine-tenths of all votes the parent company is entitled to redeem the remaining shares. The owners of the remaining shares are equally entitled to request the parent company to redeem their shares.[30]

---

26 The Swedish Code of Procedure (1942: 740) chapter 15, s. 6
27 Chapter 13, s. 3
28 Chapter 15, s. 3
29 A limited company which, itself or together with subsidiaries owns shares with at least half of all votes in another company or otherwise has a decisive influence this company.
30 Chapter 14, s. 31

If the company belongs to a group the parent company is obliged to observe the interests of the minority in the subsidiary company when establishing the group's balance sheet and the group's profit and loss account. All assets and liabilities of the subsidiary are to be included in the group's balance sheet and the profit and loss account of the subsidiary is to be included in the group's profit and loss account. The share of equity in the subsidiary owned by the minority is from the group's point of view something between long-term liabilities and equity. This is to be accounted for on the liability side in the group's balance sheet.[31]

9.2 What are the shareholder's rights and remedies when Company B exerts its control over Company A in a way that damages the interests of the latter?

The shareholder may exercise the rights and remedies mentioned above. Whether it is easier or more difficult to provide proof of any abuse and consequential loss when the majority shareholder is another company depends on the specific circumstances.

31 Chapter 11, s. 10

SWITZERLAND

Felix R. Ehrat

Bär & Karrer

Zurich and Lugano

PROTECTION OF MINORITY SHAREHOLDERS

***EDITOR* MATTHIAS W. STECHER**

SWITZERLAND

Felix R. Ehrat

Background Information

The Swiss joint stock Corporation (*Aktiengesellschaft, société anonyme, società anonima*) is the most often used legal vehicle in Switzerland, suited for any type of business activity, passive holding of domestic or foreign assets, etc. It is equally used as the legal entity of large public companies as well as of small business units, by joint ventures, by companies with purely domestic and worldwide activities, etc. Theoretically, the stock corporation can also be used for non profit making activities.[1] The law governing the stock corporation had not been changed since 1936. It is essentially contained in the Swiss Code of Obligations ("CO"), Articles 620–763. Shortfalls in the old law were already recognized in the early 1960s and the reform process started in 1968.[2] It was to last an excessively long 25 years. The new law of 4 October 1991 entered into force on 1 July 1992, with certain exceptions[3] and with certain provisions which will enter into force only after a transi-

[1] Art. 620 III Swiss Code of Obligations ("CO").

[2] See for the history of the reforms Von Greyerz, "Vom Vorentwurf zur Botschaft", in *Aktienrechtsreform, Schriftenreihe der Schweizerischen Treuhand-und Revisionskammer,* Vol. 59, 1984.

[3] CO 663e–663g which entered into force only on 1 July 1993.

tional period.[4] In the following, all references are to the new, now existing law except certain references to the old law which, however, shall be specifically marked.

Basic Objectives of the Reform

Insuring more transparency by improving the transparency of the annual accounts and the annual business report to be established by the board of directors; duty of large, respectively public companies to publish their annual accounts; more information in the Commercial Register (in particular publication of the name of the auditors); duty to disclose the number of shares represented in the general assembly by directors, independent representatives of the voting rights and professional proxy-holders.[5]

Strengthening of the protection of shareholders by improvement of the information rights of shareholders; reinforcement of subscription rights, facilitation of shareholders' claims; relaxation of share transfer restrictions.

Improvement of the structure and the functioning of the governing bodies of the corporation

General assemblies Obligation of the proxy-holder to vote the shares according to the shareholders' instructions; relaxation of the necessary quorum to take certain decisions; lowering of the influence of supervoting shares.

Board of directors Definition of certain powers which may lawfully be delegated; limitation of liability in case of lawful delegation; mitigation of the principle of joint and several liability.

Auditors Independence of the auditors; more stringent reporting duties; setting out of a minimum professional standard and requirement of special professional qualifications for auditors of listed corporations, corporations with bond issues outstanding and large enterprises as further defined by the law.[6]

Facilitation of the raising of capital by a simplification of the incorporation and the ordinary capital increase; introduction of authorized and conditional share capital; introduction of non-voting shares (participation certificates); facilitation of financial restructurings.

Avoidance of certain abuses of the corporate form by increasing the minimum share capital to SFR100,000 – and by increasing the proportion of the minimum share capital which has to be paid in; requirement of a special report by qualified auditors in the context of the incorporation and a capital increase; more stringent requirements for the acquisition of own shares and cross participations; more stringent duty to reimburse hidden profit distributions.

---

4 The most important of which is Art. 2 of section VIII of the Final Provisions of the CO providing for a transitional period of five years to adapt stock corporations existing prior to the coming into force of the new law to the new provisions.

5 CO 702 II and 689c.

6 CO 727b.

Uniform Set of Rules

It should be noted at this point that certain criticism of a general nature stems from the fact that Swiss law still governs large public companies essentially by the same set of rules as closely held small businesses,[7] even though it has to be acknowledged that there are several provisions in the new law providing for different rules in case of public companies, large companies and medium or small companies.[8]

Other Sources of the Law

Rules regarding the protection of minority shareholders are not only found in the CO but also in other rules and regulations such as the so-called Take-Over Codex (as of November 1994) and the Federal Law Act on Unfair Competition of 19 December 1986.[9] Moreover and quite importantly, the new Federal Law Act on Stock Exchanges and on Securities Trading of 24 March 1995 with its implementing ordinances which–after several delays–are now likely to enter into force in the summer of 1997 provide, *inter alia*, for important rules in the context of public tender offers.

1. Majority Requirements for Shareholders' Resolutions

1.1 What are the majority requirements in general?

In accordance with CO 703, the general meeting passes resolutions and holds elections with an absolute majority of the votes represented, unless otherwise provided for by the law or the Articles of Incorporation.

It follows from the above that decisions are taken with 50% plus one vote of all relevant votes. Relevant votes are all votes represented, that is blank votes and votes which were not tendered, too. Abstention from voting by not tendering the vote or by tendering a blank vote are therefore to be counted as no-votes.[10] Effective abstention of voting is therefore only possible by physically not participating in the vote.[11] One of the desiderata of the reform, that is to rely only on the votes actually tendered for the determination of the relevant majority was therefore not incorporated in the new law.

---

7 Böckli, p. 23 *et seq.*
8 For instance disclosure requirements, duty to issue a prospectus in case of public placements, share transfer restrictions, special audits, qualifications of auditors, etc.
9 See, *inter alia* Dieter Dubs, "Lauterkeitsrechtliche Aspekte der 'Holvis-Übernahme'", AJP 1995, pp. 899 *et seq.* where agreements regarding so-called "lock-up" clauses are examined.
10 Tanner, Neuerungen, p. 768
11 *Ibid.*

The new law has eliminated all presence requirements of the old law. *In extremis*, it would therefore be possible to take any decision by just one vote represented. It, however, remains possible to introduce other presence requirements in the articles of incorporation.

It was one of the issues under the old law, that is, to what extent the Articles of Incorporation could deviate from CO 703. The new law has not fully clarified this issue. It therefore remains an open question as to whether the Articles of Incorporation can provide for the relevance of a relative majority only or as to whether they can allow for the relevance of the votes tendered only.[12]

1.2 Which resolutions require a greater majority?

CO 704 provides for a list of decisions requiring a qualified majority. In order to reach such majority, a double test needs to be met: At least two-thirds of the represented votes and the absolute majority of the represented par values of the shares are required in order to pass a valid resolution on the listed items. Once again, the law does not rely on minimum requirements as to the presence (of votes or par values). CO 704 is unilaterally mandatory in so far as the articles of incorporation may not go lower than two thirds of the votes represented and the absolute majority of the represented par values of the shares.[13]

The decisions requiring the above-mentioned qualified majority are the following (CO 704 I):[14]

- the alteration of the object clause of the corporation;
- the introduction of super-voting shares;
- restrictions on the transferability of the registered shares, more specifically, the introduction or tightening-up of such restrictions;
- an authorized or conditional share capital increase;
- a capital increase with the company's equity, against a contribution in kind or with the intent of a subsequent acquisition of assets and the granting of special privileges;
- the restriction or cancellation of subscription rights;
- the transfer of the company's legal seat;
- the dissolution of the company without liquidation (for instance in the context of a merger).

1.3 To what extent can they be modified by the Articles of Association?

Reference to this problem has already been made above (see 1.1 above). In more general terms, CO 627 para. 11 provides that all decisions regarding a qualified majority not foreseen in the law have to be mentioned in the Articles of Incorpora-

[12] *Ibid.*, p. 770; Weber, p. 82f.
[13] Böckli, p. 685 *et seq.*
[14] *Ibid.*; Forstmoser *et al.*, pp. 224 *et seq.*

tion. CO 704 II provides that provisions of the Articles of Incorporation regarding qualified majorities for certain decisions going further than the related requirement of the law can only be incorporated into the Articles of Incorporation if the use of a (desired) higher majority is already practised. CO 704 II does not allow the lowering of the standards but only the introduction of more stringent majority requirements.[15]

2. Influence on the Decision-Making Process

2.1 Do minority shareholders have the right to call a shareholders' meeting?

The general assembly is normally convened by the board of directors, if necessary[16] also by the auditors, the liquidators or, if any, representatives of bondholders (CO 699). CO 699 III provides that one or several shareholders, jointly representing at least 10% of the share capital may call a shareholders' meeting. This is a typical minority right which, however, may be difficult to meet in large companies. When determining the relevant 10%, the non-voting share capital will not be taken into consideration.

2.2 Do they have the right to put matters on the agenda?

Shareholders representing shares with a par value of SFR1 million can – individually or jointly – request that a specific matter be put on the agenda of a general meeting (CO 699 III).[17] Subject to an appropriate provision in the Articles of Incorporation, the right to put matters on the agenda can be extended to the holders of non-voting shares (CO 656c I). When exercising their right to put matters on the agenda, shareholders have the obligation of submitting concrete proposals of which the board of directors must be notified (CO 699 III 3rd sentence).

---

15 Meier-Hayoz *et al.*, p. 24; Maute, p. 50; see, however, Tanner, Neuerungen, p. 771.

16 Forstmoser *et al.*, p. 204.

17 It is difficult to understand why the lawmaker has not also conferred this right to shareholders representing 10% of the share capital. On the basis of an assessment of the ratio legis of CO 699 III, Tanner, Neuerungen, p. 766f., is of the opinion that CO 699 III should be read to include the right of shareholders representing 10% of the share capital to put an item on the agenda of the meeting since the right to call a shareholders' meeting, the right to put matters on the agenda of such shareholders' meeting and the right to submit proposals are intrinsically linked with each other. See also Forstmoser *et al.*, p. 205.

3. Rights of Information, Independent Auditing and Supervision

3.1 To what extent do the (minority) shareholders have a right to be informed on company matters?

Every shareholder has the right to be given a written business report for each business year which has to be established by the board of directors (CO 662 I). Such written business report is composed of the following documents:

3.1.1 Annual financial statement[18]

The annual financial statement is composed of the statement of profit and loss, the balance sheet and the notes pertaining thereto (CO 662 II). The minimum information required for the statement of profit and loss is contained in CO 663, for the balance sheet in CO 663a and the contents of the notes pertaining thereto is governed by CO 663b. In addition, quoted corporations must disclose the names of important shareholders and their participations in the notes to the extent that they are known or should be known to the corporation (CO 663c I).[19] Subject to a lower threshold provided for in the Articles of Incorporation, shareholders and groups of shareholders bound by a voting agreement shall be considered important if their participation exceeds 5% of all voting rights (CO 663c II).

3.1.2 Annual report of the board of directors

The annual report as required by CO 663d presents and describes the development of the business during the fiscal year and the business and financial situation of the corporation. Contrary to the Fourth Council Directive 76/660/EEC on the Annual Accounts of Certain Types of Companies, Swiss law does not strictly require that the board of directors also mentions significant events which occurred after the close of the fiscal year. Moreover, there is no obligation for the auditors to audit the annual report of the board of directors.

Even though legal doctrine suggests that the annual report of the board of directors should account for all relevant factors having an impact on the business of the corporation[20] the reality, in particular in non-quoted and closely-held companies, is different: Here the annual report is more often a routine document with only little meaningful information contained therein.

---

18 Böckli, p. 457 *et seq.*

19 Böckli, pp. 501 *et seq.*; The New Federal Law Act on Stock Exchanges and on Securities Trading of 24 March 1995, which is likely to come into force on 1 January 1997, contains notification with obligations of important shareholders to the company. Similar obligations *vis-à-vis* of the Swiss Federal Banking Commission (in its capacity as supervisory for party) exist in respect of Swiss banks (see Art. 3 of the Ordinance to the Revised Banking Law Act).

20 See, *inter alia*, Böckli, p. 513 *et seq.*

3.1.3 Consolidated financial statement

The law imposes a duty to draw up consolidated financial statements if a corporation, either by a majority of votes or in some other manner, unites one or several corporations under one common group management (CO 663e I). There is, however, an exemption from the duty to draw up such consolidated financial statement if the group in the aggregate does not exceed two of the following conditions in two consecutive years: A balance-sheet showing assets and liabilities in the total amount of SFR10 million; revenues of SFR20 million; 200 employees as an annual average. Moreover, a so-called subholding (ie a corporation included in the consolidated financial statement of a parent corporation) might be exempted from drawing up a separate consolidated financial statement provided that the consolidated financial statement of the parent corporation has been drawn up and audited in accordance with Swiss or equivalent foreign regulations and provided it makes the consolidated financial statement of the parent corporation known to its shareholders and creditors in the same way as it makes its own annual financial statement known to them (CO 663f I). Notwithstanding such conditions, a consolidated financial statement, however, must be drawn up if the corporation has outstanding bonds, if the shares of the corporation are quoted, if shareholders representing at least 10% of the share capital request for one, and/or if it is required for a reliable assessment of the financial situation and the revenues of the corporation (CO 663 e III). Notwithstanding the possible exemptions (CO 663f I) subholdings are required to draw up a separate consolidated financial statement if there is a legal obligation to publish its own annual financial statement (as per CO 697h) or if shareholders who together represent at least 10% of the share capital demand it.

3.1.4 Disclosure of business regulations

It should be mentioned that the law imposes a duty on the board of directors to disclose the business regulations (if any) of the corporation to shareholders and creditors if they can demonstrate a legitimate interest (CO 716b II). This duty can be of particular significance in the context of contemplated liability suits against members of the board of directors or the executive management. The right to request such disclosure is not limited to the general assembly.

3.1.5 Additional information rights

At a general meeting, every shareholder is entitled to ask the board of directors for information regarding the corporation's affairs and the auditors for information regarding the procedure and the results of their audit (CO 697 I). Information shall be provided to the extent to which it is required for exercising the shareholders' rights. In can be withheld where business secrets of the corporation or any other interests of the corporation worthy of being protected would be jeopardized (CO 697 II). The books and the correspondence may only be inspected upon explicit authorization by the general assembly or on the basis of a resolution passed by the board of directors provided that the corporation's business secrets are safeguarded (CO 697 III).

3.2 Do they have the right to demand independent auditing or to initiate the supervision of company matters by an independent institution?

Every shareholder can propose to the general that specific facts should be investigated through a special audit[21] (so-called *Sonderprüfung*) provided that such special audit is a necessary part of the investigation and provided that the information rights and the right of inspection have previously been exercised by the shareholder proposing the special audit (CO 697a I). If the proposal is approved by the general , the corporation or every shareholder is entitled to ask the judge to appoint a special commissioner within a period of 30 days (CO 697a II). If the general meeting, however, rejects the proposal, shareholders jointly or individually owning at least one-tenth of the share capital or shares with a minimum par value of SFR2 million may, within three months from the date of the general meeting, request the judge to appoint a special commissioner. Certain requirements must be met in order for the appointment of a special commissioner to be made. Specifically, it must be substantiated prima facie that the founders of the corporation or its corporate bodies have breached the law or the Articles of Incorporation and, by doing so, caused the shareholders damages as a consequence of the damage caused to the corporation. If appointed, the special commissioner shall first present his report to the judge. Only afterwards does the judge submit the report to the corporation. Upon the corporation's request, he will decide whether the report infringes business secrets or other legitimate interests of the corporation and therefore may not be submitted to the shareholder(s) requesting the audit. The judge will give to the corporation and the shareholders who demanded the special audit the opportunity to express their views concerning the report and ask further questions.

The board of directors has then the obligation to submit the report and the positions taken by the parties concerned at the next general meeting. Every shareholder is entitled to receive a written copy of the report and the views expressed by the parties concerned within one year from the date of the general meeting.

The right to demand a special audit has been introduced into the new law.[22] Its objective was to give to the minority shareholders an effective tool to examine events or omissions possibly causing damages to the corporation or its shareholders. The right to request such special audit, however, has not been designed as an individual right but only as the right of a minority representing at least 10% of the share capital. The rule on the allocation of the related costs is rather favourable to the shareholder(s) requesting a special audit thereby favouring the use of the new right: CO 697g provides that the costs (including advanced payments) are to be borne by the corporation if the judge accepts the request to appoint a special commissioner. Only in exceptional circumstances, the shareholder(s) requesting the special audit shall be declared liable for the whole or part of the costs. In any event, if the general meeting consents to undertake a special audit, the corporation shall

---

[21] See Böckli, p. 985 *et seq*; Forstmoser *et al.*, p. 401 *et seq.*; Casutt, *Die Sonderprüfung im künftigen schweizerischen Aktienrecht*, 1991; Casutt, "Das Institut der Sonderprüfung", ST 1991, p. 574 *et seq.*; Pedroja, p. 774 *et seq.*

[22] Böckli, p. 985.

bear the costs (CO 697g II). Moreover, it is interesting to note that the request for a special audit does not have to be put on the agenda but may also be submitted to the general meeting, even if it may come as a matter of surprise at the meeting itself (CO 700 III).[23]

In reality, special audits will be requested in the course of the preparation of a liability claim against the board of directors or members of executive management; possibly also in the sense of a challenge to resolutions passed by the general meeting.[24]

So far, the right to request a special audit has not developed into an overly effective instrument for the protection of minority shareholders.[25] This is mainly due to rather stringent (new) case law requesting strong prima facie evidence showing that the board of directors have breached the law or the Articles of Incorporation. Moreover, the procedure is rather complicated and time consuming. The instrument as such, however, should nevertheless not be underestimated and it should not be overlooked just because there is only limited case law available so far. A request to conduct a special audit clearly has a preventive effect and is a potentially important feature of the new law.[26]

4. Capital Increases and Distributions

4.1 To what extent do (minority) shareholders have the right to participate in capital increases?

The new law has introduced important changes with regard to the increase of the share capital. While the general meeting has the power to decide on a capital increase, it is then the board of directors who has to implement the decision within three months. As a general rule, every shareholder has the right to subscribe to a number of newly issued shares corresponding to the number of all shares held by the same shareholder (CO 652b I). The resolution passed by the general assembly to increase the share capital may cancel or restrict subscription rights but only on important grounds (CO 652b II). Circumstances such as the take over of a company or parts thereof (financed by shares), a participation in another company (again financed by shares) as well as employees' participation through an increase of the share capital are considered to be important grounds (CO 652b II).

The decision to restrict or cancel subscription rights requires a special majority of two thirds of the votes represented and the absolute majority of the represented par values of the shares (CO 704 I, para. 6). It may be challenged if no important grounds, such as those that would justify the restriction as well as the cancellation, exist. Decisions relating to the restriction or cancellation of subscription rights

23 See also Watter, *Minderheitenschutz*, p. 123.
24 Pedroja, p. 775.
25 See also Böckli, pp. 1002f.
26 For a preliminary assessment see also Pedroja, p. 783.

have developed into some of the most controversial disputes under the new law, with some high profile court cases.[27]

4.2 Do minority shareholders have the right to demand dividends or other distributions?

According to CO 660, every shareholder has the right to a proportional share in the net profit of the corporation to the extent the law and the articles of incorporation provide for the distribution of profits among the shareholders. There is, however, no statutory provision which provide that the distribution of a corporation's profits be made in the form of dividends or otherwise.

Upon dissolution of a corporation, each shareholder has the right to receive a proportional share of the liquidation proceeds unless the Articles of Incorporation provide for a different use of the liquidation proceeds (CO 660 II).

It is possible to provide for the issue of preference shares in the Articles of Incorporation. The privileges pertaining thereto may be extended to cumulative or non-cumulative dividends, to a certain share of the liquidation proceeds and/or a priority rights for the subscription of new shares (CO 656). Where a company has already issued preference shares, new preference shares with priority over the existing preference shares may only be issued with the consent of an extraordinary meeting of all the holders of preference shares affected by the issuance of new preference shares as well as of the general meeting of all shareholders; these requirements, however, may be altered in the Articles of Incorporation (CO 654 II).

Any shareholder may challenge a resolution of the general meeting changing the objective of the corporation from a profit-making enterprise to a non-profit organization (CO 706 II para. 4). In that regard, any shareholder is entitled to enforce a (potentially) profit-making activity of the corporation.

5. Derivative Actions

5.1 Can (minority) shareholders enforce rights that the corporation has against other shareholders, directors, or third parties?

CO 756 provides for the right of any shareholder, as well as the corporation, to bring an action for damage caused to the corporation. The shareholder and the corporation, however, may only ask for restitution in respect of the damage to the corporation. In order to facilitate the enforcement of such right by any shareholder(s), the new law provides, in CO 756 II, the judge with a broad discretion in the allocation of costs provided that the shareholder had a legitimate cause for its action. Contrary to the general procedural rule in Switzerland according to which the los-

[27] See, for instance the court proceedings surrounding a capital increase of the largest Swiss Bank, UBS, on 29 April 1993; decision of the Swiss Federal Court 121 III 219 *et seq.*

ing party has to bear the costs and to compensate the other side for its attorneys' fees, the judge may therefore allocate the costs of the proceedings to, for example, the corporation even in the case of the shareholder losing on the merits. This has been criticised since the corporation is not normally a party to the proceedings.[28] The rule, however, reflects the determination of the lawmaker to facilitate the enforcement of these rights.

Claims of minority shareholders based upon an assignment or if the corporation is subject to bankruptcy proceedings shall not be dealt with within the given framework.

6. Other "Formal" Rights

6.1 Do minority shareholders have any other specific rights comparable to those mentioned in 2–5 above?

The new law strengthened an interesting remedy in certain specific circumstances:[29] CO 736 para. 4 provides for the possibility of a judge dissolving a corporation if shareholders representing together at least 10% of the share capital request for its dissolution on important grounds. Instead of this, the judge may now order another solution which takes due care of the existing situation and is acceptable to the parties involved. The judge might therefore order a partial buy-back of outstanding shares of the corporation at their market value if required in order to effectively protect minority shareholders. While the claim for dissolution of the corporation was already provided for in the old law,[30] the judicial possibility of "another solution" is an absolute novelty in Swiss law.[31]

Minority shareholders do not necessarily have a right to be represented on the board of directors unless provided for in the Articles of Incorporation (CO 709). The first paragraph of this same provision, however, provides that if there are several classes of shares either in relation to the right to vote or the financial rights, the articles of incorporation have to make sure that each class is represented on the board of directors by at least one representative.[32] The law, however, does not provide for a comparable right to be represented in an executive committee of the board of directors.[33]

---

28 Böckli, p. 1088.
29 See also Böckli, p. 1019 *et seq.*
30 The old law, however, required shareholders representing 20% of the share capital to effectively request dissolution.
31 Böckli, p. 1020 *et seq.*
32 Böckli, p. 759 *et seq.*
33 Böckli, p. 761.

7. Extensions of These Rights by Statute or Shareholders' Agreements

7.1 Can the Articles of Association provide for additional rights of the minority shareholders? If not, can such rights be provided for in shareholders' agreements? Are these options commonly used?

As outlined above, the Articles of Incorporation may provide for the right of minority shareholders to be represented on the board of directors (CO 709 II). This right is limited by the principle of equal treatment and the principle that the members of the board of directors are to be nominated by the general meeting (CO 698 II para. 2). A provision in the Articles of Incorporation according to which a person has to meet certain personal qualifications might therefore be problematic. Apart from this, there is, however, a considerable flexibility in so far as the Articles of Incorporation might provide for a proportional voting right, for cumulative voting (every shareholder has as many votes as there are seats in the board of directors and might freely give his votes to one or several candidates), etc.

The practical significance of CO 709 II has remained rather marginal. Most often, the same objective is achieved by appropriate provisions in shareholders' agreements (if any).

In particular, in smaller and closely held corporations, shareholders' agreements are quite common. Such shareholders' agreements normally contain rules regarding the right of first refusal in case of a sale of shares, option rights, decisions requiring a qualified majority or unanimity on the board of directors and the general meetings, the right of the parties to be represented on the board of directors, take-me-along clauses, etc. Even though a shareholders' agreement is technically irrelevant for the corporation itself, it has various advantages a few of which are the possibility of requesting specific performance, flexibility in so far as changes can be easily and speedily implemented by changing the agreement, confidentiality, etc.

8. Remedies Where a Shareholders' Resolution or Other Action Impairs the Rights of Minority Shareholders

8.1 What are the requirements for such remedies?

Any shareholder and the board of directors may challenge a resolution of the general meeting infringing the law or the Articles of Incorporation (CO 706) within two months after the date of the general meeting (CO 706a).[34] If the board of direc-

[34] Böckli, p. 1003 *et seq.*

tors is acting as claimant, the judge will appoint a representative for the corporation (CO 706a II).

Resolutions which might be challenged are, for instance, those which deprive shareholders of their rights, thereby infringing the law or the Articles of Incorporation, which revoke or restrict the rights of the shareholders without proper justification,[35] which result in unequal treatment or discrimination against shareholders in a manner not justifiable in view of the purpose of the corporation, and/or which change the objective of the corporation from the pursuit of profit to a non-profit making activity without the consent of all shareholders (CO 706 II).

Decisions of the board of directors cannot be challenged by shareholders.[36] Such decisions, however, might give rise to liability claims (CO 754 *et seq.*).

Resolutions of the general meeting which are in breach of the basic structure of the corporation or of fundamental principles of the law might be null and void.[37] Moreover, resolutions which are obviously impossible or which are against personal rights, public order or basic legal principles might also be null and void. A resolution of the general meeting which is null and void is deemed to have never been in existence and cannot be cured. There is no deadline to be observed in case of nullity of a decision of the general meeting. As long as there is a showing of a sufficient legal interest, anybody having an interest can invoke nullity (creditor of the corporation, competitors, etc) which is an important difference to the challenge of a resolution according to CO 706 which can only be invoked by a shareholder or the board of directors.

Examples of resolutions which are null and void are those which suppress or restrict the shareholders' right to attend the general meeting, its basic right to vote, its right of action or any other right which is mandatory by law, which restricts its right of control beyond what the law provides or which disregards provisions of the law which are in the interest of the protection of the share capital of the corporation.

Decisions of the board of directors might also be null and void (CO 714).[38]

8.2 When do the courts of your country accept these requirements?

As already mentioned above, resolutions passed by the general meeting have to be challenged within two months after the general meeting was held. Requests for annulment of resolutions are not subject to a strict time-limit.

8.3 What remedies are available to the claimant?

Most has already been mentioned above. In case of a challenge (contestation) to a decision of the general meeting, the shareholder(s) or the board of directors will normally request that the resolution as such be cancelled. The effect of a judgment

---

[35] For instance by improperly restricting or cancelling subscription rights; see note 20.
[36] Forstmoser *et al.*, p.361.
[37] Böckli, p. 1012 *et seq.*; Forstmoser *et al.*, p. 260 *et seq.*
[38] Forstmoser *et al.*, p. 361f.

granting claimant's request(s) is that the respective resolution of the general meeting will be suppressed with *ab initio* effect (*ex tunc*). Under Swiss law, there is no possibility of asking for a change of the resolution of the general meeting by the judge.[39] A decision of the judge granting claimants request will have effect on all shareholders (ie not only for or against claimant).

Cantonal law determines the question as to the availability of injunctive relief. This is so because procedural law is generally a matter of cantonal law in Switzerland and there is no legal basis under federal law for injunctive relief in connection with a challenge to shareholders' resolutions.

According to Article 32 II of the Federal Ordinance on the Commercial Register, it is possible to block the entry of a resolution of the general meeting into the Commercial Register. Normally, such requests are granted, subject, however, to the setting of a deadline for the commencement of the ordinary proceedings (ie for a request for injunctive relief).

In case of resolutions taken which are null and void, the claimant party will request the issuance of a declaratory judgment stating the nullity.

The extraordinary possibility of buying-out an injured shareholder has already been mentioned under para 6.1 above. The same applies with respect to the possibility of requesting the dissolution of the corporation (CO 736, para. 4).

9. Specific Protection if the Company is Controlled by Another Company

9.1 What are the rights and remedies of a shareholder of Company A when Company B gains control over it (by acquiring the majority of its shares or otherwise)?

Under Swiss law presently in force (see, however, Outlook below), several scenarios have to be distinguished.

In a non-quoted corporation, a negotiated change of control in the corporation will not trigger the application of any particular protective statutory provision nothwithstanding the possibility that minority shareholders might suffer harm as a consequence of the change of control (because the new controlling shareholder might not manage the corporation properly, might conclude transactions which are not at arm's length–which might be in particular relevant between related companies, etc). Under Swiss law, there is no general duty of trust of the controlling shareholder *vis-à-vis* the minority shareholder.[40] *In extremis*, the following, however, should be considered:[41] A majority shareholder forcing its will and decisions upon the corporation (thereby potentially causing prejudice to minority shareholders) will normally be deemed to be a corporate body of the corporation subject to the li-

[39] Böckli, p. 1099

[40] See decision of the Swiss Federal Court 105 II 128.

[41] See Watter, Unternehmensübernahmen, p. 277 *et seq.*

ability provisions applicable to the (formal) members of the board and executive management. Therefore, the controlling shareholder is subject to the same duties of equal treatment, due process, etc, as provided for by statutory law for the members of the board. This mechanism, however, will only be applicable in extreme cases.

Under Swiss law, there is no doubt that a premium paid by the buyer of a controlling share in the corporation will not have to be shared with the minority shareholders.[42] Problems do not normally arise in case of friendly tender offers for the shares of public corporations, that is tender offers supported by the board of directors of the target corporation. However, it should be emphasized that direct purchases of shares outside of the public tender are admissible, thereby potentially creating an unequal treatment of minority shareholders (who might not receive a premium which the former controlling shareholder selling its shares receives).

Also in case of negotiated take-overs and unfriendly deals regarding public corporations,[43] that is tender offers not approved by the board of directors, the position of the minority shareholders under Swiss law is weak: Presently, there is no enforceable right of equal treatment.[44] The offeree might therefore purchase shares paying an additional premium outside of the tender offer, etc. With respect to the duties of the board of directors, the general rules apply which, however, are not necessarily suited for the particular case of the unfriendly take over attempt.

9.2 What are the rights and remedies when Company B exerts its control over Company A in a way which damages the interests of the latter?

It has already been mentioned that Company B might be deemed to be a corporate body of the Company A, being subject to the general rules on liability (CO 754 et seq.). Therefore, minority shareholders might sue Company B for damages to be paid to Company A.

Outlook: The New Federal Law Act on Stock Exchanges and on Securities Trading of 24 March 1995

After certain delays, there is now a good likelihood that the new Federal Law Act on Stock Exchanges and on Securities trading of 24 March 1995 (SESTA) will enter into force in the summer of 1997. In its Articles 22–33 it contains detailed provisions regarding public tender offers for corporation which are at least partially quoted at a stock exchange in Switzerland (target companies). Amongst many other duties, there is an obligation of the offeror to submit a tender for all shares quoted

---

[42] Watter, *Unternehmensübernahmen*, p. 278.

[43] Reference may be made to the unfriendly takeover battle in 1995 involving the company Holvis.

[44] See, however, the rules and regulations of the Take-Over Codex of 1 September 1989 (as at 1 November 1994) providing for certain protective measures.

at the stock exchange if the offeror already owns one-third of the voting rights of the target company (Article 32 SESTA). The corporation has the right to increase the threshold to 49% of the voting rights in its Articles of Incorporation. The tender price has to be at least the market price and may not be lower than 75% of the highest price which the offeror has paid during the 12 months prior to the offer for shares of the target company (Article 32 IV SESTA).

The above statutory take-me-along clauses have been the subject of heated discussions during the legislative process. As a compromise between various positions, the corporations have been granted the possibility of opting out of Article 32 and Article 52 SESTA (Art. 22 II SESTA). Article 52 SESTA provides that, upon the entry into force of the law, shareholders controlling more than one-third but less than 50% of the voting rights of the target corporation are required to submit a offer for all quoted shares of the target corporation when acquiring more than 50% of the voting rights.

The above provisions which are accompanied by various information rights and disclosure obligations (*inter alia* of major shareholders) constitute a typical Swiss compromise between conflicting interests but are to be seen as an improvement of the position of minority shareholders in quoted corporations.

Concluding Remarks

Even though the position of minority shareholders still falls short compared to the standards of various others jurisdictions (such as the United States of America and England), case law has clearly improved their position and by the coming into force of the new Law on Stock Corporations and the expected coming into force of the new Federal Law Act on Stock Exchanges and on Securities Trading of 24 March 1995, in the near future, such improvements are expected to continue.

Select Bibliography

The following bibliography list is not comprehensive but should cover the most important issues mentioned in the above contribution, both under the old and the new law. Further references may be found in Brigitte Tanner, "Literaturübersicht" (as at 30 May 1992), in: AJP 1992, p. 821 *et seq.*

Böckli, Peter, *Das neue Aktienrecht*, 2nd edn, 1996.

Braun, Thomas, "Verbesserte Aktionärsinformation in der Schweiz", in *Der Schweizer Treuhänder* 1994, p. 281ff.

Bühler, Roland, "Aktienrecht 1992", in AJP 1992, p. 693 *et seq.*

Bürgi, Wolfhart F., "Das Problem des Minderheitenschutzes im schweizerischen Aktienrecht", in SAG 1957, p. 81 *et seq.*

Casutt, Andreas, *Die Sonderprüfung im künftigen Schweizerischen Aktienrecht*, Zurich 1991.

Eppenberger, Matthias, *Information des Aktionärs – Auskunfts-oder Mitteilungspflicht*, 1990.

Forstmoser, Peter, *Die aktienrechtliche Verantwortlichkeit,* 1987.

Forstmoser, Peter/Meier-Hayoz, Arthur and Nobel, Peter, *Schweizerisches Aktienrecht,* 1996.

Haymann, Eric, *Aktienübernahmevereinbarungen zwischen Mehrheits-und Minderheitsaktionären,* 1973 .

Handschin, Lukas, *Der Konzern im geltenden schweizerischen Privatrecht,* 1993.

Homburger, Eric, *Leitfaden zum neuen Aktienrecht,* 1991.

Honsell, Heinrich/Vogt Nedim, Peter and Watter, Rolf, *Obligationenrecht II, Kommentar zum Schweizerischen Privatrecht,* 1994.

Huguenin, Jacobs Claire, *Das Gleichbehandlungsprinzip im Aktienrecht,* Zurich 1974.

Maute, Wolfgang, *Die Durchführung der Generalversammlung,* Zurich 1993.

Meier-Hayoz, Arthur and Forstmoser Peter, *Grundriss des Schweizerischen Gesellschaftsrechtes,* 1993.

Meier, Robert, *Die Aktiengesellschaft,* 1994.

Mommendey, Fritz, *Einführung in das neue Aktienrecht der Schweiz,* 1993.

Müller, Roland and Lipp, Lorenz, *Der Verwaltungsrat – ein Handbuch für die Praxis,* 1994.

Nenninger, John, *Der Schutz der Minderheiten in der Aktiengesellschaft nach schweizerischem Recht,* 1974.

Nobel, Peter, *Aktienrechtliche Entscheide,* 2nd edn., 1991.

Pedroja, Graziano, "Die Sonderprüfung im neuen Aktienrecht", in AJP 1992, p. 774 *et seq.*

Stauber, Eric, *Das Recht des Aktionärs auf gesetzes-und statutenmässige Verwaltung,* 1985.

Tanner, Brigitte, "Neuerungen für die Beschlussfassung in der Generalversammlung", in AJP 1992, p. 765 *et seq.* ("Neuerungen")

Tanner, Brigitte, *Quoren für die Beschlussfassung in der Aktiengesellschaft,* 1987. ("*Quoren*")

Von Büren, Roland, "Der Konzern im neuen Aktienrecht", in *Grundfragen des neuen Aktienrechts,* 1993.

Von der Crone, Hans Caspar, "Interessenkonflikte im Aktienrecht", in SZW 1994, p.1 *et seq.*

Von Greyerz, Christoph, "Der Schutz der Minderheiten der AG de lege ferenda", in SJZ 1976, p. 53 *et seq.*

Von PlantA, Thomas, *Der Schutz der Aktionäre bei der Kapitalerhöhung,* 1992.

Watter, Rolf, "Der Minderheitenschutz im neuen Aktienrecht", in AJP 1993, p.117 *et seq.* ("Minderheitenschutz")

Watter, Rolf, *Unternehmensübernahmen,* 1990 ("*Unternehmensübernahmen*").

Watter, Rolf/Faruque, Nadine and Känzig David, *Introduction to the Law Governing the Swiss Stock Corporation,* 1993 (a publication of the law firm Bär & Karrer).

Weber, Rolf H., "Vertrags-bzw. Statutengestaltung und Minderheitenschutz", in SAV Bd. 11, 1992. p. 71 *et seq.*

Wursch, Daniel, *Der Aktionär als Konkurrent der Gesellschaft,* 1989.

Wyler, Siegfried/Watter, Rolf and Wyler, Jürg, *Swiss Company Law in the European Context,* 1994.

UNITED KINGDOM

Andrew P. Johnstone

Sinclair Roche & Temperley
London

PROTECTION OF MINORITY SHAREHOLDERS

***EDITOR* MATTHIAS W. STECHER**

UNITED KINGDOM

Andrew P. Johnstone

1. Majority Requirements for Shareholders' Resolutions

1.1 What are the majority requirements in general?

Meetings of members fall into two categories. All members may attend and vote at general meetings unless they hold shares of a class which do not confer that right. Most ordinary shares carry full voting rights. It is normally redeemable preference shares which do not. Class meetings may be attended only by holders of shares of the relevant class and are normally only convened when rights attaching to that class of share are proposed to be varied. The extent of voting rights attached to shares is governed by a company's Articles of Association ("the Articles") or the terms of issue. A majority is constituted by a holding of 50% of the voting rights, together with one further vote.

An "ordinary resolution" will be passed by a simple majority of those present in person at the meeting or, on a poll, present by proxy and who vote on the resolution. The term "ordinary resolution" is not defined in the Companies Act[1] but all

1 Companies Act 1985 as amended by the Companies Act 1989 ("the Act"). References to the Act are references to the Companies Act 1985 (as amended) unless otherwise specified.

resolutions will be ordinary resolutions unless the Act or the Articles otherwise provide. The Act provides that some resolutions require only a simple majority notwithstanding that the Articles may provide otherwise; an example is s. 303 where, notwithstanding anything in the Articles to the contrary, a director can be removed from office (subject to the giving of special notice). The purpose here is to prevent controlling shareholders from entrenching themselves in office.

1.2 Which resolutions require a greater majority?

A greater majority is required of any resolution to change the Articles or as the Act or the Articles may otherwise prescribe and requires not less than three quarters of the members entitled to vote, voting in person or by proxy in favour of the proposed resolution.

1.3 To what extent can they be modified by the Articles of Association?

In certain situations the Act or the Articles may require that a "special" (or "extraordinary") resolution be passed. On a show of hands, 75% of those voting must vote in favour of the resolution (on a poll 75% of the votes cast). The Act requires that an extraordinary resolution be passed in connection with certain aspects of winding up. The Act also requires that a number of matters be dealt with by way of special resolution, usually where constitutional change is involved, for example a change in the Articles or the company's objects as set out in its Memorandum of Association ("the Memorandum"). The Articles may, however, require that any matter be dealt with by special resolution.

The Companies Act 1989 ("CA89") establishes an elective regime whereby a private company in general meeting may, by elective resolution, vary the application of certain of the regulatory requirements of the Act. These are:

- s. 80A (election as to duration of directors' authority to allot shares);
- s. 252 (election to dispense with laying of accounts and reports before the company in general meeting);
- s. 366A (election to dispense with holding of annual general meeting);
- ss. 369(4) and 378(3) (election as to majority required to authorize short notice of meeting); and
- s. 386 (election to dispense with the appointment of auditors annually).

The resolution must be agreed to at the meeting by all the members either in person or by proxy who are entitled to attend and vote (unanimous agreement of all members and not just among those who actually attend). An elective resolution may be revoked by ordinary resolution and will cease to have effect if the company is re-registered as public.

The ability to block a resolution then will depend upon the number of shares held by a shareholder and on whether the resolution is ordinary, special, extraordinary or elective.

2. Influence on the Decision Making Process

2.1 Do minority shareholders have the right to call a shareholders' meeting?

Members who fulfil certain requirements of the Act[2] may require the directors to convene a meeting on a new resolution which they wish to be put to the members or to require the addition of a resolution at the annual general meeting which is required to be held to deal with the routine business of adopting accounts, declaring dividends, etc. Unless the company resolves otherwise, the expense incurred must be borne by the requisitioners. This may not be great where a members' resolution is simply included in the notice of meeting, but can be considerable in the case of a company listed on the London Stock Exchange.[3] The requisitionists, between them, must represent not less than one-twentieth of the total voting rights, or be at least 100 members on whose shares an average of at least £100 per member has been paid up. In practice, there are timing difficulties to be confronted by requisitionists which may restrict their theoretical rights.

The requisitionists must deposit at the company's registered office a copy of the resolution signed by all the requisitionists not less than six weeks before the meeting, or the company will not be bound to give notice of the resolution or to circulate a statement. A requisition requiring notice of a resolution will be deemed to be served in time if after the requisition has been deposited the company calls a meeting for a date less than six weeks away.

The business which may be dealt with at an annual general meeting includes any resolution of which notice is given as detailed above, notwithstanding anything in the company's Articles of Association. In connection with an extraordinary general meeting however the right is only to circulate to members entitled to receive notice of any general meeting a statement of not more than a thousand words concerning the matter referred to in any proposed resolution or the business to be dealt with at that meeting.

2.2 Do they have the right to put matters on the agenda?

At common law, no business may be conducted at a meeting unless sufficient notice of the nature of the business has been given to those entitled to receive it. The notice is adequate if it indicates the general nature of the business with enough particularity to enable a member to decide whether or not to attend. It is common for an agenda to be sent with the notice.

The responsibility for determining the contents of the agenda will normally rest with the board or its chairman. In the case of dispute the secretary should include

---

2 Ss. 376 and 377 Companies Act 1985.

3 London Stock Exchange Limited.

the item, leaving the matter for the ultimate decision of the meeting itself. In order to preserve impartiality the secretary should, at the request of a member, include any matter which can be regarded as the proper business of the meeting.[4]

Notice of a special resolution must contain the entire substance of the resolution.[5] The correction of grammatical or clerical errors is excluded. An ordinary resolution need not be set out verbatim in the notice and amendments, within the scope of the business of which notice has been given, may be validly moved.

It would appear that a members' resolution requisitioned under s. 376 may (where it is an ordinary resolution) be amended at the meeting so long as the amendment falls within the scope of the notice. While s. 376(3) requires a copy of the resolution to be served, notice of the precise wording of the resolution is not a pre-condition of validity.[6] In the case of a company listed on the London Stock Exchange proofs of notices of meetings (including newspaper advertisements, proxy forms and circulars) must be sent to the London Stock Exchange for approval.[7]

Where insufficient notice is given an individual member may apply to the court to restrain the company from acting on any resolution passed at the meeting.[8]

3. Rights of Information, Independent Auditing and Supervision

3.1 To what extent do the (minority) shareholders have a right to be informed on company matters?

Subject to certain exceptions, every member and person entitled to receive notices of general meetings must be sent a copy of the annual accounts, together with a copy of the directors' report and of the auditors' report on those accounts, for the financial year, not less than 21 days before the general meeting at which they are to be presented.[9] Every member is also entitled on demand within seven days without charge to be sent a copy of the company's latest annual accounts and report.[10]

3.2 Do they have the right to demand independent auditing or to initiate the supervision of company matters by an independent institution?

The Department of Trade and Industry may appoint investigators "to investigate the affairs of a company and report on them" in the circumstances set out in ss. 431

---

4 I. Shearman Shackleton on *The Law and Practice of Meetings*, Sweet & Maxwell 1991.
5 *Re Moorgate Mercantile Holdings Ltd* [1980] 1 All ER 40 and s. 378(2) Companies Act 1985.
6 Cf. *Moorgate Mercantile Holdings Ltd.*
7 The Listing Rules: para. 9.1.
8 *MacConnell* v. *E Prill & Co Ltd* [1916] 2 Ch 57.
9 Section 238 (1)–(3) Companies Act 1985.
10 Section 239 (1)–(3) Companies Act 1985.

The Department of Trade and Industry may appoint investigators "to investigate the affairs of a company and report on them" in the circumstances set out in ss. 431 and 432 of the Act. These include an application made by not less than 200 members or members holding at least 10% of the issued share capital. In practice, such an appointment is very rare, particularly in private companies.

4. Capital Increases and Distributions

4.1 To what extent do (minority) shareholders have the right to participate in capital increases?

A company must be authorized by its Articles to alter the share capital conditions of its Memorandum.[11] In the case of an increase of capital this authorization is commonly Article 32(a) Table A. S. 121(4) requires that the powers be exercised in general meeting. This can be altered by the passing of a special resolution.

If the increase of capital is connected with a company whose shares are listed on the London Stock Exchange it is necessary to file a circular with the Listing Department, prior to any final printing. Where 10% or more of the voting capital will remain unissued there must be included in the circular a statement that no issue will be made which would effectively alter the control of the company without the prior approval of the company in general meeting.

The ability of a company or its directors to issue shares to persons other than existing members is curtailed by s. 89 (in addition to any pre-emption provisions on transfer or issue of shares contained in the Articles).

Section 89(1) states that, subject to certain exceptions, a company proposing to allot equity securities:

- "shall not allot any of such securities on any terms to a person unless it has made an offer to each person who holds relevant shares to allot to him on the same or more favourable terms a proportion of those securities which is as nearly as practicable equal to the proportion in nominal value held by him of relevant shares;" and
- "shall not allot any of those securities to a person unless the period during which any such offer may be accepted has expired or the Company has received notice of the acceptance or refusal of every offer so made."

One important qualification is contained in s. 89(4). The pre-emption provisions are not applicable if the equity securities are, or are to be, wholly or partly paid up otherwise than in cash (eg, a share for share exchange).

Shares may be allotted under s. 89 by renounceable letters of allotment, and this is required in the case of listed companies.

[11] *Mutual Life Insurance Co of New York* v. *Rank Organisation Ltd* [1985] BCLC 11.

Section 92 of the Act makes the company and any officer who knowingly authorizes or permits a contravention jointly and severally liable to compensate any person to whom an offer should have been made for any loss, damage, costs or expenses which that person has sustained.

4.2 Do minority shareholders have the right to demand dividends or other distributions?

Except in so far as the Memorandum, Articles or terms of issue provide otherwise an ordinary shareholder is entitled to receive dividends when declared (subject to priority enjoyed by preference shareholders).[12] Unless the Memorandum or Articles provide or imply otherwise, a dividend is not payable until it has been declared. It has been held that members are entitled to have profits distributed so far as is commercially possible and that directors who fail to make the appropriate recommendation would be exercising their powers for an improper purpose. Such an abuse is, potentially, unfairly prejudicial under s. 459 of the Act.[13]

Any company (public or private) can only make distributions out of its "accumulated realized profits" so far as not previously distributed or capitalized, less "accumulated realized losses" so far as not previously written off in a reduction or reorganisation of capital.[14] Under Table A and most other forms of Articles the power to pay dividends lies with the company in general meeting which may declare dividends, but not exceeding the amount recommended by the directors. In practice it is the directors who will propose any dividend.

5. Derivative Actions

5.1 Can (minority) shareholders enforce rights that the company has against other shareholders, directors, or third parties?

The rule contained in *Foss* v. *Harbottle*,[15] in essence, is that a shareholder cannot go to court to complain of a wrong done to his company. This is because a shareholder does not have a proprietary interest in the underlying assets of the company. Any action of a third party which reduces the value of the underlying assets will not lead to a shareholder having a personal action against the wrongdoer, unless

---

12 Boyle and Sykes (eds.) *Gore Browne on Companies* Vol. 1, 44th edn. (London, 1996), Jordans.

13 *Re Sam Weller & Sons Ltd* [1989] 3 WLR 923.

14 "Accumulated realized profits" and "accumulated realized losses" means that profit for a particular year becomes irrelevant, the profit and loss account being regarded as continuous for this purpose. No distinction is made between capital profits and revenue profits. Unrealized profits are not distributable, they must be realized before dividends are paid. Profits are recognized as realized only when realized in the form of cash or of other assets the ultimate cash realization of which can be assessed with reasonable certainty. S. 273 Companies Act 1985.

15 (1843) 2 Hare 461.

that shareholder can show that the action also infringed a personal right belonging to that shareholder. A shareholder then, may have suffered demonstrable harm in that the value of his shares has been diminished by the wrong doing, but under the rule, if the company will not sue, then the shareholder's loss must go unredressed. The problem is in determining in what circumstances a minority shareholder should be allowed to bring proceedings on *behalf* of the company. Such an action is called a "derivative action".

The rule in *Foss* v. *Harbottle* is currently in the spotlight in the UK. On 22 December 1994, the Minister for Corporate Affairs, Mr Jonathan Evans, announced that he had invited the Law Commission, in consultation with the Scottish Law Commission, to carry out a review of shareholders' remedies with particular reference (*inter alia*) to that rule. The Law Commission published a consultation paper (No. 142) entitled *Shareholder Remedies* during 1996 requesting comments before 22 January 1997. At the time of writing it is considering these responses.

The rule in *Foss* v. *Harbottle*[16] does not exclude a minority shareholder from bringing an action in respect of acts which are *ultra vires* the company or illegal. Members can bring an action to restrain the doing of an act which is beyond the company's capacity. Ratification of such acts is permitted only by special resolution.[17]

A derivative action may be brought only where one of the exceptions to the rule applies, for example where it is claimed that fraud has been committed and the alleged wrongdoers are in control of the company and preventing the company from suing in its own name. Such an action must be distinguished from a personal action brought by a shareholder, claiming a remedy in his own right for a wrong done to him personally. A typical example would be a claim for a dividend declared but not paid. Problems arise where there is an overlap, where the same act is a wrong done both to the company and to the individual shareholder who is complaining. The law in the area has not developed because the rulings and the cases on the question are not consistent.

6. Other "Formal" Rights

6.1 Do minority shareholders have any other specific rights comparable to those mentioned in 2–5 above?

Section 4 of the Act provides that "the memorandum and articles, when registered, bind the company and its members to the same extent as if they respectively had been signed and sealed by each member, and contained covenants on the part of each member to observe all the provisions of the memorandum and articles". The membership contract which is the result of this provision has certain special features. It gives members the ability to enforce the company's constitution and to enforce any of their rights that are contained there. It was at one time the case that a

---

16 *Ibid.*
17 S. 35 Companies Act 1985 (as amended).

member could not sue for damages for breach of his membership contract while remaining a member.[18] However, s. 131 CA89 alters the Act to provide "a person is not debarred from obtaining damages or other compensation from a company by reason only of his holding or having held shares in the company or any right to apply or subscribe for shares or to be included in the company's register in respect of shares". Section 4 has been interpreted as only creating rights and duties *qua* member. The leading case is *Hickman* v. *Kent or Romney Marsh Sheep-Breeder's Association*[19] where the court held that the section only applied to members in their capacity as members.

The contract cannot therefore be invoked in disputes between officers and the company; *Eley* v. *Positive Government Life Security Assurance Company*.[20] The Articles there provided that Eley should be the solicitor to the company. He was a member of the company but, it was held, could not enforce the relevant Article in his capacity as an officer.

There are certain provisions of the Act that enable dissident shareholders to object to particular courses of action. Section 5 of the Act provides that application may be made to the court to cancel a change of object within 21 days of the passing of the resolution. The objection may be made by the holders of not less than 15% in nominal value of the company's issued capital or any class of it. An example is *Re Cyclists Touring Club*,[21] where the court upheld an objection to a change of object to allow the club to cater for motorists. The court accepted that the interests of cyclists and motorists might conflict. An identical procedure exists for objecting to the alteration of conditions set out in the memorandum which could have been contained in the Articles.[22]

Where a company is proposing to vary the rights that attach to a particular class of share it needs to follow a procedure set down in the company's constitution or obtain the sanction of either the shareholders who hold three-quarters of the nominal value of the issued shares of that class or an extraordinary resolution passed at a separate meeting of the holders of that class.

Where a private company passes a special resolution to make a payment out of capital to redeem or purchase shares, any member of the company, other than one who consented to or voted in favour of the resolution, may within five weeks of the date on which the resolution was passed apply to the court for cancellation of the resolution.[23]

Section 54 of the Act permits an objection by the holders of 5%of the nominal value of the company's share capital, where a company passes a special resolution to re-register as a private company.

---

[18] *Houldsworth* v. *City of Glasgow Bank* [1880] 5 App Cas 317.
[19] [1915] 1 Ch 881.
[20] [1876] 1 Ex D 88.
[21] [1907] 1 Ch 269.
[22] S. 17(3) Companies Act 1985.
[23] S. 176 Companies Act 1985.

7. Extension of These Rights by Statute or Shareholders' Agreements

7.1 Can the Articles of Association provide for additional rights of the minority shareholders? If not, can such rights be provided for in shareholder's agreements? Are these options commonly used?

The Articles are essentially concerned with a company's internal management and administrative structure. They regulate the company's affairs and constitute a contract between each member and the company.[24] They can therefore be used to provide additional rights for minority shareholders and the Articles will commonly regulate the following matters:

- share capital and class rights, together with permitted alteration requirements;
- allotment, transfer and transmission of shares;
- meetings of members and directors including quorum requirements, exercise of voting rights, appointment of alternates and proxies;
- powers of directors and delegation thereof;
- administration matters such as the keeping of minutes, common seal, giving of notices, winding up; and
- accounts, including preparation and audit, declaration and payment of dividends.

Anyone acquiring shares in a private company without gaining control is well advised to obtain some form of additional contract direct with the other members. The agreement may be with the company or with some or all of the other shareholders. It may cover any aspect of the company's business and activities including, *inter alia*, dividend distribution, appointment of directors, general principles of management and transfer of shares. Such an agreement will be subject to variation only with the consent of the parties, by contrast with the Articles. The remedy for breach is an action against the shareholder concerned, not against the company. A shareholders' agreement may also include, or entirely consist of, voting agreements. A vote constitutes a shareholder's property and he may bind himself to vote in a particular way.

Any attempt to use a shareholders' agreement to fetter the power to alter the Articles is arguably invalid. In *Russell* v. *Northern Bank Development Corporation Limited*,[25] the Northern Ireland Court of Appeal held that a provision in a shareholders agreement to the effect that no further share capital was to be created without the written consent of each of the parties to the agreement, including the company, was unlawful as it fettered the company's statutory powers. On appeal to the House of Lords[26] it was held that the shareholders may lawfully agree between

[24] S. 22 Companies Act 1985.
[25] [1991] BCC 517.
[26] [1992] BCC 578.

themselves as to how to exercise their voting rights, but that where the company is a party to the agreement its statutory powers could not be fettered by any such agreement.

8. Remedies Where a Shareholders' Resolution or Other Action Impairs the Rights of Minority Shareholders

8.1 What are the requirements for such remedies?

8.2 When do the courts of your country accept these requirements?

A member of the company may petition for an order on the ground that the affairs of the company are being or have been conducted in a manner which is unfairly prejudicial to the interests of members generally (including at least himself) or that any actual or proposed act or omission of the company is or would be so prejudicial.[27]

This area of company law has seen the most radical changes in recent years. The Cohen Report (1944)[28] recognized that provision for such abuse could not be made in every case, but accepted the principle that there should be a remedy other than by way of a winding up or a derivative action. The only available method then of enabling these two contradictory objects to be achieved was to grant to the courts a wide discretion. This discretion is a strand which runs throughout the legislation regarding unfair prejudice.

During 1948–1980, there were only two successful petitions brought by minority shareholders under the old minority remedy. The reform carried out by the Companies Act 1980 (s. 75), consolidated into the Companies Act 1985, created one of the most vibrant areas of company law. In the new minority remedy section, the link with winding-up has been swept away and a single act or omission or threatened future conduct can now be the basis for a petition. Personal representatives can sue. A new remedy also applies in cases of unfair prejudice, far easier to show than oppression, which requires a course of deliberate conduct. The most common example of the minority seeking relief is where an undertaking to a member that he would have a say in the management of the company has been breached. This usually involves his removal from the board of directors.

A host of cases suggest that exclusion from management can be used as the basis of a s. 459 petition.

It has been held that there is no rule requiring the petitioner to come to court entirely blameless. The fact that he may also have acted inequitably was only relevant in relation to whether the conduct was unfair and in relation to what relief should be granted. It did not bar him from bringing a petition.[29]

---

27 S. 459 Companies Act 1985.

28 *Tolley's Company Law* Issue 16 1994, Stephen Barc (ed.) para. S4047.

29 *Re London School of Electronics* [1985] 3 WLR 474.

Note that exclusion from management in the case of a public company will not generally found a successful petition under s. 459.[30]

Previously, if all members were unfairly prejudiced, that is, they all suffered equally, no petition could be brought. This position led to an amendment of the law in the CA89. It is now provided that a petition may be brought if the conduct is "unfairly prejudicial to the interests of its members generally, or of some part of its members".

The question of whether there has been unfair prejudice is an objective one, not a matter of intent.[31]

There need be no effect on the value of a person's shareholding for there to be unfair prejudice. In *Re A Company number 004475*[32] Lord Grantchester QC suggested that before there could be unfair prejudice, there had to be an adverse effect on the value of a person's shares. However, in *Re R A Noble & Sons (Clothing) Limited*,[33] it was said that the conduct could be unfairly prejudicial even though the value of a person's holding had not been adversely affected.

Only members of the company or personal representatives have *locus standi* to present a petition. In *Re A Company number 007828* of 1985[34] it was held that persons who were not members of the company but who had the benefit of a purported agreement between themselves and the majority shareholders to transfer shares to them had no *locus standi* to present a petition.

8.3 What remedies are available to the claimant?

8.3.1 Discretion of the court

The court has a wide discretion in making an order. Section 461(2) of the Act sets out specific examples of possible orders. These are that a court may make an order regulating the conduct of the company's affairs in the future, it may require the company to refrain from doing, or continuing to do, an act complained of, or it may require a company to do an act which the petitioner had complained it has omitted to do. The court can authorize civil proceedings to be brought in the name and on behalf of the company by such person or persons and on such terms as it may direct, and it may provide for the purchase of the shares of any members of the company, by other members, or by the company itself, which would involve a reduction of the company's capital. The examples of the orders set out in this sub-section are without prejudice to the generality of the discretion that the court has to award whatever remedy it considers appropriate. The court may also make an order forbidding the alteration of the Memorandum or Articles.

---

30 *Re Blue Arrow Plc.* [1987] 3 BCC 618.
31 *Re R. A. Noble & Sons* (Clothing) Ltd [1983] BCLC 273.
32 [1983] 2 All ER 36.
33 *Ibid.*
34 [1986] 2 BCC 98, 951.

8.3.2 Purchase of shares

The most common order under s. 461 is the order for the purchase of shares. The problem which then arises is that prices are usually discounted to take account of the fact that the vendor does not have control. On occasion the court may order that the respondents purchase the shares from the petitioner, although this is rare. In *Re Bird Precision Bellows Limited*,[35] Nourse J considered that it was erroneous to assume that a minority shareholder in a *quasi* partnership company was selling freely. If the sale was not from a willing vendor the shares should be valued on a pro-rata basis with no element of discount. On the other hand, if the holding has simply been acquired as a minority holding with no participation in management rights or if the minority has been blameworthy to some extent, then the value of the holding will be discounted as a minority shareholding.

The other controversial feature of valuation is the date when the valuation is to be made. There is no fixed rule on this matter. The date of valuation may be the date of the purchase order, but it could also be the date when the unfairly prejudicial conduct began. Another possibility is a valuation of the shares on the date the petition is presented. The court has accepted that compensation should take account not merely of matters such as prospective dividends and the financial value but also of matters such as prestige. For instance, prestige is a relevant factor in valuing football club shares.[36]

The court could order that the petitioner receive, in effect, damages as compensation for any diminution in the value of his shares caused by the unfairly prejudicial conduct.

8.3.3 Winding up

The just and equitable ground for winding-up a company is contained in s. 122 (1)(g) of the Insolvency Act 1986 ("IA"). Under s. 125 (2) IA the mere fact that there is another available remedy does not preclude the making of a winding-up order, unless the petitioner is acting unreasonably in not pursuing that other remedy. This statutorily reverses previous judicial reluctance to make winding-up orders where there is another available remedy. The most obvious alternative is an order under s. 459 of the Act and an offer to buy the petitioner's shares at an independent valuation. Indeed, s. 459 is a more flexible remedy but there are unusual cases where a court will make a winding-up order instead.

The winding-up petition is presented by a contributory. It seems that any member may be a contributory. A contributory can only present a petition where the shares in respect of which he is a contributory, or some of them, were originally allotted to him, or have been held by him and registered in his name for at least 6 months during the 18 months before the commencement of the winding up, or have devolved upon him through the death of a former holder. This is extended so that

---

35 [1984] Ch 419.

36 *Nuneaton Borough AFC Ltd.* [1989] 5 BCC 792.

where a person who has had his shares purchased or redeemed by the company in the past year may be liable to contribute to the company's assets, and may apply.

The leading case is *Ebrahimi* v. *Westbourne Galleries*.[37] The appellant and Nazar carried on a partnership as carpet dealers in equal shares. They formed a company to take over the business. Ebrahimi and Nazar were the shareholders with 500 shares each and the first directors. Nazar's son, George, was appointed a director and each of the two original shareholders transferred to him 100 shares. The company was highly profitable. No dividends were paid. The profits were distributed by way of directors' remuneration. The parties fell out. Nazar and George disagreed with Ebrahimi and Ebrahimi was removed by them as a director. Ebrahimi then sought, *inter alia*, an order to wind-up the company on the just and equitable ground. Ploughman J held that although Ebrahimi had been lawfully removed from office, Nazar and George had acted wrongfully in abusing their power and excluding Ebrahimi from office, since the business had started on the basis that both Ebrahimi and Nazar were participating managers. The Court of Appeal reversed the decision but the House of Lords reversed the Court of Appeal.

Lord Wilberforce considered the scope of s. 122(1)(g) of the Act and noted that "the members of the company are in substance partners or quasi partners and [that] a winding-up may be ordered if such facts are shown as could justify a dissolution of partnership between them".

The just and equitable winding-up would therefore be appropriate and has been ordered in the following circumstances:

- Deadlock: in *Re Yenidje Tobacco Co Limited*,[38] deadlock existed between two director shareholders who were the only directors and shareholders. This case is an authority only for the resolution of a total deadlock.
- Lack of probity of directors: in *Loch* v. *John Blackwood Limited*,[39] the judicial committee of the Privy Council hearing an appeal from the West Indian Court of Appeal (Barbados) considered a case where a director had given grounds for loss of confidence in his probity and had shown that he regarded the business as his own. The director had omitted to hold general meetings, to submit accounts or to recommend dividends.
- Breakdown of mutual trust and confidence: in *Re Zinotty Properties Limited*,[40] the company was formed by A and B to develop a particular site. The shares were held by the petitioner, which was a company controlled by A and by another company which was controlled by B and his business associate C. A was not made a director although he was entitled to assume that he would be made a director. B and C were made directors. When the development was completed, the company was not dissolved (contrary to the original intention) but continued to carry on business without A's knowledge or consent. Some of the company's cash was lent to a company in which C had an interest and to the exclusion of any benefit to A. The court held that it was just and equitable that the company be wound up.

---

37 [1972] 2 All ER 492.
38 [1916] 2 Ch 426.
39 [1924] AC 783.
40 [1984] 3 All ER 754.

- Failure of substratum: *Re German Date Coffee Company*.[41] The company had as its main object the exploitation of a German patent for making coffee from dates. The company never obtained a patent. The court ordered a winding up on the just and equitable ground. It was immaterial that the company had subsidiary objects that could have been achieved. However, if there is a main activity which can still be carried out, a winding-up order will be refused even if the company's original business has ceased.[42]
- Exclusion from management: this was the principle put forward in *Ebrahimi* v. *Westbourne Galleries*.[43] In *Tay Bok Choon* v. *Tahansan Sdn Bhd*,[44] a shareholder director who had contributed a significant amount of capital to the company was held entitled to have the company wound up when he was removed from office.

9. Specific Protection if the Company is Controlled by Another Company

9.1 What are the rights and remedies of a shareholder of Company A when Company B gains control over it (by acquiring the majority of its shares or otherwise)?

In reality, in large public companies only a small proportion of shareholders attend and vote at general meetings. It is possible for a shareholder who holds significantly less than 50% to exercise control.

Thus the City Code on Takeovers and Mergers[45] requires under Rule 9 that any person who acquires, whether by a series of transactions over a period of time or at one time, shares which (taken together with shares held or acquired by persons acting in concert with him) carry 30% or more of the voting rights of the company, is required to make an offer on the same terms to acquire the rest of the equity share capital.

Similarly, a person who holds between 30% and 50% of the company's voting rights who acquires in any period of 12 months more than 1% of the voting rights is also required to make a mandatory offer.

Where a take-over offer is completed and the bidder has achieved a certain rate of acceptance, both the bidder and the dissentient minority can require that the bidder acquires shares of the minority on the terms of the offer under ss. 428 to 430 of the Act.

---

41 [1982] 20 Ch D 169.
42 *Re Kitson & Co Ltd.* [1946] All ER 435.
43 *Ibid.*
44 [1977] 3 BCC 132 (Malaysia).
45 The City Code on Takeovers and Mergers and the Rules Governing Substantial Acquisitions of Shares, The Panel on Takeovers and Mergers.

9.2 What are the shareholder's rights and remedies when Company B exerts its control over Company A in a way which damages the interests of the latter?

No specific protections are available to minority shareholders in this instance. The rule in *Foss* v. *Harbottle*,[46] as mentioned above, will apply to this situation two distinct principles, that of corporate personality and the internal management rule. Together they are a procedural obstacle to the enforcement of minority shareholders' rights. The first part of the rule is that the proper plaintiff in an action in respect of a wrong alleged to be done to a company is, prima facie, the company. The second part of the rule is that the court will not interfere with the internal management of companies acting within their powers and has no jurisdiction to do so.

The result is that a minority shareholder (even one which is itself a company) can rarely bring an action against those in control of the company in his or its own name. Equally, it is likely to be difficult, if not impossible, for him to bring an action in the name of the company. There is authority to suggest that where the right to use the company's name in an action lies with the directors, a general meeting has no power to override the decision of the board and to adopt it for itself.[47] Even where the Articles do give the shareholders the power in general meeting to commence litigation in the name of the company this will still require an ordinary majority. The exceptions to the rule have been discussed above, including the statutory exception contained in ss. 459 and 461(2)(c) of the Companies Act 1985. But for practical reasons the development of exceptions to the rule by the courts has been limited; it prevents suits from being brought by large numbers of plaintiffs and avoids the futility of a successful action being immediately overturned by a resolution of the company passed in general meeting which ratifies the action complained of. The rule of the majority has to some degree to be preserved to enable the business of the company to be conducted and not subverted by a minority attempting to protect its own interests.

---

[46] *Ibid.*

[47] *Breckland Group Holdings Ltd* v. *London & Suffolk Properties Ltd* (1988) 4 BCC 542.

aija

UNITED STATES

Catherine Habermehl, David R. Koepsell

Altreuter & Habermehl

Buffalo, New York

PROTECTION OF MINORITY SHAREHOLDERS

***EDITOR* MATTHIAS W. STECHER**

UNITED STATES

Catherine Habermehl, David R. Koepsell

Introduction

Corporate matters are, as a general proposition, creatures of contract governed in various degrees by the separate and distinct corporate statutory and decisional laws of each of the 50 states, the District of Columbia, and the federal government. While not purporting to create a comparison of all the state and federal provisions applicable to minority shareholders' rights, we do hope to provide a sampling of the protective devices implemented – with varying degrees of success – across the land in the continuing effort to fairly address certain universal concerns associated with corporate ownership.

The old story, so often told, of a prominent eastern newspaperman's reply to the question of what the shares in his company were worth, is very apt: "There are 51 shares that are worth $ 250,000. There are 49 shares that are not worth a _____." (*Humphreys* v. *Winous Co.*, 165 Ohio 45 (1956), 133 NE2d 780, quoting an address of John H. Doyle before the 1893 annual meeting of the Ohio State Bar).

1. Majority Requirements for Shareholders' Resolutions

1.1 What are the majority requirements in general?

Majority mandate remains the norm in corporate governance. The majority shareholders elect the directors who in turn – also by majority vote – choose the officers and employees, set compensation, determine business policies, and manage the operation. Unless otherwise altered by contract, by-law, or statute, the majority rules.

Although majority rule may be a hard-and-fast concept, determining just exactly what constitutes "a majority" can be more equivocal, and provides a good starting point for a discussion on the protection of minority shareholders' rights. Traditional concepts of majority rule can be affected by adding, to what would otherwise be a simple mathematical formula, issues such as voting rights and quorums.

New York shareholders, for example, are permitted to transact certain business at shareholders' meetings only if there is a quorum of shareholders present. The statutory quorum requirement is satisfied by the presence of a majority of all those shareholders entitled to vote.[1] Once a quorum is present, the corporate action subject to the vote of shareholders can be approved, with certain exceptions, by a majority of votes cast at that meeting, even if the number sufficient enough to qualify as a majority falls far short of the amount that equals a majority of all outstanding stock.[2] To illustrate, in a corporation with 100 shareholders, a shareholders' meeting may go forward as long as at least 51 shareholders are present in person or by proxy. If 26 of those shareholders agree on a certain proposal it will pass. Business can be transacted, therefore, even though the 26 shareholders number falls far short of the 51 that would constitute a majority of *all* shareholders.

Limiting voting rights to only certain classes of stock certificates is another method used to impact on voting allocation and strength. Two classes of stock can be issued, one that puts voting rights as a priority, and the other that focuses only on earnings and assets distribution. The second, called preferred shares, have no voting rights and do not get counted when determining quorums.[3] It is also possible to create within one class of stock an equal right to profit but different qualifications on voting rights (called common voting and common non-voting stock).[4]

Because shareholders exercise their influence over corporate matters most effectively through the election of directors (generally accomplished through a plurality of

1 Unless otherwise provided for in the certificate of incorporation or by-laws. See New York's Business Corporations Law (BCL) §608; see also, Delaware Code Ann. (DCA) §216.

2 BCL §614; note that if voting is done by class of stock, then a quorum would be a majority of holders of that particular class of shares. See also DCA §216.

3 Here it is necessary to briefly explain the concept of preferred shareholders and class distinction. The preferred shareholders are considered and treated more as passive investors, who instead of wishing to voice opinions on directorships and fundamental changes to the corporate structure (the matters normally left to the vote of shareholders) elect to take priority on payoff and stand first in line over the class of common stock holders when distributions are made. Because of their election, the preferred shareholders would not be counted in the majority vote.

4 See Internal Revenue Code §1361(c)(4) for the impact on Subchapter S election.

votes), majority control can also be influenced by methods of distributing votes for this purpose. Cumulative voting allows shareholders to accumulate votes and cast them for any one or more directors to be elected. It is an alternative to straight voting, where each share is entitled to one vote for each director to be elected, which allows any shareholder or group of shareholders with 51% or more of shares to place the board. With cumulative voting, each shareholder is entitled to one vote per share of stock, multiplied by the number of directors to be elected. The shareholder may cast all votes for a single director or may distribute them among the number of directors that can be seated. This allows shareholders to elect directors in some proportion to the number of shares held. It also gives smaller shareholders a chance to have some impact on the make-up of the board by casting all their votes for a particular candidate. Majority shareholders cannot so easily combat this sort of block voting where several directors are up for election. Cumulative voting for directors is mandatory in some states (required by state constitution or statute) and discretionary in others (provided for only if set forth in the certificate of incorporation or by-laws).[5]

Having qualified and quantified majority status, the next matter to address is which issues are most typically resolved by majority shareholder vote? In addition to the election and removal of directors, some jurisdictions provide for obtaining judicial assistance by majority vote. Shareholders in New York can petition a court for judicial dissolution of the corporation when certain conditions exist. Where shareholders believe that the corporation's assets are not sufficient to discharge liabilities, a resolution to so petition may be adopted by a majority of the shareholders.[6] A majority of shareholders generally vote on whether to adopt, amend or repeal the initial by-laws of a corporation as set up by the incorporators at the organizational meeting or the by-laws adopted, amended or repealed by an authorized board.[7] Amendment of the certificate of incorporation is generally authorized by vote of the board, followed by vote of the holders of a majority of all outstanding shares entitled to vote.

Although election of corporate officers is traditionally a function of the corporate directors, shareholders may elect the officers if the certificate of incorporation so provides.[8] Majority vote controls, and when officers have been elected by shareholders, only a majority shareholder vote can remove them.[9]

Shareholders may also be able to control whether directors or officers can be issued a right or option to purchase shares. In New York, if the issuance of such a right or option is an incentive to service or continued service, such issuance must be authorized at a meeting of shareholders by the vote of the holders of a majority of all outstanding shares entitled to vote thereon, or be authorized by and consistent with a plan adopted by such a vote of the shareholders.[10]

A good example of the care that must be taken when establishing voting rights and majority status is set forth in the case of *In re Laser Tech, Inc.*[11] Laser Tech,

---

[5] BCL §618.
[6] BCL §1103.
[7] BCL §601.
[8] BCL §715.
[9] BCL §716.
[10] BCL §505.
[11] 35 A.D.2d 994 (2d Dept. 1970).

Inc. had 355,000 corporate shares issued and outstanding. One shareholder who held 127,500 shares called a special shareholders' meeting for the purpose of removing, without cause, two directors who together owned 127,500 shares. Another 100,000 shares were publicly held. Holders of 283,950 shares were present at the meeting, and 158,450 of those shares voted in favour of removal. The chairman of the meeting, however, declared that the removal had not passed, because the proposition had not been supported by a majority of the outstanding stock. The lower court disagreed, finding that no more than a majority of outstanding stock present at the meeting was required by the applicable statutes. The appellate court in turn reversed, opining that the corporate by-laws, read in conjunction with the applicable state statutes, made it clear that the removal of a director without cause could only be accomplished by a majority vote of all the outstanding corporate stock.[12]

First, the court noted that by statute, a director could only be removed without cause if, and in the manner that, the certificate of incorporation or by-laws so provided. Laser Tech's by-laws provided that any one or more of the directors were removable without cause by vote of the shareholders holding a majority of the outstanding stock of the corporation entitled to vote, present in person or by proxy, at any special meeting of the shareholders. The court distinguished this language from §614 of New York's Business Corporation Law, which grants majority voice to *those present* at the meeting. Second, and perhaps more importantly, the court made special note of the fact that "interests to be served differ from corporation to corporation", therefore there must be strong adherence to the position expressed in the by-laws. The court made no attempt to hide its utmost concern for the preservation of the rights of the holders of the 100,000 shares of publicly owned stock, especially given the dominance of the three major shareholders. The court read the by-laws as insisting upon the presence or participation of those outside shareholders in order to prevent major changes at meetings at which their interests were not represented.

1.2 Which resolutions require a greater majority?

Those resolutions dealing with substantive changes in the corporate structure can generally only be accomplished by a greater than majority percentage vote. In those circumstances, most state statues require a two-thirds majority vote of shareholders to approve board resolutions covering

- merger or consolidation of domestic corporations;
- corporate guarantees not in furtherance of corporate purpose;
- the sale or lease or exchange of all or substantially all the assets of the corporation if not made in the usual or regular course of the business;
- a share exchange between two domestic corporations; and
- authorization to dissolve.[13]

---

12 *Ibid.*

13 BCL §§903, 908, 909, 913, 1001.

Other states, such as Delaware, demonstrate a more management-friendly orientation, and permit merger or consolidation of domestic corporations with a simple majority vote by shareholders of both corporations.[14]

1.3 To what extent can they be modified by the Articles of Association?

The relationship between corporate owner (shareholders) and corporate management (directors and officers) is essentially contractual. Therefore, many modifications of the majority rule of governance can be negotiated. For example, the certificate of incorporation or corporate by-laws may provide for a quorum of less than a majority (albeit generally not lower than a certain percentage, such as one-third, of those shareholders entitled to vote). Conversely, the certificate of incorporation could provide for a greater than majority quorum, a so-called "supermajority".[15] This is also why it is often said that whether your intent is to protect minority shareholders' rights or silence the minority stock owner's voice, you are never at a greater position of strength than at the beginning of establishing a business.[16] The clearest limitation on the right to negotiate voting rights is by state constitution or statute. Where the law sets forth certain minima, those cannot be reduced by inclusion of lesser provisions in the by-laws or articles. Negotiated modifications can be seen in provisions which raise the number of votes required to amend the Articles of Incorporation or by-laws, change the classification of a stock, and issue new stock

2. Influence on the Decision-Making Process

2.1 Do minority shareholders have the right to call a shareholders' meeting?

There is generally held an annual meeting of shareholders at which the election of directors takes place. Other matters may be placed on the agenda, but issues of a fundamental nature cannot be raised unless that matter has been included in a notice of the annual meeting. For the annual meeting, management controls the topics listed in the notice. The notice must comply with applicable state statutes, the articles and the by-laws.

Special meetings of the shareholders may be called by such person or persons as may be so authorized by the certificate or incorporation or the by-laws. At that

---

[14] DCA §251.

[15] BCL §608(b).

[16] An amendment to the certificate which alters the greater requirement must be supported by two-thirds of holders of all outstanding shares entitled to vote – or an even greater amount if the certificate so specifies, BCL §616.

meeting, only the business related to the purpose set forth in the notice can be discussed.[17] Individual corporate by-laws and meeting protocol would govern who is entitled to choose the topic and send notice, but states do provide some minimum requirements that permit minority shareholders to insist upon a meeting. For example, New York allows 10% of shares entitled to vote in an election of directors to demand the call of a special meeting for the election of directors if a certain amount of time has passed and the annual election still has not occurred. If shareholders of a corporation believe that the corporation's assets are not sufficient to discharge liabilities or that a dissolution would be beneficial to the shareholders, a meeting to adopt a resolution stating such may be called by 10% of all outstanding shares entitled to vote (although the Articles of Incorporation can authorize a lesser proportion). The resolution need only be adopted by majority. If the concern is over a deadlock among directors or shareholders, then a petition for dissolution may be presented at the request of 50% of all outstanding shares. Where fraud or negligence on the part of the directors is suspected, then the petition need only be supported by 20% of all outstanding shares.[18]

Minority shareholders do have, to a limited extent, the right to control what does *not* belong on the agenda. In addition to insisting upon strict compliance with the rule that only stated business can be discussed at special meetings, federal proxy rules can play a part. Proxy regulations require that certain information be provided to shareholders before a vote can be taken on the issue. If the proxy solicitation is misleading or otherwise erroneous, a minority shareholder can take advantage of the threat of federal agency assistance and a private right of action to table discussions.

2.2 Do they have the right to put matters on the agenda?

Shareholders have a right to put matters on the agenda only if there is statutory basis for calling a special meeting (see above, 2.1), or if individual by-laws or meeting protocols so dictate.

3. Rights of Information, Independent Auditing and Supervision

3.1 To what extent do the (minority) shareholders have a right to be informed on company matters?

In keeping with the philosophy that control by management is distinct from the ownership interest in obtaining a return on investment, the information available to

[17] BCL §602.
[18] BCL §§1103, 1104, 1105.

shareholders is generally limited. Shareholders of large, publicly traded corporations have access to continually updated items of information prescribed by federal securities law.[19] This information includes outstanding securities, compensation, key contracts, options to purchase securities, bonus and profit sharing plans, and overall financial structure. With the closely held corporation, however, state statutes rarely guarantee anything more than a right (other than to notice of matters to be addressed at special meetings, heretofore addressed) to inspect certain books and records after a particular triggering event. If a dispute arises, a shareholder may have no choice but to go to court to litigate the issue. State statutes generally list only the minimum that must be readily available to shareholders. Certificates or by-laws can always provide for more extensive disclosure.

In Alabama, for example, there is a right to inspect all corporate books and records only if the shareholder has held stock for at least six months or owns 5% of any class of stock. The request must be done in writing and state the purpose for the inspection.[20] If a corporate officer wrongly believes the purpose is improper or otherwise wrongly refuses to allow the inspection, the officer must pay the shareholder 10% of the value of the shares. In Florida, the right extends to relevant corporate books and records of account, minutes, and records of shareholders. What is "relevant" could become a point of contention. Other states require the request to be in writing and submitted a period of days before the actual inspection or copying of records.

Another means available to acquire certain financial information is the Internal Revenue Code. The Internal Revenue Service imposes a special tax on a corporation that too greatly accumulates its earnings instead of distributing dividends to shareholders. This provides a basis for a derivative action (the directors violated their duty of loyalty to the company by subjecting it to IRS scrutiny and unnecessary taxation), and also creates a valid purpose enabling minority shareholders to obtain financial information to which they may not otherwise have access under state law or by-laws. There are also informational filings that must be made to the federal tax authorities regarding corporate earnings and key personnel compensation.

An officer may refuse to permit inspection if he or she believes the request is not made for a proper purpose, including harassment, idle curiosity, or misappropriating important corporate information for personal gain. Requests will not be considered improper, however, if premised on a need to know whether earnings and profits support a claim for dividend distribution, how to value shares, or vote on a matter that is the subject of a special meeting, or the remuneration of officers, directors, and majority shareholders. There is nothing that prohibits the shareholder from reviewing these documents with legal or accounting assistance under the theory that access to information is meaningless if that information cannot be understood.

---

19 Securities and Exchange Act of 1934, §§12, 13.

20 Code of Alabama, Corporations, Partnerships and Associations §10-2B-16.02(b).

3.2 Do they have the right to demand independent auditing or to initiate the supervision of company matters by an independent institution?

If the extent of waste, overreaching, fraud, or arbitrary and capricious behaviour on the part of directors or officers or majority shareholders so warrants, a court can order the business into receivership and liquidation. Upon a showing of irreparable loss or material injury to the corporation or its assets, the court has discretion to appoint a temporary receiver, or other form of custodian in charge to manage the business for a period. A court may also elect to retain closer jurisdiction over a particular claim for a period of years, providing the minority shareholders ready access to a familiar tribunal without preventing the management from continuing with valid business operations over which custodians may have had less exposure. The difficulty with the court retaining jurisdiction is that this depends upon whether the litigants are assigned a court willing to keep a case on its docket.

There is nothing that would preclude a company from including in its by-laws a provision for periodic access and auditing, with audited reports and financial statements being provided to the shareholders on a regular basis. It is also possible to list in those provisions the name of an independent auditing company to be used. Anything shy of an agreement like this would require initiating litigation upon a good faith belief that some improper event has occurred.

4. Capital Increases and Distributions

4.1 To what extent do (minority) shareholders have the right to participate in capital increases?

Shareholders generally only have the right to participate in capital increases to the extent of their pre-emptive rights. Pre-emptive rights give to existing shareholders the option of purchasing new stock issued by the corporation and thereby maintaining current proportions of power. Careful consideration must be given to the various state laws. Some states limit preemptive rights, others offer no statutory basis but allow for rights if granted in the certificate of incorporation, while the remainder do provide a statutory basis with room to expand upon their use through Articles of Incorporation or by-laws. One reason for the difference of opinion on this matter is that pre-emptive rights – as helpful as they are in maintaining a balance of power – can cause a delay in the public issuance of stock or otherwise hinder financing options.

Arkansas precludes the use of pre-emptive rights with respect to shares issued as compensation to directors and officers, shares issued within six months of incorporating, or shares exchanged for property.[21] Louisiana requires the shareholder to ex-

[21] Arkansas Business and Commercial Law 4-27-630 (3).

ercise the right within 15 days of notice of the issuance.[22] New York extends no rights to treasury shares (shares reacquired by the corporation which remain uncancelled in its treasury). In Alabama, the price is to be set by the directors.[23] Even in states where these are not required, the same limitations may be set forth in the articles of incorporation.

A look at those few state laws should provide the reader with a sense of how pre-emptive rights can be circumvented. Rights cannot be exercised if the new stock is issued when the minority holder cannot afford it or does not have the time to liquidate the cash for purchase. There are also pre-emptive rights for issuance of treasury stock (reissued stock). Directors or officers can elect to take compensation (an issue, if left to the shareholders, generally subject only to majority vote) in shares. Stock could also be sold to others in exchange for property such as real estate, an event which may be difficult to challenge as violating the business judgment rule.

4.2 Do minority shareholders have the right to demand dividends or other distributions?

There is no automatic right to dividend distribution unless minimum dividend levels have been set in the articles or by-laws. Dividends can be fixed at a specific rate by those articles. Otherwise, corporate directors are given wide latitude concerning how earnings are to be retained and, relatedly, whether dividends should be dispersed. The minority shareholder does have an ally, if necessary, in the IRS. The IRS can impose a tax penalty on any entity that "stores" too much of its profit. Directors, therefore, must be careful not to act in such a manner as to impose the penalty and invite a derivative suit.[24] Those directors wishing to squeeze out minority shareholders or minimize the value of a minority shareholder's stake must be aware that an active pursuit by the board along these lines could amount to a federal securities violation as well.[25]

5. Derivative Actions

5.1 Can (minority) shareholders enforce rights that the company has against other shareholders, directors, or third parties?

Derivative actions are permitted, and may be brought against directors and third parties – and other shareholders if that shareholder has had any influence over a

---

22 Louisiana Statutes Annotated, Corporations and Associations §12:72.

23 See *supra*, note 20, §10-2b-6.30.

24 See, eg *United States* v. *Byrum*, 408 U.S. 125, at 137–141 (1972).

25 Rule 10b-5.

wrongful act against the corporation. In New York, the actions are governed by statute, which is "broad and covers every form of waste of assets and violation of duty whether as a result of intention, negligence, or predatory acquisition".[26] Waste and self-dealing are bases for attack because New York requires majority shareholders – not just directors – of closed corporations to conform to the high standards of a fiduciary relationship.[27] Some states recognize an enhanced fiduciary duty in close corporations; a duty that amounts to a strict good faith standard, and analogize the relationship of the directors and shareholders to partners in a partnership.[28] Delaware recognizes the claim for "an indirect injury [to a shareholder] as a result of the wrong done to the corporation".[29] As a general matter, this type of suit is available where there has been a violation of a duty of care whether it be gross negligence, mismanagement, self-dealing, excessive compensation, or usurpation of corporate opportunity.

An interesting aspect of derivative claims can arise where a case is brought in federal court. Federal Rule of Civil Procedure 23.1 governs derivative actions by shareholders. This rule allows shareholders to initiate actions on behalf of their corporations if they allege: "(1) that the plaintiff was a shareholder or member at the time of the transaction of which the plaintiff complains or that the plaintiff's share or membership thereafter devolved on the plaintiff by operation of law, and (2) that the action is not a collusive one to confer jurisdiction on a court of the United States which it would not otherwise have". The complaint must also allege in what way the plaintiff has sought correction of the complained-of problems. The hurdles are fairly well expressed in the statute, and are mirrored in most state derivative action laws. The purpose is to prevent strike suits by minority shareholders and to minimize undue interference in corporate management.[30] Potential litigants must be aware that a conflict of interest may disable a shareholder from "fairly and adequately" representing the interests of the other shareholders;[31] however, demands on the board to resolve or correct a claimed problem need not be made where such demands would prove futile.[32]

There are other procedural rules that may apply in the action, such as providing a security bond or having the settlements and attorney's fees subject to judicial review. One advantage to those bringing derivative suits is the potential for having attorney's fees paid for by the corporation and not the watchdog shareholder. In a recent federal decision, the court held that a corporate plaintiff need not allege damages to itself. It was enough to state that a corporate fiduciary entrusted with potentially valuable information appropriates that information for his or her own use "even though, in doing so, he causes no injury to the corporation."[33] "An action

---

[26] BCL §§626 and 720, *Rapoport* v. *Schneider*, 29 N.Y.2d 396, 400 (1972).

[27] See *Street* v. *Vitti*, 685 F.Supp 379 (S.D.N.Y. 1988).

[28] See *Donahue* v. *Rodd Electotype Co. of New England, Inc.*, 367 Mass 578, 328 N.E.2d 505 (1975).

[29] *Lewis* v. *Spe\ncer*, (Chancery, CA 8651), aff'd 577 A.2d 753 (1990).

[30] *In re Ionosphere Clubs, Inc.*, 17 F.3d 606 (2d Cir. 1994).

[31] *Ryan* v. *Aetna Life Ins. Co.*, 765 F.Supp 134 (S.D.N.Y. 1991).

[32] *Grobow* v. *Perot*, 539 A.2d 180, 186 (Del. 1988).

[33] *Zaciva Communications Corp.* v. *Horowitz*, 826 F.Supp 86 (S.D.N.Y. 1993), quoting from *Diamond* v. *Oreamuno*, 24 N.Y.2d 494, 301 N.Y.S.2d 78 (1969).

for breach of fiduciary duty is a prophylactic rule intended to remove all incentive to breach - not simply to compensate for damages in the event of a breach."[34] These sentiments, however, may not be embraced in all jurisdictions.

6. Other "Formal" Rights

6.1 Do minority shareholders have any other specific rights comparable to those mentioned in 2–5 above?

Perhaps the most daunting of available rights potentially available to a minority shareholder are those made available under federal law. Although application is limited, its availability is helpful inasmuch as it provides a basis for venue within the federal court system and the potential for federal agency oversight.

The cornerstone of the federal action is Rule 10b-5 under the Securities Exchange Act of 1934. It is, in essence, a broad, anti-fraud provision which comes as close to being the federal corporate law as the US legal system will allow.[35] Its purpose is to provide a private right of action as a means of challenging deceptive acts which create a detriment to investors. In order to prove securities fraud, a claimant must show that the defendant, with scienter, made misrepresentations of material facts or failed to disclose material facts, and that the plaintiff relied on those misrepresentations or omissions and suffered a loss as a result of the misrepresentations or omissions.[36] Federal courts reluctant to intervene in matters which they deem belong to the individual states will cite *Santa Fe Indust. Inc.* v. *Green.* [37] This case limited the applicability of s. 10(b) to cases which involve fraud or deception. Other courts are more inclined to interject, personify the business, express great concern (not as much over the loss to the hapless shareholder, but over the injury to the corporation itself), and consider "unfairness to minority shareholders" as evidence of deception.[38]

Other federal provisions include sections of the Securities Act of 1933 and the Securities Exchange Act of 1934 which regulate proxy solicitation in companies with registered securities; mergers; statements issued to entice purchasers of stock; going private transactions; tender offers; and officers' or directors' purchases of stock. Actions can also be brought under the federal Racketeer Influenced and Corrupt Organization Act (RICO). To establish the requisite pattern of racketeering activity prohibited under the act, a plaintiff must show, *inter alia*, that the acts complained of extended over a long period of time or that the defendant's activities

---

[34] *ABKCO Music, Inc.* v. *Harrisongs Music, Ltd.* 722 F2d 988 (2d Cir. 1983).

[35] Eg The *Erie* doctrine.

[36] Securities Exchange Act of 1934, Sec. 10(b), as amended, 15 USCA §78J(b); *Burke* v. *Jacoby*, 981 F2d 1372 (2d Cir. 1992).

[37] 430 US 462 (1977).

[38] See, eg, *Frankel* v. *Slotkin*, 984 F2d 133 (2d Cir, 1993) ("A corporation is injured when it is fraudulently induced into issuing its own securities for less than their fair value because of misappropriation of inside information").

are not isolated or sporadic. The claim is available against corporate directors and officers. The claim usually fails when it is based on a defendant's narrowly directed actions toward a single fraudulent end with a limited goal, lasting over a limited period of time. In "closed-ended" allegations of RICO violations, such as this, efforts at covering up the initial fraudulent act are inadequate to establish the continuity element. Furthermore, a recent federal case held that shareholders are prohibited from bringing individual suits under RICO unless they can demonstrate a direct harm to them in addition to an economic injury to the corporation. The court noted that "minority shareholders have been granted standing under RICO when a majority shareholder violated a fiduciary duty owed directly to plaintiff, in addition to committing fraud on the company which caused plaintiff's stock to depreciate in value".[39] A prosecution can also be made under the auspices of federal mail and wire fraud statutes, provided the shareholder can allege a scheme to defraud and an intent to do actual harm.[40]

7. Extension of These Rights by Statute or Shareholder's Agreements

7.1 Can the Articles of Association provide for additional rights of the minority shareholders? If not, can such rights be provided for in shareholders' agreements? Are these options commonly used?

The contractual nature of the relationship between management and owners has been discussed throughout the responses above. If a special provision for particular minority representation is agreed to by a majority of shareholders, the provision can be included in the Articles of Incorporation or by-laws. Additional protection, certainly, can be set forth in a shareholders' agreement. These agreements are generally limited to voting rights issues, but can be much more expansive. They may include:

- how shares are to be voted in the election of directors;
- who are to be appointed officers;
- restrictions on the power of majority shareholders to change articles or by-laws;
- limitations on which shareholders can be employees and the terms of their employment;
- limitations on shareholders' rights to work for other businesses;
- matters concerning dividends and use of earnings;
- multiple signature requirements for contracts, loans, or checks; and
- mechanisms for conflict resolution, including buyouts and mandatory arbitration.[41]

---

[39] *Chanoff* v. *US Surgical Corp.*, 857 F.Supp 1101 (D.Conn. 1994).
[40] *US* v. *Harris*, 805 F.Supp 166 (S.D.N.Y. 1992).
[41] *Business Strategies*, p.6725, para. 1137, Shareholder Agreements.

It is worth emphasizing that if any portion of a shareholders' agreement arguably serves to undercut the function of the directors, a review of state statutes must be made to determine whether there must be a corresponding limitation in the Articles of Incorporation. In other words, sometimes the agreement will not be enough.

Shareholders may also enter into voting agreements, whereby they agree to vote their stock as a block.

8. Remedies Where a Shareholders' Resolution or Other Action Impairs the Rights of Minority Shareholders

8.1 What are the requirements for such remedies?

Remedies would be available if the claimant successfully brings a derivative, direct, or federal statute-based action. As discussed, a derivative action brought by a shareholder in the name of the corporation would require a showing of some violation of the duty of care owed to the corporation by one who has a fiduciary responsibility. In a direct action, an individual would bring a claim in his or her name alone for enforcement of shareholders' rights involving a proposed merger, recapitalization, redemption (or similar transaction), a request to inspect books, a failure to call a meeting or otherwise hamper voting rights, a violation of pre-emptive rights, or the ability to compel dividends, force a dissolution, or enforce an employment agreement.[42] The nature of the claim may be contractual, for which a showing of breach would be adequate to require the breaching party to provide restitution.

Where the nature of the claim relates to fiduciary relationships or misrepresentation, however, deference to the business judgment rule makes it incumbent upon the aggrieved party to show malfeasance or other form of impropriety. Courts have expanded upon the notion of a fiduciary relationship among shareholders so that, even where the majority can point to some legitimate business purpose, the minority may demonstrate a breach where that objective was achievable through some alternative route less harmful to the minority.[43]

8.2 When do the courts of your country accept these requirements?

The exact elements that must be pleaded and proved would be governed primarily by state law of contract and fraud.[44]

---

42 See, Finkelstein, *Delaware Law of Corporations and Business Organizations* § 13.6.

43 *Wilkes* v. *Springside Nursing Home, Inc.*, 310 Mass. 842, 851–52 (1976).

44 See, eg *Balsam* v. *Pure Tech Intern.*, 864 F.Supp 1440 (S.D.N.Y. 1994) (involving fraud).

8.3 What remedies are available to the claimant?

There are generally four types of remedies available–appraisal, reversal of the improper transaction, damages, and dissolution of the corporation. Injunctive relief may be available regardless of what the ultimate remedy will be. Appraisal is typically considered available whenever the majority effects a fundamental change in the corporation (eg merger or consolidation). Dissolution, however, is considered a drastic remedy available only where the actions of the majority shareholders are found to be oppressive.[45]

It is the general rule that, because a shareholders' derivative suit seeks to vindicate a wrong done to the corporation through enforcement of a corporate cause of action, any recovery obtained is for the benefit of the injured corporation.[46] Where, however, the plaintiff sues in an individual capacity to recover damages resulting in harm, not to the corporation, but to individual shareholders, the suit is personal, not derivative, and it is appropriate for damages to be awarded directly to those shareholders. Under either theory, damages and equitable relief, such as rescission or dissolution, are available. Furthermore, the derivative and direct actions are not mutually exclusive remedies.[47]

Claimants are entitled to seek temporary restraining orders and preliminary injunctions if they can demonstrate the likelihood of success on the merits, irreparable harm absent the relief requested, and a balance of the equities in their favour.[48] Where a provision is illegally adopted in conflict with the statutory law, an injunction is appropriate regardless of the extent of the harm.

The injunctive relief could include requiring corporate action, for example directing the withdrawal of certain banking resolutions, and might require the movants to provide a suitable undertaking.

9. Specific Protection if the Company is Controlled by Another Company

9.1 What are the rights and remedies of a shareholder of Company A when Company B gains control over it (by acquiring the majority of its shares or otherwise)?

Generally, the sale of substantially all of the corporate assets triggers the right of dissenting shareholders to an appraisal. While appraisal rights are always available

---

45 See, C. Murdock, "The Evolution of Effective Remedies for Minority Shareholders and its Impact Upon Valuation of Minority Shares", 65 *Notre Dame L.R.* 425 (discussing concept of "oppression").

46 *Glenn* v. *Hoteltron Systems, Inc.*, 547 N.Y.S.2d 816, 74 N.Y.2d 386, (N.Y. 1989).

47 Moreover, "[t]he fact that a particular act of directors may constitute a wrong to the corporation which may be righted ordinarily on behalf of the corporation does not bar a stockholder from having redress if that act effects a separate and distinct wrong to him independently of the wrong to the corporation. Redress of this latter wrong is available to him personally despite the right of a present stockholder to redress the wrong in a derivative action so far as it relates to the corporation", 539 N.Y.S.2d at 69.

48 *Bank of New York Co., Inc.* v. *Irving Bank Corp.*, 139 Misc.2d 665 (N.Y.Sup. 1988).

to those shareholders who may object to a corporate consolidation or merger, this is not an available form of relief if the sale of assets is deemed part of the regular course of business, such as with an inventory-intensive operation. Some states also deny the right of appraisal in asset sales where the selling corporation retains control of a certain amount of assets.[49] As previously mentioned, minority shareholders may also be entitled to have the sale, or other transaction by which control is transferred, approved by a supermajority. If the transfer was made by stock sale, and prior to the sale the corporation purchased the minority shareholders' stock at a price substantially lower than the price to be obtained upon sale of the business to a third party, a fraud-based claim may be available too that would permit recovery of damages for the difference.

9.2 What are the shareholder's rights and remedies when Company B exerts its control over Company A in a way which damages the interests of the latter?

An attack on a controlling company can come from two fronts. First, minority shareholders of the controlling company may be afforded standing under the double derivative theory, allowing them to sue to correct any damage done to the subsidiary. Under this theory, plaintiffs must establish that a stockholder controls a subsidiary, and there is no independence between the parent stockholder and subsidiary. "[I]t can not be expected that the controlling stockholder will authorize a suit on behalf of the subsidiary against itself for harm to the subsidiary".[50]

However, as for the minority shareholder of Company A, a derivative action can be maintained against Company B as controlling shareholder with the same limitations applicable to derivative actions in general. Actions against the directors and officers of the controlling corporation would require a showing of the requisite fiduciary relationship between those officers and the subsidiary, something that might require an successful showing of alter ego overreaching.

10. Dissenters' Rights under the Model Business Corporation Act

We would be remiss not to discuss the various rights and remedies made available by the Model Business Corporation Act (MBCA). The MBCA, like other model codes, is an attempt to formulate, out of a mish-mash of common law, a consistent

---

[49] "Is a fistfull of dollars an answer? A critical look at dissenters' rights under the revised model business corporation act", 12 *Journal of Law and Commerce*, 211 Spring 1993.

[50] *Pessin* v. *Chris-Craft Industries, Inc.*, 181 A.D.2d 66, 586 NYS 2d 584 (1992).

and fair model statutory scheme which might be acceptable and applicable in all US jurisdictions. Needless to say, the Act has not been adopted by everyone nor without some revision. However, as a model code, it offers some vision of what the future of minority shareholders' right might look like.

In general, the MBCA offers dissenters' appraisal rights for any situation in which the majority shareholders effect a fundamental change in the corporation.[51] Essentially, this means there are such rights whenever a shareholders' vote is required. The Act specifically denies dissenters' rights, however, when a corporation's assets are sold for cash which is to be distributed within the year to the shareholders.[52] Significantly, the Act eliminates the Stock Market exception noted above.[53]

A dissenter must, in order to prevail under the Act, not have voted in favour of the proposed action and he or she must, within 30 to 60 days of receiving notice of the proposed changes, file a written notice of his or her intent to demand payment.[54] The dissenter's notice must be given before a vote is actually taken or else he becomes unable to be paid for his shares.[55] Within 10 days of the corporate action, the corporation must send a "dissenter's notice" to those who dissented from that action. This notice must indicate to the shareholder where and when his demand for payment must be sent and in what manner the shares will be exchanged.[56] If the shareholder fails to comply with the requirements of the notice, he loses his rights as a dissenter. If the dissenter complies with the notice, then it must pay the dissenter the amount which it considers to be the fair market value of the dissenter's shares and include with the payment corporate financial statements and other explanatory materials.[57] Clearly, this provision is designed to reduce the need for intervention by the courts through judicial valuation proceedings. If the dissenter does not agree with the corporate valuation he may then make his own determination of value and interest due and demand payment.[58] Finally, if the parties are unable to compromise, the corporation must commence a judicial valuation proceeding.[59]

The Model Business Corporation Act is designed to streamline dissenter's actions and to keep them, for as long as possible, from bogging down the courts. In so doing, the Act makes dissent an exclusive remedy, except that dissenters may yet maintain actions for fraud and illegality, and sometimes breach of fiduciary duty.[60] To prevent frivolous actions on the part of dissenters, the MBCA provides that costs associated with appraisal proceedings are chargeable to dissenters who are found to have acted in bad faith.[61]

---

51 M.B.C.A. §13.02 (1984).
52 *Ibid.* §13.02 (a)(3) (1984).
53 Compare Model Business Corp. Act §§80, 81 (1969) (revised 1978).
54 M.B.C.A. §13.21(a) (1984).
55 *Ibid.*
56 *Ibid.* at §13.23 (a).
57 *Ibid.* at §13.25.
58 *Ibid.* at §13.28 (a).
59 *Ibid.* at §13.30 (a).
60 *Ibid.* at §13.02 (b).
61 *Ibid.* at §13.31 (b) (1984).

Appendix: the Limited Liability Company

A discussion of minority shareholders would not be complete without an analysis into the relatively new form of business organization that is crossing the country at a rapid pace.

The limited liability company is a hybrid form of business which combines limited liability with pass-through income taxation. It is said to have attributes similar to the *Limitada* and the *Gesellschaft mit beschränkter Haftung*, as well as the holding companies of the United Kingdom.

Instead of stock certificates, the individual members (which can be individuals, corporate entities or partnerships) receive a membership interest reflective of their entitlement to share in the profits of the business. The business is governed by Articles of Organization which can be amended by a majority in interest of the members entitled to vote thereon, and management is vested in the members, unless the articles provide for management by manager or class of managers. The majority in interest of members entitled to vote shall constitute a quorum, although the operating agreement (the by-laws equivalent) may provide for a greater quorum or a lesser quorum which may not be less than one-third in interest of members entitled to vote.

As the name implies, the liability of members and managers of an LLC is limited. Members and managers are not liable for the debts, obligations, or the liabilities of a properly formed LLC. As well, judgments do not reach the members or managers unless a state's regulations provide otherwise. LLC members or managers are generally not properly named as parties in proceedings against an LLC unless the object of such a suit is the enforcement of a member's rights or liability regarding the LLC.[62] Interested manager transactions are not void or voidable so long as the interest is disclosed and the transaction fair. Finally, members must be wary of liability for certain promises to contribute and for excess distributions.[63]

---

[62] See, Lubaroff and Schurr, *Forming and Using Limited Liability Companies and Limited Liability Partnerships* (Practicing Law Institute 1994), at 163.

[63] *Ibid.* at 164.

ANNEX I: COMPARATIVE TABLES

Nathalie Everaert
Matthias W. Stecher

PROTECTION OF MINORITY SHAREHOLDERS

EDITOR MATTHIAS W. STECHER

Austria

1.	**Majority requirements for shareholders' resolutions**	
1.1	General majorities	Simple majorities are required for the adoption of resolutions in both types of company
1.2	Resolutions requiring greater majorities	
	Joint stock company	A majority of three-quarters of the share capital is required for many resolutions, notably the modification of the Articles of Association, and capital increase or decrease
	Private limited company	(a) A majority of three-quarters is required in specific cases: notably, the amendment of the Articles of Association (b) Unanimity is required for the modification of the objects of the company, the constitution of a merger, or an increase in the shareholders' obligations (c) A majority of 90% is needed in two cases of transfer of the company's assets
1.3	Modification of majorities	The majority requirements may be increased by the Articles of Association
2.	**Influence on the decision-making process**	
2.1	The right to call a meeting	
	Joint stock company	A majority of 5% of the share capital may call a shareholders' meeting by indicating in writing the purpose and reasons. Should the management board refuse to convene the meeting, the shareholders may obtain a judicial order
	Private limited company	A minority of 10% may call a shareholders' meeting under the same conditions as stated above
2.2	The right to put matters on the agenda	
	Joint stock company	A minority of 5% is entitled to request certain matters on the agenda if this is done in specific delays before the general meeting
	Private limited company	A minority of 10% may request in a signed petition items to be included on the agenda. (This must be done in the three days following the announcement of the general meeting.)
3.	**Rights for information, audit and supervision**	
3.1	Information	
	Joint stock company	(a) Every shareholder has the right to examine, within the 14 days prior to the annual meeting: the accounts, the financial statement, the reports on the supervisory board, the situation report and the profit distribution proposal
	Private limited company	(b) The shareholders at the general meeting may consult the register of shareholders and holders of personal shares

Austria cont.

3.2	Auditing and supervision	The shareholders have an automatic right to information concerning the annual accounts and the report on the situation of the company. They equally have the right of access to the books and documents of the company in the same conditions as above In general, a minority of 10% of the share capital may ask the court for an examination of the company's affairs
4.	**Capital increase and dividend payment**	
4.1	Participation in the capital increase	
	Joint stock company	Every shareholder has a pre-emptive right proportionate to the amount of shares already owned. This right exists however only in the case of ordinary capital increases. The exclusion of this right requires a majority of 75%
	Private limited company	The shareholders have the same right as above, unless specified otherwise in the Articles of Association
4.2	Right to demand dividends	
	Joint stock company	Every shareholder has the right to a distribution of the net profit shown in the annual account. They can also raise a claim against any resolution deciding upon the transfer of net profit to reserves
	Private limited company	Every shareholder has the right to a distribution of the net earnings shown in the balance sheet
5	**Derivative actions**	
	Joint stock company	In principle, the shareholders do not have the right to derivative actions. A minority of 10% may demand that the company raise a claim against certain persons, however these claims remain asserted by the company itself and not by the shareholders
	Private limited company	The shareholders do not have the right to derivative action. A minority of 10% (or representing the nominal amount of 10 million schillings) may present on behalf of the company claims against the managers and members of teh supervisory board
6.	**Other "formal" rights**	
	Joint stock company	The minority shareholders are granted many additional statutory rights in both the joint-stock company and the private limited company. For example: (a) A minority of 5% can ask for a judicial order to remove a liquidator (b) A minority of 5% can file for a final examination of the accounts and the balance of liquidation (c) The same minority may file for the annulment of a decision of the general meeting
	Private limited company	(a) A minority of 10% can file for a judicial dismissal of a member of the supervisory board (b) A minority of 10% can file for the appointment of an independent liquidator (c) Any shareholder can file for the dismissal of a manager for an important reason

Belgium

1.	**Majority requirements for shareholders' resolutions**	
1.1	General majorities	The common majority of 50% + 1 vote applies if no other specific majority or quorum was agreed upon
1.2	Resolutions requiring greater majorities	(a) The modification of the Articles of Association and the reduction of capital require a quorum of 50% and a majority of 75% (b) The modification of the purpose of the company requires a quorum of 50% and a majority of 80%
1.3	Modification of the required majorities	The Articles of Association can provide for specific majorities and quorums. They may also limit the exercise of voting rights if this is done without discrimination. However, the statutory provisions may only be extended and not reduced
2.	**Influence on the decision-making process**	
2.1	The right to call a meeting	The shareholders representing 20% of the capital may request a meeting. The board of directors must comply within a reasonable period
2.2	The right to put matters on the agenda	The shareholders can decide on the items for the agenda of the meeting they have called
3.	**Rights for information, audit and supervision**	
3.1	Information	Each shareholder has the right to obtain a copy of: (a) the balance sheet (b) the accounts of the company (c) the annual report (d) the directors' report (e) the auditors' report The request must be addressed to the board of directors, who must comply. However, the directors do not have to answer questions if this would be contrary to the interests of the company
3.2	Auditing and supervision	
	Large companies	These have an obligation to nominate a public accountant as an independent auditor
	Small companies	Each shareholder has the right to ask for a public accountant to have an audit performed
4.	**Capital increase and dividend payment**	
4.1	Participation in the capital increase	All shareholders have a preferential right to participate in a capital increase. They must exercise this right within 15 days after the opening day of subscription
4.2	Right to demand dividends	The individual shareholder has no right concerning the distribution of dividends. The shareholders' meeting decides by common majority on the distribution of dividends upon the proposal of the management
5.	**Derivative actions**	
5.1	Derivative action against other shareholders	The shareholders do not have the right to bring derivative actions against other shareholders. Shareholders nevertheless have the possibility of a direct claim against another shareholder for breach of duty

Belgium cont.

5.2	Derivative action against directors	This action is possible for minority shareholders holding at least 1% of the share capital (and who have not previously given discharge to the director during the shareholders' meeting)
5.3	Derivative action against third parties	Claims against third parties can only be introduced by the company
6.0	**Other "formal" rights**	The new Reparation Act has provided the minority shareholders with two new rights
6.1	Lock-out	Shareholders holding at least 30% of the shares can force other shareholders to sell their shares for a price determined by the court. This action is only accepted by the courts if there is a fundamental disagreement between the shareholders. The courts decide strictly on the basis of the interests of the company
6.2	Opt-out	A shareholder may ask the court to force another shareholder to purchase his shares The shareholders have other rights such as the possibility to have the decisions of the shareholders' meeting declared void on the basis of irregularity, breach of the Articles of Association, abuse of power of *ultra vires*
7.	**Extension of rights**	
7.1	By the Articles of Association	Examples: right to appoint directors, higher majority for certain shareholders' resolutions or resolutions of the board of directors, pre-emptive rights, etc
7.2	By shareholders' agreements	This option is commonly used. Note that shareholders' agreements must at all times be in the interest of the company
8.	**Actions impairing minority rights**	
8.1	Requirements	For dissolution: fundamental misbehaviour of one (or more) shareholder(s) which makes the continuation of the company practically impossible For the appointment of directors: Action obviously harming the interests of the minority
8.2	Examples	Serious and continuous impairment of minority shareholders' interests would be considered "justifiable serious reason"
8.3	Remedies	(a) Dissolution: only in severe cases (b) Appoinment of a judicial director by the court (often by way of preliminary relief)
9.	**Controlled companies**	
9.1	Gaining of control	In case of a public take-over bid, Co. B is obliged to acquire the shares of minority shareholders if Co. B acquires over 90% of the shares in Co. A
9.2	Wrongful exercise of control	No specific protection

Finland

1.	**Majority requirements for shareholders' resolutions**	
1.1	General majorities	Most decisions are made by a simple majority of the votes cast. In case of parity, the chairman has the deciding vote
1.2	Resolutions requiring greater majorities	(a) Resolution amending or modifying the Articles of Association require a majority of two-thirds of the votes cast and the approval tow-thirds of the shares represented at the meeting (b) Certain decisions require an unanimous approval of all the shareholders. (For example: the reduction of the preferential rights, an increase in the shareholders' obligations) (c) Other decisions (liquidation, or merger) require a greater majority
1.3	Modification of the required majorities	The Articles of Association may modify the majorities, but not reduce statutory majority requirements
2.	**Influence on the decision-making process**	
2.1	The right to call a meeting	Shareholders owning at least one-tenth of the shares have the right to call a general meeting. This is done by means of a written request specifying the purpose of the meeting. It is not possible to request a meeting concerning an issue that has already been discussed at another general meeting
2.2	The right to put matters on the agenda	Every shareholder has the right to put matters on the agenda of the meeting. This must be done in a written request addressed to the board of directors in a reasonable delay before the date of the meeting
3.	**Rights for information, audit and supervision**	
3.1	Information	Shareholders do not have the right to be informed on company matters continuously. They have no right to examine the company's book-keeping or agreements They do however have the right to request information about company matters during the general meeting. The board of directors may refuse this request if it causes prejudice to the company
3.2	Auditing and supervision	(a) The shareholders representing one-tenth of all shares or one-third of the votes at the general meeting may request an extra auditor. This auditor may not however provide individual shareholders with the information he has gathered during the audit (b) The shareholders holding the same majorities as above may ask for a special examination of the company's accounts for a specific matter or period of time
4.	**Capital increase and dividend payment**	
4.1	Participation in the capital increase	All shareholders have a preferential right in relation to the number of shares they already own This right may only be limited by a resolution of the general meeting which must be justified by the company's interests and significant economic motivations
4.2	Right to demand dividends	The minority shareholders representing 1/10 of the share capital have the right to demand dividends. This is done by a request at the general meeting before the decision on the allocation of the profit

Finland cont.

	The general meeting will be obliged to distribute at least 1/2 of the sum of the profits for the remaining financial period, after completing the necessary transfers and deductions required by the law and the Articles of Association
5. Derivative actions	All derivative actions must be decided upon at the general meeting. If a discharge from responsibility has been granted or no action for damages has been taken, the shareholders representing one-tenth of the share capital or one-third of the shares represented at the meeting may bring a derivative action on behalf of the company against the directors or other shareholders. They may not however enforce these rights against third parties
6. Other "formal" rights	(a) The law provides that every shareholder may be accompanied by an adviser at the general meeting (b) Shareholders representing one-tenth of the share capital may demand that certain decisions (for example: the adoption of the income statement and balance sheet) be adjourned to another meeting (c) Shareholders representing one-tenth of the share capital may require the election of an authorized auditor
7. Extension of rights	
7.1 By the Articles of Association	Examples: Some (but not less than half) of the directors may be elected other than by the shareholders' meeting; specific rights in the election of the managing director
7.2 By shareholders' agreements	Commonly used, specifically to determine the composition of the management or the guidelines for the company's administration
8. Actions impairing minority rights	
8.1 Requirements	Manifestly unjustified benefit at the expense of other shareholders; undue benefit to a shareholder at another shareholder's expense
8.2 Examples	Influencing the accounts in a way to make the distribution of profits impossible; exploitation of the services of the company by the majority; issuing new shares at a very high price which the minority cannot afford
8.3 Remedies	(a) Avoidance of a resolution (b) Preliminary injunction preventing the implementation of the resolution/action (c) Damages (intent need not be proved) (d) Dissolution (only for extremely serious reasons where there are no alternatives) (e) Buy-out of the aggrieved shareholder (only for serious reasons).
9. Controlled companies	
9.1 Gaining of control	If Co. B holds more than 90% of the shares of Co. A the minority shareholders of Co. A have a right (but also an obligation if Co. B demands so) to sell their shares to Co. B. (This rule applies also to private companies) The same right applies to minority shareholders of a publicly listed company where the shareholders of Co. B exceed 2/3 of the aggregate votes of the shares of Co. A (the threshold may be lowered by the Articles of Association)
9.2 Wrongful exercise of control	No specific protection

France

1.	**Majority requirements for shareholders' resolutions**	
1.1	General majorities	
	SA	Majority of votes by present or represented shareholders. Extraordinary or special meetings require two-thirds of the votes present or by proxy
	Sàrl	Absolute majority on first consultation, and majority of votes cast upon second consultation. Articles and by-laws amendments require three-quarters of the interest shares
1.2	Resolutions requiring greater majorities	Unanimous votes for increases in shareholder liability or transformation into a simplified stock company
1.3	Modification of the required majorities	
	SA	Legal majority requirements are imperative
	Sàrl	Articles and by-laws may require an absolute majority vote for the second meeting but may not impose a greater majority for extraordinary resolutions
2.	**The right to put matters on the agenda**	
	SA	Shareholders holding 5% of the registered capital, when registered capital is less than FFR5m, or capital percentage of 0.5 - 4% when registered capital is greater than FFR5m may put a resolution on the agenda
	Sàrl	No specific provision
3.	**Rights for information, audit and supervision**	
3.1	Information	
	SA	At any time, documents regarding corporate management from up to three years prior must be made available to any stock holder. Any shareholder may submit written questions to be answered by the board of directors during the meeting
	Sàrl	Rights modelled on those of corporate shareholders
3.2	Auditing and supervision	Any shareholder or associate holding one-tenth of the registered capital may petition the court for the appointment of an expert to report on management operations
4.	**Capital increase and dividend payment**	
4.1	Participation in the capital increase	
	SA	Every shareholder has a proportional pre-emptive subscription right. This right may be cancelled by a two-thirds majority in an extraordinary general meeting
	Sàrl	An authorization procedure may be required for a transfer of shares to a non-associate

France cont.

4.2	Right to demand dividends	Minority shareholders have no right to demand dividends unless there is abuse by the majority or a shareholders' agreement provides for a guaranteed dividend
5.	**Derivative actions**	Minority shareholders cannot act on behalf of the company against other shareholders, or third parties. Actions may be filed by any shareholder against directors if company representatives fail to assert the company's rights
6.	**Other "formal" rights**	Corporation shareholders may veto resolutions requiring unanimous votes of shareholders, and may apply to the president of the Commercial Court for dissolution of the company. Minority shareholders holding one-third plus one of the shares may oppose any amendments to the Articles and by-laws
7.	**Extension of rights**	
7.1	By the Articles of Association	Public policy widely institutionalizes governance by the majority. However, a greater right to information or to appoint management experts may be provided by the Articles and by-laws. Preferred shares with rights such as priority dividends, preferential rights in the winding up bonus, and representation in the board of directors may also be created
7.2	By shareholders' agreements	Shareholders' agreements may organize power distribution or management consistency through voting agreements. Ownership stability, protection of minority shareholders during a power change, pre-emption and withdrawal rights may also be covered. Public policy rules for stock companies apply to these agreements
8.	**Actions impairing minority rights**	
8.1	Requirements	Minority shareholders may file suit for majority abuses, which include resolutions against the general corporate interest for the sole benefit of the majority. The breach of equality must be conscious and purposeful
8.2	Examples	Examples include exorintant executive compensation, and the systematic appropriation of profits into reserves
8.3	Remedies	(a) Annulment of the abusive resolution (b) Damages
9.	**Controlled company**	
9.1	Gaining of control	Specific protection of minority shareholders is only organized by the set of rules governing listed companies
9.2	Wrongful exercise of control	Minority shareholders may criticize the exercise of power subsequent to a takeover, through a claim of majority abuse. The acquisition of the company by majority shareholders may not be opposed on the grounds of "special advantage"

Germany

1.	**Majority requirements for shareholders' resolutions**	
1.1	General majorities *GmbH and AG*	Simple majority of the votes. No quorum is required
1.2	Resolutions requiring greater majorities *GmbH*	A three-quarters majority is required for the modification or amendment to the Articles of Association or to dissolve the corporation
	AG	The modification of the Articles of Association requires a simple majority of the votes and a majority of three-quarters of the share capital represented at the meeting (eg, capital increase and dissolution of the corporation)
1.3	Modification of the required majorities *GmbH*	Greater majorities and quorums may be provided for in the Articles
	AG	Modification of the majorities by the Articles of Association is only possible if expressly stated in the law
2.	**Influence on the decision-making process**	
2.1	The right to call a meeting *GmbH*	The shareholders representing one-tenth of share capital can demand a meeting for specified reasons. The shareholders must state these reasons on the agenda of the meeting
	AG	The shareholders representing one-twentieth of the share capital may call a meeting. If faced with a refusal of the directors, the shareholders may seek a court order
2.2	The right to put matters on the agenda	Shareholders representing one-tenth of the share capital may demand that certain items be added to the agenda of the meeting
3.	**Rights for information, audit and supervision**	
3.1	Information *GmbH*	Every shareholder has the right to request information on the business and financial situation of the corporation. This request can be refused by the managers if it is deemed potentially detrimental to the corporation

Germany cont.

	AG	Every shareholder may request information, yet only during the meeting and to the extent of what is necessary for a clear evaluation of an item on the agenda. The board of directors may refuse only in limited situations
3.2	Auditing and supervision *GmbH*	This right does not exist
	AG	The shareholders may appoint a "special auditor" at the general meeting with a simple majority vote. Shareholders representing one-tenth or DM 2 million may request the court to appoint a special auditor
4.	**Capital increase and dividend payment**	
4.1	Participation in the capital increase *GmbH*	A majority of three-quarters is required for all capital increases and all exclusions of the right to participate in capital increases (this must be justified by the interests of the company)
	AG	The same majorities apply for all capital increases. The right of participation in the capital increase is expressly regulated by the statute. The same conditions as for the GmbH apply for the eventual exclusion of this right
4.2	Right to demand dividends *GmbH*	This right does not exist, except for if the shareholder can prove that the non-payment is contrary to the interests of the company
	AG	This right does not exist, yet the shareholders are automatically entitled to at least 4% unless the company's interests justify the non-payment
5.	**Derivative actions** *GmbH*	The shareholders have the right to a derivative action (*actio pro socio*) against other shareholders. This right only exists if the majority shareholders have not pursued the claim. The claim must be based on shareholder relations. The shareholders cannot, however, pursue any derivative actions against third parties or the directors
	AG	There are no derivative actions available to the minority shareholders. The shareholders representing one-tenth of the capital shares may demand that the corporation pursue certain damage claims against the founders of the corporation or the managers. The minority shareholders have a general right to challenge shareholder resolutions by means of a complaint filed with the court

Germany cont.

6.	**Other "formal" rights**	
	GmbH	(a) Shareholders of one-tenth can file a complaint against the corporation with the intent to dissolve the corporation (b) In case of a liquidation, the same minority might request a court-appointed liquidator
	AG	(a) The same minority can demand a vote at the general meeting concerning the election of the members of the supervisory board (b) The same minority (or those representing a nominal value of DM 2 million) may intervene in the decisions concerning the discharge of the members of the board of directors
7.	**Extension of rights**	
7.1	By the Articles of Association	
	GmbH	The Articles of Association may provide for numerous additional rights (eg concerning the transfer of shares and pre-emptive rights)
	AG	The Articles of Association may only deviate from the law if the statutory provisions expressly allow such modifications
7.2	By shareholders' agreements	
	GmbH	Shareholders' agreements play a minor role
	AG	Shareholders' agreements may also be used, but cannot affect the validity of the vote and the shareholders' resolution
8.	**Actions impairing minority rights**	
8.1	Requirements	The protection of minority shareholders' rights is based on the theory of "fiduciary duty", under which every shareholder is legally obligated to consider the legitimate interests of other shareholders

Germany cont.

8.2	Examples	
	GmbH	In general, the courts recognize a breach of fiduciary duty when the actions of a shareholder (eg actions taken to dissolve the company or the refusal to participate in a capital increase) are unjustified and detrimental to the interests of the corporation and the other shareholders (see report)
	AG	The principle of fiduciary duty plays only a limited role
8.3	Remedies	(a) Avoidance of a resolution (b) Damages (c) Obligation to act
9.	**Controlled company**	
9.1	Gaining of control	
	GmbH	Unanimity is required for the validity of a contractual concern. If a smaller majority suffices, dividend guarantees and an optional repurchase of shares is possible
	AG	A three-quarters majority is required for the validity of a contractual concern. The *de facto* concern requires a simple majority and a three-quarters majority of the shares represented. Dividend guarantee or redemption of shares must be provided for
9.2	Wrongful exercise of control	
	GmbH	The dominant company may not exercise any influence to the detriment of the dependant company
	AG	The minority shareholders have the right to a derivative action against the dominant company

Ireland

1.	**Majority requirements for shareholders' resolutions**	
1.1	General majorities	
	Ordinary resolutions	Simple majority 50% plus one vote present or by proxy
	Special resolutions	75% of the votes cast in person or by proxy
1.2	Resolutions requiring a greater majority	Certain resolutions qualify automatically as special resolutions and therefore require a 75% majority, eg, the modification of the Articles of Association and the alteration of the objects of a company's Memorandum of Association
1.3	Modification of the majority requirements	The Articles of Association may provide for specific resolutions with prescribed majorities, yet the statutory provisions must be adhered to
2.	**Influence on the decision making process**	
2.1	The right to call a meeting	Two or more shareholders holding not less than one-tenth of the share capital may call a meeting (unless the Articles of Association provide otherwise). The directors are obliged to convene an extraordinary general meeting on the demand of shareholders holding at least one-tenth of the share capital. The High Court also has the power, under the Companies Act 1963, to convene a general meeting if necessary
2.2	The right to put matters on the agenda	All shareholders and other persons entitled to attend and to vote at general meetings have the right to put matters on the agenda. Certain notice requirements must be adhered to
3.	**Rights for information, audit and supervision**	
3.1	Information	There are a number of statutory rights concerning rights to notices and information. For example, each shareholder has the right to receive copies of the balance sheets and directors' and auditors' reports and to inspect the register of directors and secretaries' shareholdings
3.2	Auditing and supervision	A simple majority of 50% plus one is required to appoint or to remove auditors. There is no statutory right of a shareholder to an independent audit. However, certain shareholders may initiate an investigation of the company's affairs. The shareholder may also obtain a judicial order for the investigation if the company's affairs have been conducted in a fraudulent, unlawful manner
4.	**Capital increase and dividend payment**	
4.1	Participation in the capital increase	The shareholders have a pre-emptive right to the allotment of new shares based on the ratio of existing shares. This right may be exluded in the Articles of Association
4.2	Right to demand dividends	There is no legal obligation to pay dividends even if there is a sufficient profit unless it is provided otherwise in the Articles. The company in the general meeting may declare dividends but no dividend can exceed the amount recommended by the directors. Section 205 of the Companies Act 1963 grants to any member a right of action in cases where that member claims that the affairs of the company are being exercised in an oppressive manner. The court has a large discretionary power in this area

Ireland cont.

5.	**Derivative actions**	Generally, the company is the only proper person to institute proceedings in the case where a wrong has been committed against the company. Individual shareholders cannot overturn a decision adopted by the majority. Derivative actions are, however, possible in the case of (a) Illegal acts commited by the company (b) A violation of the majority requirements (c) An infringment of shareholders' rights (d) A fraud committed by the majority (e) If the court deems the action to be justified The shareholders must establish that the company is entitled to relief and that the action falls within the exceptions to the rule
6.	**Other "formal" rights**	Many statutory rights exist in favour of minority shareholders, eg: (a) Application to the High Court to prevent an *ultra vires* act commited by the company (b) Application to the High Court for the cancellation of an alteration made to the objects of the company (c) Application to the court for an investigation of the company's affairs
7.	**Extension of rights**	
7.1	By the Articles of Association	Examples: right to appoint or to remove directors, right to veto on certain company decisions May also provide for additional rights, specifically veto powers.
7.2	By shareholders' agreements	Courts have shown a willingness to enforce shareholders' agreements
8.	**Actions impairing majority rights**	
8.1	Requirements	(a)"Oppression" – burdensome harsh and wrongful conduct (b) Disregard of members' interest in the capacity of a member
8.2	Examples	Exclusion from the management, directors' non-consultation with the shareholders may constitute oppression. Conduct does not need to be unlawful or in bad faith
8.3	Remedies	Court may make such order as it sees fit, directing/prohibiting any act, cancelling/varying a transaction, buy-out, etc
9.	**Controlled companies**	
9.1	Gaining of control	If Co. B acquires more than 80% of the shares of Co. A, the dissenting shareholders of Co. A can demand (or can be forced if the terms are fair) that Co. B acquire their shares
9.2	Wrongful exercise of control	Minority shareholders can apply to the High Court to have Co. A wound up if "this is just and equitable" or if the company's affairs are being exercised in manner oppressive to any member or in disregard of his interests as a member. This remedy is appropriate specifically for small private companies

Italy

1.	**Majority requirements for shareholders' resolutions**	
1.1	General majorities *Ordinary resolutions*	Simple majority 50% plus one present or by proxy (at least half of company's capital must be present)
	Second call	Simple majority present or by proxy
1.2	Resolutions requiring a greater majority	Extraordinary meetings: votes representing more than half of the company's capital on first and second call for serious matters. For other matters, on second call, votes representing more than one-third of the company's capital
1.3	Modification of the majority requirements	Statutes and Articles of Association can admit or request higher majorities, but never lower majorities. Statutes can never require a unanimous vote of shareholders or majorities equivalent to unanimity
2.	**Influence on the decision making process**	
2.1 2.2	The right to call a meeting; and The right to put matters on the agenda	Shareholders that represent at least one-fifth of the whole company's capital can demand the directors to convene the meeting The request needs to contain the items to be listed on the agenda. Directors have the right not to accept such a request when its purpose is to discuss items contrary to law, impossible or out of competance of the meeting
3.	**Rights for information, audit and supervision**	
3.1	Information	The board of auditors, being an impartial body, shall guarantee correct management by the directors. If there is no board of auditors, each partner has the right to receive from directors news on the development of the company's businesses and to inspect the corporate books
3.2	Auditing and supervision	Shareholders representing one-third of the capital of a company without a board of auditors have the right to request at their own expense, on a yearly basis, a check of the company's management (auditing, control of balance sheet and accountancy)

Italy cont.

4.	**Capital increase and dividend payment**	
4.1	Participation in the capital increase	The shareholders have a pre-emptive right to the allotment of new shares. This can be excluded when the capital increase has to be deliberated with assets in nature, or if there is a motivated interest of the company demanding the exclusion, with the favourable vote of at least half of the company's capital
4.2	Right to demand dividends	Shareholders have no individual right to the distribution of profits
5.	**Derivative actions**	There is no possibility for the shareholders to enforce rights of the company. The shareholder may act directly against directors when their behaviour, as office managers of the enterprise, has caused damage directly to shareholders' assets
6.	**Other "formal" rights**	No rights other than those in points 2 and 5
7.	**Extension of rights**	
7.1	By the Articles of Association	It is not common to make extensions of rights by the Articles of Association
7.2	By shareholders' agreements	Shareholders' agreements may organize a "voting trust", which shall not be prejudicial to "the primary interest of the company which is guaranteed by imperative rules"
8.	**Actions impairing majority rights**	
8.1	Requirements	It may happen that a meeting resolution is prejudicial to the positions and to the rights of the minority shareholder
8.2	Examples	Decisions of the meeting majority to: exclude in a definitive way the distribution of the profits to the shareholders; exclude or render more burdening the withdrawal of shareholders' capital increase; exclude the shareholders' right of option
8.3	Remedies	The absent or dissenting minority shareholders can contest the meeting resolutions that can be cancelled within three months from the date of the resolution
9.	**Controlled companies**	
9.1 9.2	Gaining of control and Wrongful exercise of control	Italian law does not provide specific protection in the cases mentioned

Netherlands

1. Majority requirements for shareholders' resolutions	
1.1 General majorities	Shareholders' resolutions are usually adopted by an absolute or simple majority of the votes. Quorums may be required by the law. Unanimity and the presence of the entire issued capital at the meeting is required under specific circumstances such as an irregularly convened meeting, or topics that have not been included in the notice covening the general meeting
1.2 Resolutions requiring a greater majority	(a) The conversion of a NV or BV into another legal entity (b) A legal merger (c) The exclusion of preferential rights in a NV (d) Capital reduction if less than half of the issued capital is present at the meeting
1.3 Modification of the majority requirements	The law and the Articles of Association may provide for larger majority requirements
2. Influence on the decision making process	
2.1 The right to call a meeting	Netherlands law does not provide for a general right. Normally, the board of directors and the supervisory board may call a shareholders' meeting, but the Articles of Association may vest this authority in others. One or more shareholders representing at least 10% of the share capital may request the board of directors to convene a meeting. If the board chooses not to comply, the request may be enforced by the president of the District Court. If the board fails to call an obligatory meeting, the District Court may authorize any individual to call a meeting prescribed by the law or the Articles of Association
2.2 The right to put matters on the agenda	The shareholders have no right *per se* to put matters on the agenda
3. Rights for information, audit and supervision	
3.1 Information	Shareholders are entitled to receive the company's annual accounts, but in general are not entitled to receive any other documents from the company. Shareholders may also ask questions during the shareholders' meetings. The management may refuse to respond to questions in the interest of the company

Netherlands cont.

3.2	Auditing and supervision	Shareholders representing at least one-tenth of the issued capital may assert an inquiry right. They may request the Enterprise Chamber of the Amsterdam Court of Appeals to appoint one or more persons to conduct an investigation into the affairs of the company. This request must be justified by serious reasons (such as apparent mismanagement). If such reasons are apparent, the Enterprise Chamber may also enforce certain sanctions
4.	**Capital increase and dividend payment**	
4.1	Participation in the capital increase	Every shareholder has a preferential subscription right proportional to his total shareholding. This right may be limited in a BV company by the Articles of Association and by the general shareholders' meeting in both a BV and NV The preferential right does not apply (a) To certain statutorial exceptions (b) To employee shares (c) To shares on which the payment is made in kind (d) To the holders of preferred shares concerning new ordinary shares and vice-versa
4.2	Right to demand dividends	Shareholders are entitled to a dividend, yet the Articles of Association and the shareholders meeting may determine the destination of the profits. A minority shareholders' right to dividends may never be excluded and the shareholders may contest the profit allocation on fairness grounds
5.	**Derivative actions**	The shareholders have no right to derivative actions under Netherlands law. Recent case law has confirmed that in the case of damage caused to the company by a third person, only the company will be entitled to claim any damages. A shareholder may only exceptionally assert the company's rights against other shareholders, directors or third parties if these persons have commited a wrongful act against the shareholder. Also, the principles of reasonableness and fairness may, under certain circumstances, cause for action by the management
6.	**Other "formal" rights**	(a) The Articles may designate the right to make nominations for the appointment of directors to specific types of shares. Such shares may be owned by minority shareholders (b) Shareholders representing at least one-third of the share capital may file a claim with the District Court to force the transfer of another shareholder's shares on the grounds of damage caused to the company by this individual (c) The civil code provides for the protection of minority shareholders in the case of a buy-out claim exercised by the majority shareholders (owning at least 95%). The court will refuse such a claim in the minority shareholders will as a result suffer financial damage, or if the claim targets priority shares

Netherlands cont.

7.	**Extension of rights**	
7.1	By the Articles of Association	Examples: greater voting powers; right for binding nomination for the appointment of managing directors or supervisory directors; veto rights (eg, on the amendments of the Articles of Association, restriction of the powers of the board or managing directors). Transfer of shares may be subject to an approval (only in private limited companies) or a right of first refusal. Different rights can be attributed to the shares of different classes ("letter shares")
7.2	By shareholders' agreements	Validity of pooling agreements specifically those providing for "preliminary meetings" in which certain shareholders agree on their voting on the shareholders' meeting
8.	**Actions impairing majority rights**	
8.1	Requirements	Avoidance: breach of the reasonableness and fairness principle and interest of the claimant. Buy-out: shareholder can no longer be reasonably required to keep his shares

Netherlands cont.

8.2	Examples	Avoidance: decision of the majority is exclusively based on their own interests rather than those of the company Buy-out: dividend policies are detrimental to the minority; interests of the company have been subordinated to those of the majority
8.3	Remedies	(a) Avoidance (b) Buy-out (c) In an action against another shareholder requiring him to take over the claimant's shares, claimant may additionally claim damages
9.	**Controlled companies**	
9.1	Gaining of control	No specific protection
9.2	Wrongful exercise of control	No specific protection

Spain

1. Majority requirements for shareholders' resolutions	
1.1 General majorities	
SA	A simple majority vote and a quorum of 25% is required
SL	A simple majority vote (provided that these votes represent at least one-third of the share capital) is required
1.2 Resolutions requiring a greater majority	
SA and SL	For any modification of the by-laws (the issue of bonds, modification of share capital) a quorum of 50% at the first meeting and 25% at the second meeting is required
1.3 Modification of the majority requirements	
SA	The by-laws may restrict the right to attend a meeting and limit the voting right of individual shareholders
SL	The by-laws may provide for higher majorities or quorums, but may not limit the right to attend a general meeting
2. Influence on the decision making process	
2.1 The right to call a meeting	Any shareholder can request an ordinary general meeting. Shareholders representing 5% may call an extraordinary general meeting
2.2 The right to put matters on the agenda	Shareholders who have called a meeting under 2.1 have the right to include any matter on the agenda
3. Rights for information, audit and supervision	
3.1 Information	Shareholders may obtain the annual accounts, directors' report and auditors' reports. They may ask questions
3.2 Auditing and supervision	For companies not obliged to audit their annual accounts, shareholders representing 5% of the share capital can request an audit
4. Capital increase and dividend payment	
4.1 Participation in the capital increase	The shareholders have the right to subscribe to new shares in proportion to the shares owned
4.2 Right to demand dividends	The shareholders cannot demand dividends; the general meeting is the only competent authority in this matter. Non-voting shares can have the right to dividend equal to 5% of the nominal share value

Spain cont.

5.	**Derivative actions**	Shareholders representing 5% of the share capital can bring derivative actions against the administrators. Shareholders may not, however, enforce the company's rights against other shareholders or third parties
6.	**Other "formal" rights**	(a) Shareholders representing 1% can request the presence of a notary at the annual general meeting (b) Shareholders representing 5% can request the suspension of resolutions which are judicially reviewed (c) Shareholders representing 20% can seek government intervention to ensure the continuity of the company
7.	**Extension of rights**	The Articles of Association may provide for additional rights. Shareholders' agreements are not commonly used for this purpose in Spain and cannot in any case bind the company or third parties
8.	**Actions impairing majority rights**	
8.1	Requirements	Resolution that is contrary to the law or the Articles of Association or harms the company's interests. Resolutions on certain matters (eg, a change of the company's object, of the system for the transfer of shares etc) give the shareholders who have voted against them the right to be bought out
8.2	Examples	Resolution awarding the chairman a remuneration higher than the profits, approval of balance sheet without proper accounting.
8.3	Remedies	(a) Avoidance of a resolution (b) Action for damages against the company or the board of directors (c) Preliminary relief eg, the suspension of a resolution
9.	**Controlled companies**	
9.1	Gaining of control	Where Co. B is a listed company and intends to reach a holding of at least 25 or 50% in Co. A, it must make a public bid open to all shareholders
9.2	Wrongful exercise of control	No specific protection

Sweden

1.	**Majority requirements for shareholders' resolutions**	
1.1	General majorities	Absolute majority of the votes is normally required. The chairman has the casting vote in case of parity
1.2	Resolutions requiring a greater majority	(a) A majority of two-thirds of the votes cast and a majority of two-thirds of the shares represented at the meeting are required in case of minor amendments to the Articles of Association. (Please see report for further details) (b) A resolution implying changes in the rights of shares or certain categories of shares may require an even greater majoirty (eg, the unanimous approval of all shareholders)
2.	**Influence on the decision making process**	
2.1	The right to call a meeting	Shareholders representing one-tenth of all the shares may request the board of direcrtors to convene a meeting for a specified objective. The board shall issue a convening notice within 14 days
2.2	The right to put matters on the agenda	Any shareholder has the right to put matters on the agenda by submitting a written request to the board of directors in reasonable time before the general meeting
3.	**Rights for information, audit and supervision**	
3.1	Information	Each shareholder has inquiry rights during the shareholders' meeting. The board of directors shall furnish the information unless it deems this disclosure damaging to the company. If the directors refuse the request for the above reason, the information will be sent to an auditor and the shareholders will have access to the auditor's report. In companies with no more than ten shareholders, each of them is entitled to acquaint himself with the books, accounts and other documents
3.2	Auditing and supervision	Shareholders representing one-tenth of all shares or one-third of the shares represented at the meeting may appoint an independent auditor or special examiner. Shareholders representing one-tenth of all shares may request the election of an authorized public accountant as auditor
4.	**Capital increase and dividend payment**	
4.1	Participation in the capital increase	Principal rule: all shareholders have a preferential right to sign for new shares, convertible and simple debt instruments with a right of option in relation to the number of shares they already own
4.2	Right to demand dividends	In principle, the distribution of dividends will be decided upon at the shareholders' meeting. However, shareholders representing at least one-tenth of all shares may request that the shareholders' meeting declare a dividend of at least half of the distributable net profit. (The majority cannot, however, be obliged to pass a resolution on a dividend exceeding 5% of the equity)

Sweden cont.

5.	**Derivative actions**	
5.1	Derivative action against other shareholders	This action is possible for the owners of at least one-tenth of all shares if another shareholder has caused damage to the company by participation in a gross violation of corporate law or the Articles of Association
5.2	Derivative action against the directors	This action is equally possible if a director commits a deliberate or gross violation of the law or the Articles of Association, causing damage to the company or to the shareholders
5.3	Derivative action against third parties	Action for damages in favour of the company may be instituted by owners of at least one-tenth of all shares but these are liable for all costs for the action but equally entitled to reimbursement to the extent that the costs are covered
6.	**Other "formal" rights**	(a) The Swedish Companies Act of 1975 provides a general clause prohibiting any resolution which gives undue advantage to a shareholder or a third party and is therefore detrimental to the company or other shareholders (b) Shareholders representing one-tenth of all shares may ask the court to order a compulsory winding up of the company or the redemption of the claimant's shares if another shareholder has abused his influence and participated in an infringement of the Articles of Association
7.	**Extension of rights**	
7.1	By the Articles of Association	Examples: appointment of directors, higher majorities for certain resolutions
7.2	By shareholders' agreements	More commonly used to strengthen the rights of minority shareholders
8.	**Actions impairing majority rights**	
8.1	Requirements	Undue advantage to a shareholder to the detriment of another shareholder. A deliberate or negligent violation of the law or Articles of Association
8.2	Examples	(not covered)
8.3	Remedies	(a) Avoidance of a resolution (b) Damages (c) Dissolution of the company where the shareholders intentionally misused their influence in the company
9.	**Controlled companies**	
9.1	Gaining of control	If Co. B acquires more than 90% of the shares of Co. A, the dissenting shareholders may demand the purchase of their shares. (This rule also applies to private companies)
9.2	Wrongful exercise of control	No specific protection

Switzerland

1.	**Majority requirements for shareholders' resolutions**	
1.1	General majorities	The absolute majority of the votes present is required unless otherwise provided by the Articles of Incorporation
1.2	Resolutions requiring a greater majority	The Swiss Code of Obligations provides for eight specific resolutions requiring a majority of at least two-thirds of the votes represented and the absolute majority of the represented par value of the shares. For example: (a) The modification of the Articles of Incorporation (b) The introduction of supervoting shares (c) An authorized or conditional capital increase
1.3	Modification of the majority requirements	The Articles of Incorporation can provide for greater majorities and quorum requirements. However, the modification itself requires that use of the (desired) higher majority is already practiced
2.	**Influence on the decision making process**	
2.1	The right to call a meeting	Shareholder(s) representing at least 10% of the shares may call a general meeting
2.2	The right to put matters on the agenda	Shareholders who represent a par value of SFR 1 million may put matters on the agenda
3.	**Rights for information, audit and supervision**	
3.1	Information	Each shareholder has the right to be informed about the business report (composed of the annual financial statement, the annual report and the consolidated financial statement); the participation of important shareholders in public companies; the auditor's report. At the general meeting, every shareholder may also address questions to the board of directors concerning the company's affairs
3.2	Auditing and supervision	Shareholders can request an audit if this is necessary to exercise their rights and if their right for information and inspection have already been used in an attempt to gather the information needed
4.	**Capital increase and dividend payment**	
4.1	Participation in the capital increase	As a general rule, every shareholder has the right to subscribe to a number of newly issued shares corresponding to the number of all shares held by the same shareholder. Under certain conditions, subscription rights can be restricted or cancelled, such decision requiring a special majority in the general meeting
4.2	Right to demand dividends	Every shareholder has the right to claim a proportional share in the net profit and/or a share in the proceeds from teh eventual liquidation of the company. An enforceable right to demand dividends in the absence of a respective resolution of the general meeting, however, does not exist. Any shareholder may challenge a resolution of the annual meeting which bars the pursuit of profit without consent of all the shareholders

Switzerland cont.

5.	**Derivative actions**	According to Article 756 of the Swiss Code of Obligations, each shareholder as well as the company may seek to bring an action for damages caused to the company. Claims in bankruptcy proceedings are not dealt with here
6.	**Other "formal" rights**	A judge may not only dissolve a corporation if shareholders representing together at least 10% of the capital so request but he could also order other solutions such as a partial buy-back of outstanding shares at their market value if required in order to effectively protect minority shareholders
7.	**Extension of rights**	
7.1	By the Articles of Association	Examples: Right to be represented on the board of directors; cumulative voting in the election of the board members
7.2	By shareholders' agreements	Shareholder agreements are quite common specifically in smaller and closely-held corporations. Examples: right of first refusal, option rights, qualified majorities or unanimity, right to be represented on the board of directors, etc
8.	**Actions impairing majority rights**	
8.1	Requirements	Resolution deprives shareholders of their rights or revokes or restrict their rights without proper justification, or results in an unequal treatment of or discrimination against shareholder
8.2	Examples	Breach of the basic structure of the corporation, impossibility, breach of public order, etc
8.3	Remedies	(a) Avoidance (b) Buy-out (only in exceptional cases) (c) Dissolution (only in exceptional cases) (d) Declaration of nullity
9.	**Controlled companies**	
9.1	Gaining of control	No specific protection at this time (the rights of minority shareholders of publicly listed companies will be expanded if the planned legislation comes into force - envisaged for Summer 1997
9.2	Wrongful exercise of control	A majority shareholder (Co. B) who forces it will and decisions upon Co. A may be deemed a quasi-director of the latter and therefore, be liable in the same way

United Kingdom

1.	**Majority requirements for shareholders' resolutions**	
1.1	General majorities	Ordinary resolutions are passed by a simple majority either present or by proxy. All resolutions are ordinary unless provided otherwise by the Articles of Association or the Companies Act 1985
1.2	Resolutions requiring a greater majority	(a) Extraordinary resolutions require a majority of 75%. The Articles may require any matter to be dealt with by a special resolution (b) Elective resolutions, requiring unanimity, may be used to vary the application of certain regulatory requirements contained in the Companies Act 1985
1.3	Modification of the majority requirements	The Articles of Association govern the voting rights originally attached to each type of share. The Articles also determine whether a resolution is to be classified as ordinary or extraordinary
2.	**Influence on the decision making process**	
2.1	The right to call a meeting	Members with at least one-twentieth of the voting rights or 100 members whose paid up stock each represents 100 GBP, have the right to call a general meeting of the shareholders. They may require the directors to convene a meeting on a new resolution or require the addition of a resolution at the annual general meeting
2.2	The right to put matters on the agenda	If proper notice has been given, an item for the agenda can be included in the notice. Several cases have addressed this issue
3.	**Rights for information, audit and supervision**	
3.1	Information	Twenty-one days before the annual general meeting, all members are entitled to receive a copy of: the annual report; the directors' report; the auditors' report. Each member is also entitled to receive copies of the accounts upon written demand within seven days
3.2	Auditing and supervision	The Department of Trade and Industry may appoint investigators to examine the company's affairs if asked to do so by at least 200 shareholders or shareholders representing at least 10% of the share capital
4.	**Capital increase and dividend payment**	
4.1	Participation in the capital increase	The capital stock may be altered by the passing of a special resolution (majority of 75%). Section 89 of the Companies Act 1985 provides for a pre-emptive right for all shareholders. However, the pre-emption provisions are not applicable if the equity securities are wholly or partly paid up otherwise than in cash. In private companies, the pre-emptive rights may be excluded by the Memorandum or the Articles of Association
4.2	Right to demand dividends	Any company can only make dividend payments out of the difference between its "accumulated realized profits" and "accumulated realized losses"

United Kingdom cont.

5.	**Derivative actions**	The rule contained in *Foss* v. *Harbottle* governs derivative actions. In general, the shareholders do not have a proprietary interest in the underlying assets of the company therefore may not go to Court to complain of a wrong done to the company. The proper plaintiff is the company. The shareholder may only bring an action for the violation of his personal rights or interests. Exception: a derivative action may be brought where it is claimed that fraud has been committed and the alleged wrongdoers are preventing the company from suing in its own name
6.	**Other "formal" rights**	The Memorandum and Articles contain covenants on the part of each member to observe all the provisions contained therein. The shareholders may therefore enforce the Articles to exercise any of the rights there set out. Shareholders representing at least 15% of the share capital may apply to the Court to cancel a change of object (within 21 days). Any shareholder may apply for the cancellation of certain special resolutions (for example: the purchase or redemption of a company's own shares). The shareholders have the right to restrain the company from entering into a transaction which would otherwise be *ultra vires* and to hold the directors liable.
7.	**Extension of rights**	
7.1	By the Articles of Association	They may regulate class rights, transfer of shares, quorum requirements, exercise of voting rights, powers of directors, etc
7.2	By shareholders' agreements	Shareholders' agreements are quite common. They govern, *inter alia*, dividend distribution, appointment of directors, general principles of management, transfer of shares
8.	**Actions impairing majority rights**	
8.1	Requirements	The unfair prejudice to the benefit of some of the shareholders. The prejudice may be caused by a single act, an omission or threatened future conduct
8.2	Examples	Breach of an undertaking to a member that he would have a say in the management; exclusion from management
8.3	Remedies	The Court has a wide discretion in making an order, eg: (a) regulate the conduct of the company's affairs (b) require or restrict the company from doing an act (c) buy-out of a shareholder by another shareholder or the company (most common remedy)
9.	**Controlled companies**	
9.1	Gaining of control	Any person who acquires shares carrying 30% or more of the voting rights, or already holds between 30% and 50% of the voting rights and acquires in any 12 month period more than 1% of the voting rights in a public company is required to make an offer on the same terms to acquire the rest of the equity share capital
9.2	Wrongful exercise of control	No specific protection

United States

1.	**Majority requirements for shareholders' resolutions**	
1.1	General majorities	General majority rules can be affected by issues such as limitations on voting rights and quorum requirements. For example: statutory quorum requirements may result in the adoption of a resolution by a majority that falls short of the majority of all outstanding stock
1.2	Resolutions requiring a greater majority	Greater majorities are usually required for resolutions dealing with substantive changes in the corporate structure (eg, mergers or sale of the company's assets)
1.3	Modification of the majority requirements	These modifications are usually negotiated between the shareholders, directors and officers. The certificate of incorporation and by-laws can provide for lower or higher quorums. However, state statutes may set restrictions on minimum voting rights
2.	**Influence on the decision making process**	
2.1	The right to call a meeting	An annual shareholders' meeting is generally held, at which the election of directors takes place. The management controls the matters on the agenda of this meeting. Special meetings may be called by persons designated in the certificate of incorporation or the by-laws
2.2	The right to put matters on the agenda	Minority shareholders have, to a certain extent, the right to control what does not belong on the agenda. This is done through insisting upon strict compliance with the general rule that only stated business can be discussed at special meetings and the application of federal proxy rules. Shareholders only have an active right to put matters on the agenda if there is a statutory basis for calling a special meeting
3.	**Rights for information, audit and supervision**	
3.1	Information	The right to information is limited by the distinction between the management and ownership in a corporation. Shareholders of a large corporation have access to the information specified by federal security law. Regarding closely held corporations, state statutes only guarantee a right to inspect certain books or records after specific events. The by-laws may extend these rights
3.2	Auditing and supervision	The court may order a business into receivership and liquidation or appoint a temporary receiver. By-laws may provide for periodic access and auditing and the communication of the financial statements to the shareholders
4.	**Capital increase and dividend payment**	
4.1	Participation in the capital increase	Shareholders have the right to participate in capital increases to the extent of their pre-emptive rights. Some state statutes limit pre-emptive rights, while others permit them if provided for in the by-laws

United States cont.

4.2	Right to demand dividends	There is no automatic right, unless minimum dividend levels have been provided for in the by-laws. Directors have wide discretion unless restricted by the IRS
5.	**Derivative actions**	Derivative actions may be brought against directors, third parties and other shareholders. These actions are governed by state statutes. This type of suit is possible in the case of a violation of a duty of care, (eg gross negligence, mismanagement). The shareholder bringing the action must comply with the state statutes who mostly attempt to minimize interference in corporate management
6.	**Other "formal" rights**	Federal law provides shareholders with other formal rights (despite a reluctance concerning federalization of corporate laws): (a) Rule 10(b)5 SEC 1934 provides for a private right of action as a means of challenging deceptive acts which create a detriment to investors (b) Other federal provisions are contained in sections of the Securities Act of 1933 and the "Federal Racketeers Influenced and Corrupt Organization Act" (RICO)
7.	**Extension of rights**	
7.1	By the Articles of Association	Special provisions for particular minority representations can be included in the Articles of Association or by-laws
7.2	By shareholders' agreements	Examples: rights regarding the election of directors, appointment of officers, restrictions of the power of majority shareholders to change the Articles of Association or by-laws
8.	**Actions impairing majority rights**	
8.1	Requirements	Violation of a fiduciary duty
8.2	Examples	Undermining minority shareholders' pre-emptive rights (New York State law), withholding material information from the claimants
8.3	Remedies	(a) Appraisal (b) Reversal of the improper transaction (c) Damages (d) Dissolution of the company (only where the action of the majority is oppressive) (e) Injunctive relief
9.	**Controlled companies**	
9.1	Gaining of control	If the acquisition of a majority of shares succeeds because a controlling block of stock was used and a premium was paid for such a block, a court may, in some jurisdictions, require the block holders (ie sellers) to redistribute among the minority holders the premiums they received
9.2	Wrongful exercise of control	The minority shareholders of Co. A may sue Co. B for any damage done to the subsidiary if thereis no independence between the parent stock holders and the subsidiary ("double derivative theory")

ANNEX II: THE ROLE OF THE TAKEOVER PANEL IN THE UNITED KINGDOM

Noel P. Hinton

PROTECTION OF MINORITY SHAREHOLDERS

EDITOR MATTHIAS W. STECHER

ANNEX II: THE ROLE OF THE TAKEOVER PANEL IN THE UNITED KINGDOM

Noel P. Hinton

1. The Panel

The Takeover Panel ("the Panel") in the United Kingdom is the regulatory body which issues and administers the City Code on Takeovers and Mergers ("the Code"). It was set up in 1968. The concept was proposed by the Governor of the Bank of England and the Chairman of the Stock Exchange in response to mounting concern about practices unfair to shareholders which had featured in a number of controversial takeovers.

The purpose of the Panel is best described by an extract from the Code's Introduction:

> "The Code and the Panel operate principally to ensure fair and equal treatment of all shareholders in relation to takeovers. The Code also provides an orderly framework within which takeovers are conducted. The Code is not concerned with the financial or commercial advantages or disadvantages of a takeover. These are matters for the company and its shareholders. Nor is the Code concerned with those issues, such as competition policy, which are the responsibility of government."

The Panel is basically concerned with takeovers of public, and certain private, companies – in other words, most transactions that involve a change in control of companies the shares of which are held by the public.

If the three paragraphs above explain in broad terms what the Panel is trying to achieve, the Code is the mechanism for achieving the objective.

2. The Twin Approach by the Code

There are two particular areas of the Code to which I would wish to draw the reader's attention. These two sections are entitled "General Principles" and "Rules" and the relationship between them is fundamental to an understanding of the way the Panel operates. Perhaps I could explain by using another quote from the Introduction to the Code:

> "The Code is based upon a number of General Principles, which are essentially statements of good standards of commercial behaviour. These General Principles apply to all transactions with which the Code is concerned. They are, however, expressed in broad general terms and the Code does not define the precise extent of, or the limitations on, their application. They are applied by the Panel in accordance with their spirit to achieve their underlying purpose; the Panel may modify or relax the effect of their precise wording accordingly.
>
> In addition to the General Principles, the Code contains a series of Rules, of which some are effectively expansions of the General Principles and examples of their application and others are provisions governing specific aspects of takeover procedure. Although most of the Rules are expressed in more detailed language than the General Principles, they are not framed in technical language and, like the General Principles, are to be interpreted to achieve their underlying purpose. Therefore, their spirit must be observed, as well as their letter, and the Panel may modify or relax the application of a Rule if it considers that, in the particular circumstances of the case, it would operate unduly harshly or in an unnecessarily restrictive or burdensome, or otherwise inappropriate, manner."

This approach – and I would suggest it can best be summed up by the word "flexibility" – is simply designed to enable the Panel to deal with the unexpected events and problems that can – and frequently do – occur during takeovers.

3. The General Principles

It may be helpful to mention some of the General Principles. There are ten in all, but the following four are particularly relevant.

3.1 Similarity of treatment for all shareholders in an offer

All shares of the same class have the same economic interest in the company; each share receives the same dividend. Obviously, the more shares an individual owns, the more power he has with regard to the company, but in a general offer it would seem illogical to permit shareholders to receive different offers from the offeror simply because they own different numbers of shares. In the USA many years ago I understand it was possible to construct an offer in such a way that the first 50% who accepted received, say, $5 a share, the next 10% $4 a share, the next 10% $3 a share, and so on. Not surprisingly, rather than considering the merits of the offer, shareholders were involved in a mad scramble to make sure they received $5 a share, rather than a smaller sum.

To deal with these matters, we have adopted this General Principle so that no matter when you accept an offer within the prescribed time scale whether on Day 1 or Day 59, and no matter whether you are the chairman or a small shareholder, you know you will be treated in exactly the same way as all other shareholders who accept.

3.2 Sufficient time and information

Shareholders should be given sufficient time, and sufficient information, in which to make an informed decision.

There must be no doubt about this. It is, after all, a critical time in a company's life: shareholders should have the appropriate information before they make their decision. Looked at from the opposite end, it is also equally fair that the target company should not be under siege for too long. Therefore, there has to be a finite timetable for offers.

3.3 A transparent market in the relevant shares

In the UK we believe that it is important during a bid to have an open and informed market in the shares of the offeror and the offeree company. Accordingly, we accept that, during a bid, the offeror and the offeree companies can operate in the market, along with all other participants, provided that there is adequate disclosure of all relevant dealings. We therefore require public disclosure of all relevant dealings by the principals and their associated parties by 12 noon on the day after the dealing took place. Further, any independent party who comes to own more than 1% of relevant shares also has to make a public disclosure. On this basis the market is well informed and can make up its own mind what should happen to the quoted share price: the share price itself then provides a useful barometer for shareholders to assess the merits of the offer.

The Panel is able to monitor share dealings through a link with the Stock Exchange computer. This, *inter alia*, enables the Panel to see whether shareholders are approaching critical levels, ie requiring disclosure, or to see if there are any suspicious dealings, for example, purchases above the offer value. Given that the Panel believes in transparency, it will not surprise you to learn that we do not allow disclosures to be made under "nominee" names. It is of no use to the market if an off-shore holding company is disclosed as the new owner of some shares in the target company. We want the market to be informed of the true beneficial owner of such shares. You may wonder whether the non-statutory nature of the Panel is an impediment to this. The facts probably speak for themselves. Since this particular Rule was introduced in its stricter form in 1987, there has been one occasion when a stockbroker made a disclosure on behalf of a client, using only a nominee name. As it happens, the Executive had been in touch with the broker beforehand to say that it had noted that one of the broker's clients was approaching the disclosure threshold. The Code makes it clear that considerable responsibility is placed on the intermediaries to ensure that their clients are aware of it. In this particular case, instructions to deal had been given by the majority owners of the broker, a well-known Swiss bank. When the broker in London asked head office in Switzerland for the name of the beneficiary, no reply was forthcoming. I understand the telephone wires between London and Switzerland got rather hot that day. However, there was no success and, as a result, five minutes after the broker had put out the disclosure in the name of a nominee company, the Panel put out a statement explaining that the Code had been breached. Very shortly thereafter, a Swiss lawyer got in touch with his European client, not resident in the UK, to explain the problem. The client contacted the Panel, and an appropriate disclosure was made, albeit 24 hours late. I cannot say whether the transaction was at all relevant to the success or otherwise of the bid, but it is a useful indicator that even non-residents of the UK wish to comply with the Code.

3.4 Frustrating action by management

This is sometimes an emotive subject but, to our way of thinking, the principle is straightforward. As you can see from the other three General Principles I have mentioned, during a takeover the regulatory system in the UK places particular emphasis on the protection and interests of the shareholder. It is, after all, the shareholder who receives the offer and who has to decide whether or not to accept it. At the same time, it is equally clear that management of the target company is employed to manage that company. What the Code effectively says is this: the management should always be in a position to manage the company as it sees fit but, during the relatively short period of a takeover bid, if the management of the target company proposes significant changes to the company, then shareholders should be consulted since they should have the right, in such circumstances, to decide whether their assets (ie the shares) are better employed by acceptance of the offer or by agreeing to management's new proposals.

Perhaps I can illustrate this with an example. For the purposes of this example I have obviously ignored the impact of any other rules and regulations, such as Stock Exchange Listing Requirements. Let us suppose the target company has five factories of equal size, all of which produce motorcycles. The offeror is very interested in acquiring a motor cycle company. Halfway through the bid, the target company announces that it is selling two of the five factories, since it believes the motor cycle sector is in difficulties and it is going to buy two computer-making factories of equal size since it believes that this particular sector is a growth area. It may well be a perfectly justifiable commercial decision but the offeror has made what it describes as "a very generous offer" for motor cycle factories. It is not interested in computers and could, in the UK, if it chose, withdraw its offer on the basis of a material change in the condition of the target company. But that is not really the point since shareholders in the target company have received this generous offer and are in the process of deciding whether or not to accept. As I have outlined above, in the UK we would require this proposal to be put to shareholders. They then have the choice. On the one hand, they can consider the merits and attractiveness of the offer and decide whether or not to accept the cash or the shares; on the other hand, they can decide whether they believe their management has spotted a gap in the market which would enable profits (and therefore dividends) in the target company to increase significantly, provided it remains independent. It is therefore *their* decision whether to support the board or to accept the offer. Accordingly, they are able to express this decision at an extraordinary general meeting during the course of the offer. That is the broad basis for the UK's approach. I can confidently say that such problems have always been overcome in the UK, following discussions between the Panel Executive and the two relevant companies.

This is one General Principle which might well apply before an offer has been announced if the board of the offeree company has reason to believe that a bona fide offer might be imminent. In such circumstances the target company (or indeed the offeror) could well be consulting the Panel to decide what could or should be done. And, indeed, "consultation" is another key word.

4. The Decision-Making Process

If the Code is the mechanism, who is it who operates this wonderful device? There are two answers to this question.

4.1 The Executive

The day-to-day work of the Panel is carried out by the Executive which is a very small group numbering under 30. Those with executive responsibilities (15 of the 30) are from different disciplines (such as accountancy, stockbroking and the legal profession) and in the main on secondment from City firms for periods of two years, although 3 of the 15 are permanent. The mix of permanent staff and secondees is one of the great strengths of the Panel. The permanent members provide essential continuity and yet, all the time, others are coming in with up-to-date practical experience of current practice and thinking and stimulating new ideas.

The Executive gives rulings and guidance on the interpretation of the Code. It tries to avoid giving *ex parte* rulings, but sometimes because of the need for secrecy this has to be done. Strict confidentiality in the work is of course of paramount importance.

One of the cornerstones of the system is advance consultation. The Executive is very often asked about an offer before it takes place, perhaps on a no names basis, to make sure it gives rise to no problems. Similarly, prior consultation before action during a bid is very common, particularly in a contested bid. We welcome this as it is much easier to consider problems before the event rather than after. We prefer fire prevention to fire fighting!

Much of the work involves meetings, often at very short notice, and telephone conversations with merchant bankers, stockbrokers, lawyers, accountants or company directors who require guidance or a ruling on either an intended offer or one which is already in progress. The Executive's decisions are almost always relayed by word of mouth and not in writing; this is because speed is essential and also because by and large we know and have a reasonably close relationship with the great majority of inquirers. Rulings are generally given either immediately or within about 24 hours and a record is made of all discussions relating to such rulings. In a normal week the Executive would give perhaps 100 rulings, some major, some minor.

4.2 The Panel

If any party disagrees with an Executive ruling, it may appeal to the full Panel which will hear the argument from both parties, as well as from the Executive, and decide whether or not to uphold the decision or allow the appeal. The full Panel is made up of a Chairman, two Deputy Chairmen and three independent members (all appointed by the Governor of the Bank of England) and the Chairmen or nominees of each of the 11 member bodies (principally organizations whose members are involved in the takeover field either as shareholders, as corporate finance practitioners, or as the offerors or offeree companies). The full Panel meets whenever necessary to hear appeals against the Executive's decisions and in addition has a routine meeting four times a year at which the Executive reports on recent activity. In recent years there have only been four or five appeals a year.

As time is usually critical we try to assemble a full Panel within about 48 hours of notification of an appeal. The procedure before the full Panel is fairly informal and legal representation in the strict sense is not normally allowed. Decisions are promulgated very quickly and usually a public statement is issued.

The full Panel is also the body empowered to revise the Code, either to clarify it or to amend it to take account of new concerns or changed market practices.

4.3 The Appeal Committee

The Executive may deal with a disciplinary matter where the party which is to be subject to disciplinary action agrees the facts and the action proposed by the Executive. If such agreement is not forthcoming, the person against whom disciplinary proceedings have been instituted by the Executive would appear before the full Panel which would decide if there has been a breach of the Code and, if so, what action should be taken.

If the Panel decides to take disciplinary action, the offender has a right of appeal to the Appeal Committee, which consists of a permanent Chairman (a former senior judge) and two others drawn from the member bodies. The Appeal Committee meets rarely–less than once a year on average. There are a number of other circumstances in which a right of appeal may lie from the full Panel to the Appeal Committee.

5. Judicial Review

I should add that, while that exhausts the appeal procedures within the Panel system, it is possible to go beyond the Panel system and ask for judicial review of the Panel's decision by the courts. This was established by the judgment in the *Datafin* case in December 1986.

As I am sure you all know, until a few years ago, judicial review, certainly in the United Kingdom, was concerned primarily with the decisions of government departments and local authorities. In December 1986, the Court of Appeal's decision in the landmark *Datafin* case significantly expanded the types of bodies whose decisions could be reviewed by the courts. Before *Datafin*, only those bodies whose powers were derived from statute or the royal prerogative were subject to judicial review. Since *Datafin*, what matters is not only the source of a body's powers but also whether those powers are of a public nature and have a public effect,

In the *Datafin* case the Court of Appeal held that the Panel was subject to review by the courts. The particular application in the Datafin case was dismissed, but nevertheless this important point of principle was decided. The court held that although the Panel is a self-regulatory body without any direct statutory base it is supported and sustained by a periphery of statutory powers and penalties, it operates wholly in the public domain and performs public law functions in prescribing and operating the Code. Therefore the court held that an interested party can apply to the court for leave to seek judicial review of a decision of the Panel.

The Court of Appeal accepted that this could create a number of practical problems for the Panel and the parties affected by its decision. It therefore laid down guidelines as to how the court's jurisdiction should be exercised. The effect of these guidelines should be that, unless the Court of Appeal is overruled, the courts are unlikely, except in extreme cases, to interfere with the Panel's decision.

As it appears that the courts would be slow to interfere with Panel decisions, acknowledging the necessity for speed and certainty in the context of a current takeover, the potential use of judicial review as a tactic in takeovers has been considerably restricted.

The *Datafin* guidelines may be summarized as follows:

- the courts will give the Panel great latitude in interpreting the Code;
- the courts are unlikely to intervene unless the Code is interpreted in conflict with the fundamental principle of achieving equity between shareholders or contrary to the ordinary meaning of the words used in the Code;
- the courts are unlikely to interfere with Panel decisions unless the Panel has acted unfairly such that the applicant has suffered real injustice;
- the courts will normally be reluctant to intervene unless the applicant has first exhausted the Panel's own appeal procedures, unless the complaint is based on procedural irregularity;
- the Panel's decisions should be treated as valid and binding unless and until set aside by the courts;
- the relationship between the Panel and the courts should be historic rather than contemporaneous; and
- it is in effect supervisory, long stop jurisdiction only.

The *Datafin* decision has not significantly impacted on the way the Panel has operated in the last few years. Since *Datafin* there have been three unsuccessful attempts to judicially review decisions of the Panel. I should mention at this stage this is against the background of about 6,000 takeovers in the last 27 years, as well as roughly the same number again of transactions discussed with the Executive but which never came to fruition.

6. Relationships with Other Regulatory Bodies

Perhaps at this point, I should also mention the relationship of the Panel with other regulatory bodies (all statutorily backed).

The Financial Services Act 1986 brought major changes to the regulation of the financial markets in the UK. The Act does not, by and large, extend to the regulation of takeovers, and so the scope of the Panel's work has remained largely unaltered. In particular, for good reason, the Panel remains non-statutory and the Code does not derive its authority from the Act. However, the work of the Panel can no longer be seen in isolation; it now has to be seen in the context of the new structure. The Panel has always worked closely with the Bank of England and the Stock Exchange and, as mentioned earlier, has access to the Stock Exchange system of surveillance of market-dealing, which enables it to monitor closely dealings during the course of a bid. In addition, the Panel is now expressly authorized, by statutory instrument, to receive restricted information obtained by other regulatory authorities under the Financial Services Act 1986 and the Banking Act 1987.

The Securities and Investments Board (SIB), established under the Financial Services Act, and relevant Self Regulating Organizations (SROs) require practitioners to cooperate with the Panel in its investigations and the sanctions of the SIB and SROs are available for use against practitioners if breaches of the Code are such as to show them not to be "fit and proper" to carry out their businesses. Again, SIB and SROs have adopted "cold-shoulder" rules requiring investment businesses not to act for a person whom they have reason to believe would not comply with UK practice and standards in takeovers. It is reasonable to add that this statutory buttressing is welcome but, prior to the adoption of the Financial Services Act, the Panel had always had extremely high levels of cooperation from all concerned when it was investigating matters.

7. Conclusion

I have tried in this text to explain what the Panel is trying to achieve and how it goes about its business of regulating takeovers. I have not given any details about the Rules but have considered the underlying philosophy and approach of the Code. Obviously the Rules in the Code deal with several issues, such as the appropriate timetable, the amount of information that should be made available to shareholders and the requirements relating to disclosure of share dealings.

In conclusion, perhaps I should emphasize a number of keywords: speed, flexibility and certainty. Given the timetable, the regulator of takeovers needs to make decisions rapidly. Obviously the decisions should be based on provision of all necessary information. Flexibility is required to deal with the unexpected that certainly can and does happen during takeovers. I am not trying to suggest that the Panel gives dispensations from the requirements of the Code during every offer. The majority of offers simply follow the Rules: in those cases where a dispensation is considered, it will be against the standards imposed by the General Principles. A dispensation that conflicts with the General Principles is virtually impossible to imagine. Finally, I have mentioned "certainty". In the context of takeovers, certainty is provided by the knowledge of offerors, offeree companies and shareholders that they can rely on rulings of the Panel.

I explained earlier the relationship between the courts and the Panel. Perhaps I should conclude by mentioning an article in the *Wall Street Journal* which compared takeover regulation in the United Kingdom with that of the United States. It concluded that, in the United Kingdom, it was better to be a shareholder; in the United States, it was better to be a lawyer. It will not surprise you that I believe the position in the UK to be preferable.

INDEX